The Dwarf Who Moved

PETER WILLIAMS QC

The Dwarf Who Moved
And other remarkable tales from a life in the law

HarperCollins*Publishers*

Two verses of the poem 'A Rope for Harry Fat'
reproduced by permission of the Estate of James K Baxter

HarperCollins*Publishers*

First published in 2014
by HarperCollins*Publishers* (New Zealand) Limited
Unit D1, 63 Apollo Drive, Rosedale, Auckland 0632, New Zealand
harpercollins.co.nz

Copyright © Peter Williams 2014

Peter Williams asserts the moral right to be identified as the author of this work. This work is copyright. All rights reserved. No part of this publication may be reproduced, copied, scanned, stored in a retrieval system, recorded, or transmitted, in any form or by any means, without the prior written permission of the publisher.

HarperCollins*Publishers*
Unit D1, 63 Apollo Drive, Rosedale, Auckland 0632, New Zealand
Level 13, 201 Elizabeth Street, Sydney NSW 2000
A 53, Sector 57, Noida, UP, India
77–85 Fulham Palace Road, London W6 8JB, United Kingdom
2 Bloor Street East, 20th floor, Toronto, Ontario M4W 1A8, Canada
195 Broadway, New York NY 10007, USA

A catalogue record for this book is available from the National Library of New Zealand

ISBN 978 1 7755 4047 2 (hbk)
ISBN 978 1 7754 9084 5 (ebook)

Front cover photograph by Sara Orme;
back cover photograph from the *Auckland Star*, early 1960s
Cover design by Hazel Lam, HarperCollins Design Studio
Typeset in Sabon LT Std by Kirby Jones
Printed and bound in Australia by Griffin Press
The papers used by HarperCollins in the manufacture of this book are a natural, recyclable product made from wood grown in sustainable plantation forests. The fibre source and manufacturing processes meet recognised international environmental standards, and carry certification.

Contents

Foreword by Associate Professor Bernard Brown	7
Dedication	15
Introduction	17
The Red Bicycle	21
The Bloodbath	33
Isabelle	44
The Boarding House Years	52
The Farmer Who Detested Scientology	61
The Fist Through the Judas Hole	69
The Boy Who was Tortured	77
The Schoolgirl Who Lied to the Court	83
Natural Justice at Te Awamutu	88
A Chance Encounter	95
The 'Lost' Hotel Register	103
The Exotic Stripper Whom the Judge Found Appealing	110
The Dwarf Who Moved	118
He Laughed with the Wind and the Sky	123
The Most Courageous Man	137
The Jurors Who Used Sledgehammers on the Loghaulers	146
Dynamiting the Wall of the Wellington High Court	153
Polling the Jury	162
She Killed Her Baby	166

The Planted Shell-case	173
The Girl Who Identified the Wrong Accused	184
The Police Sergeant Who Came to Dinner	191
He Chopped Her Head Off	198
Mr Uganda	206
Yelash Sues the Prime Minister	214
The Careless Accountant	221
Among the Poets	226
Fishing with Joe	234
The Highest Court in the Country	241
The View from the Penthouse Suite	251
Death by Fire	257
The Fijian Escape	263
In Cruel Solitude	273
The Great Evangelist	280
The Howard League	285
He Saw the Stars	293
Acknowledgments	299
Index of Names	301

Foreword

In my early years as a law lecturer I would accompany my students to the Auckland courts – to the Hogarthian Magistrates Court in Kitchener Street and the (misnamed) Supreme Court, solemn and bewigged, at Waterloo Quadrant. Both courts were forbidding; neither was especially exciting – except for one presence: my students and I, and the public galleries, stiffened in attention whenever a particular advocate appeared. That was Peter Aldridge Williams – distinctive in voice, looks and learning. Drama was afoot. And fifty years later, on selective occasions, it still is.

Peter Aldridge Williams is the definitive defendant's alter ego, the popular ideal of what a defending lawyer should be, should look like and what he should do in court. He is counsel for the accused, the people's champion in the adversarial lists. As a distinguished retired judge said to me recently, 'If – in that nightmare situation – you found yourself in trouble with the law and pleaded guilty, an Allen Nixon or David Lange or half a dozen others could be relied on for an eloquent plea in mitigation of sentence. If your plea was not guilty, your only possible choice would be Peter Williams.' And with respect, Your Honour, I unhesitatingly concur.

As a court-watcher over five decades, I rate Peter Williams QC the most effective defence barrister our legal system has experienced. Effective not only due to his success ratio – with which lawyers are not supposed to concern themselves – but because he was, and is, exciting and resourceful and visionary.

The excitement factor shows through Peter's own modestly related accounts of trials in this book. A lot of his resourcefulness is fuelled by his vision – his legal imagination. In the second retrial of a late 1970s Gisborne cannabis case, which was removed to Wellington, the jury had come back into court and its foreman had returned on its behalf the verdict, 'Guilty.' Peter Williams, defending, had noted two women jurors wiping away tears and that they had appeared perturbed as they had filed back from the jury room. Conscious of the fact – indeed the law – that it is the verdict reached in court rather than that reached in the jury room which represents the final and true verdict ('of you all'), Peter immediately requested the judge to conduct a poll of the jurors as individuals. Polling the jury is a hen's-tooth rarity in the Common Law. The judge complied, however, and the two women jurors stated, there and then, that they did not agree with the announced verdict. It should never be taken for granted that a juror or jurors might not change their mind between the jury room and courtroom. The accused was put on trial a third time and was acquitted.

This kind of alertness is part and parcel of Peter's trial lawyer prowess and was, once again, displayed vividly at the early 1970s Supreme Court trial in Auckland of a man charged with the murder of a drug dealer 'heavy' who had a reputation for battering non-paying clients with a club. In terrified expectation of such a home visit, the accused had sequestered himself inside with a gun. The dealer had turned up, made a lot of threatening noise and, as he turned away, the still trembling accused shot at him – not a propitious basis for a successful self-defence or provocation plea. The Crown made maximum use of that fact.

During his cross-examination of the late dealer's young girlfriend, Peter Williams noticed her contorted knuckles. By skilful questioning, he elicited that the fingers of both hands had been broken, and on different occasions, by the deceased dealer. The unified gasp of astonishment from the jury matched that from the public gallery. Later the jury returned its verdict of not guilty of murder or of manslaughter. They took only a few minutes. Indeed, I would not have been wholly surprised if they had added a rider that the prisoner should be recommended for the OBE! Effectively, defence counsel had put the deceased on trial. Effectively, the latter had received his comeuppance twice over.

A good defence, like a well-conducted prosecution, ultimately depends on thorough preparation. That occurs away from the limelight and involves as much energy (and more time) than forensic jousting at the public trial. That holds true for the lower courts, too – and it is axiomatic of appeal hearings. No more pointed example was the 1980s arrest and subsequent events affecting a man named Terry Clark (also known later as 'Mr Asia'). Clark had been charged with possession of and trafficking in a substantial quantity of class A drugs. In the face of what appeared to be an indefensible case, Peter Williams and his fellow barrister Kevin Ryan were left with the sole option of exploiting any possible weaknesses in the Crown's case. (The prosecution of course is duty bound to prove all material parts of their case beyond reasonable doubt.)

The Crown was overconfident. Not least about a possibly frail Department of Scientific and Industrial Research drug-testing procedure which was merely a screening test, but had been wrongly reported as a definitive test. Also, two witnesses were vulnerable. One was a corporal of police from Queensland who surprisingly was presented wearing a kind of summer khaki outfit which, to Kiwi eyes, appeared rudely militaristic. And the other was a woman witness with a reputation as a female Titus Oates (a perjurious informer). For all that, the case against Clark loomed large and strong.

Peter asked me to draft a change of venue application from Auckland to Wellington. Clark was well known in Auckland circles and would not have had even the appearance of a fair trial here. The application succeeded. I still did not appreciate the full implication of the transfer to Wellington, but Peter, its architect, did. It was the era of the (Muldoon) public service salary stagnation, and no Wellington jury would be bereft of members directly or indirectly affected – or, rather, disaffected – by that. And Peter Williams and Kevin Ryan put a lot of effort into jury selection (including challenges). That jury, for whatever reasons, and one can only guess, acquitted Clark. Perhaps it didn't appreciate or believe the Queensland corporal of police or the morally impugned woman witness. Add a likely protest mentality (at that time) of a Wellington jury panel and an answer may emerge.

It must be added, too, that Peter Williams had been focal in the later curial and ex cathedra manoeuvring to achieve a pardon for Arthur Allan Thomas in the Crewe case. The importance of the Thomas case is highlighted in a chapter of this book. Peter was hitting one of the highest peaks of his career at this time. Juries are fascinated by the star qualities of such an advocate. Such an advocate must not only be well prepared for court; he or she has to be brave. The police were not quiet or gentlemanly about their antipathy to the lawyer – above all lawyers – who threw doubt on their handling of the Thomas investigations. To my dismay, I listened to a public address (to which I replied privately) by senior appellate judge Sir Alfred North, in which he had castigated Peter Williams and others for their 'crusade' on behalf of Thomas. Earlier, Sir Alexander Turner, President of the Court of Appeal, had written an article highly critical of the jury polling matter (referred to earlier).

Many cases of the hundreds that P A Williams conducted were defences of sad and derelict persons; they were arguably more sinned against by society than sinning. Numerous such casualties of life he befriended and helped to find their way back into decent, useful lives. They fuelled Peter's resolve to re-create the Howard League of Penal Reform, an organisation that achieves positive results and practical reforms. These are explained in more detail in a subsequent chapter.

I recollect, not without anguish, a late middle-aged woman charged with the attempted murder of her cruel, neglectful husband. She had endured years of his callous, drunken behaviour on a remote farm. She had no friends, no money, and no access to shopping, even to basic toiletries. One night she awaited his inebriated return from a pub, threw petrol over him and applied a match.

The court accepted Peter Williams's plea of insanity on her behalf. For him that was nowhere near the conclusion of his brief. There was a moral dimension. He and I had visited the woman over Christmas on remand at Mt Eden's female wing, where, touchingly, she said how much she appreciated 'at last' some company: 'The girls here do speak to me.' Peter sought the cooperation of both the Crown and defence psychiatric expert witnesses, Henry Bennett and Laurie Gluckman, and approached the judge. It was agreed – and that judge did not own a reputation as a glowing humanitarian – that she would be placed in the care of Dr Bennett and stay with his family until adjudged fit to be released. After less than a year, that order was made.

Not all Peter's cases were conducted in the criminal courts. He built a strong reputation as a defamation lawyer. The Exclusive Brethren case was another illustration of exquisitely careful preparation backed by accomplished courtroom performance. A group of Brethren based in Motueka had 'excluded', as their religious practice required in this particular instance, an errant member who months later took his own life. An article in the Christchurch *Press* claimed the death was due to named Motueka members' concerted pressure on him.

Those individuals sued *The Press* for defamation. They, with supporters, flew to Peter's home in Remuera to seek his counsel. After inquiry, he established the deceased suffered, independently of the alleged pressures, from a life-threatening malady. I, as a researcher, was gifted the services of a young woman in the group who, scarfed and rosy-faced, typed and telephoned for me prodigiously for three weeks.

Before the High Court in Christchurch the libelled plaintiffs won. I thought it was a case that could have gone either way. A crucial decision made by Peter well before the trial was to gain the services of a leading Oxford professor as an expert witness on comparative religions. If a fulcrum of the merits needed a justifiable tilt, this expert, Dr Wilson, provided it. That, with the medical evidence, carried the day.

I must declare a personal reward here. A few weeks after the verdict a group of Auckland Brethren arrived at my door with a gift of two bottles of whisky, distilled at the Exclusive Brethren's still in Scotland. I had no idea Brethren partook. One gathers it is much more sparingly than I proceeded to partake.

Personal reminiscences have to close. That is hard because Peter and his trials have been important in my life and in my still developing legal imagination.

Suffice to conclude that as an advocate he was not cut in the fashion of any predecessor I know of. He had his own inimitable style – not only in terms of preparation and of elegant, dramatic delivery, but also in his eminently decent human approach to every client. That clientele ranges from a defamed District Court judge to one of the most demonised defendants in our criminal history. The former, for an unfathomable reason, was not championed by the Solicitor-General in the proceedings; the latter, Peter Fulcher, a recidivist offender who tried briefly to go straight was surprised by more than twenty charges laid by the Christchurch police from passport application injunction to keeping a noisy terrier. At a difficult time for him, P A Williams QC travelled to the South Island on the early morning flight, successfully defended all charges against Fulcher and returned the same day to prepare for a High Court trial starting the next day.

Fulcher, like numerous other personae dramatis who feature in this book, probably was not made of the stuff of reformability. A lot of others were. Wearing his Howard League hat, or seafaring skipper's cap, Peter Williams helped recover a lot of lives. Some, such as Ron Jorgensen, an underworld figure later discussed in the book, whose artistic talent Peter encouraged, were welcome at his home and on his yacht.

This book is very well written by an acknowledged wordsmith. It goes without need of my elaboration that it is exciting and colourful, humane and insightful. *Res ipsa loquitur.*

Bernard Brown
Law Faculty, University of Auckland

Dedication

For the last eight years I have suffered from cancer and have been subjected to sometimes brutal treatments including chemotherapy, radiation therapy, and a numerous battery of drugs. It was during this period that I wrote the manuscript for this book.

I wish to dedicate these writings firstly to my partner, Heeni Phillips, an Auckland barrister whose Ngati Hine upbringing has granted her great determination and compassion. She has been my mainstay and support throughout these years.

I want to include in this dedication my late mother and father, Mavis and Jim, who supplied me with the genes to enable me to write, occasionally, whilst suffering from my illness. My mother, whose maiden name was Pearce, had the stoicism provided by her Irish ancestors, who had endured the cruelties and hardships imposed by the English conquest of Ireland.

Introduction

In a letter to Emma Wedgwood, Charles Darwin wrote in 1838, 'I believe you will humanise me.' My fond hope in writing this book is that it may have at least a tendency to humanise its readers, by granting a deeper understanding of the legal process and the characters involved.

The facts have not been varnished over and the plain truth is that both our legal system and its partner, the penal system, still remain in the early days of social evolution.

In 1966, Karl Menninger, perhaps the greatest American psychiatrist of our generation, wrote as follows in *The Crime of Punishment*:

> *Included among the crimes that make up the total are those which we commit, we non-criminals. These are not in the tabulations. They are not listed in the statistics and are not described in the president's crime commission studies. But our crimes help to make the recorded crimes possible, even necessary; and the worst of it is we do not even know we are guilty.*

Crimes prevalent in New Zealand committed by society and deemed non-criminal would include such things as tobacco sales, apparently justified by its revenue production; the holy alliance between sport and the encouragement to consume alcohol; government tolerance of large-scale poverty, particularly among children; and the greed of a social plutocracy. Some of this hypocrisy is illustrated in these stories, such as 'She Killed Her Baby' and 'Mr Uganda'.

These vignettes, however, have not been written merely to encapsulate some examples of moral dereliction but in reality are glimpses of the past that have remained dormant yet intact in my memory. I am in my seventy-ninth year and have spent about sixty of those practising as an advocate in Her Majesty's Courts. During that time, I have witnessed great social changes, some of which have been reflected in the catalogue of crimes set out in the statute books. Until recently, I believe this metamorphosis has been in the public interest but more latterly, with a conservative government, we have witnessed regression.

As a young lawyer in the 1960s I witnessed during each court day at least ten to twenty men being brought before the courts for the offence of being drunk in a public place. Some of these individuals had been located under the Grafton Bridge in Auckland or other rough shelters for the homeless and usually they were quite ill. Watching these semi-comatose prisoners being lectured by sanctimonious magistrates on the evils of alcohol was indeed a sad pantomime.

Abortion was then also an offence. I remember one case in particular where a woman taxi driver with dependent children attempted to terminate her pregnancy using Lifebuoy soap and a knitting needle. She became seriously ill, and was then hospitalised and treated for blood poisoning. On her release, this unfortunate woman was immediately arrested and indicted in the courts.

Consensual sex between adult homosexuals was also an offence. People accused of homosexuality were usually ill-treated at the police station and punished by the courts at times to perniciously lengthy prison sentences.

Today, however, all these so-called criminal acts have been decriminalised. But on the other hand, sentences have been increased across the board. Important defences, such as provocation, have been struck out from the statute books, and the infamous 'Three Strikes' sentencing legislation has been introduced with its cruel and inhumane potential.

Although decreases in crime should be striven for, we are now finding out that much petty crime is better dealt with without the strict judicial processes. Many cases in the past just did not need to be brought before the courts. Years ago, I acted for a woman who practised the 'art' of fortune telling using tea leaves. At a social function where five or six women met to socialise and partake in tea and cake, one of the women present made some harmless prophecy after reading the state of the tea leaves in the various empty cups. One of the recipients of these predictions was married to a police officer and when she got home she told her husband about a prophecy made by the fortune teller. As a result, the tea leaves reader was arrested and brought before the courts, on the basis of anachronistic legislation.

On another occasion, I acted for a husband and wife who had about fourteen or fifteen children. They had recently rented a house where some of the children had found toys belonging to the previous tenant and proceeded to play with them. The parents were charged with receiving stolen property.

I could go on and on. Today, in an effort to lessen the incidences of recorded crime, our police have been ordered to warn people rather than invariably arresting and I am sure that this will have favourable consequences.

On the lighter side, I reiterate that most of my stories, although having a legal background, are recorded for their human interest. My journey from being a country boy to a city trial lawyer includes naiveté and many crossroads. Some of these are well illustrated in the pages of this book.

I have indeed been fortunate in at times obtaining encouragement from the Chief Registrar, Mr Mason, of the Supreme Court (as it then was), George Skelton, and Justice Terrence Gresson. I was also inspired by such lawyers as Frank Haigh, Sir Owen Woodhouse, and Sir Duncan McMullin. I wish also to pay tribute to Sir Edmund Thomas and Justice Ailsa Duffy for their judicial recognition of compassion and fairness.

The Red Bicycle

A boy floated down the river on a log. It was a bright summer day and the world was good. The banks were covered with willow trees, with their delicate light green foliage, some of them leaning their branches into the stream, forming a canopy that was incomplete, allowing the sun to stream in. The boy drifted down on his log with a waterproof box bobbing along behind him, which contained his clothes. The box was attached by a cord to the khaki shorts he was wearing.

Sometimes he would move slowly over the dark deep pools, where at times he would see a trout, almost stationary, a metre or two below the surface, waiting for something to happen. Then there would be the rapids, where the water was so shiny and silvery, streaming over the pebbles, with the sunlight giving it luminosity. Here, sometimes, he would have to alight from the old trunk as it jammed against the shingle, and he would slide down the rapids with the log tumbling behind him. Then again to ride the log with a wonderful, joyful sensation, the sunlight streaming onto his back, his body full of warmth and full of pleasure. The euphoria of childhood, the bliss of youthful things, the exuberance of being in harmony with nature, and the sheer pleasure of doing something just for the delight of it.

Near the bridge, he left the log and let it float alone towards the sea. It would now meet its own future, eventually becoming a piece of decayed wood adrift on some remote beach.

The boy put his clothes on slowly and then looked around. He always had his mind on finding something of value that the stream might provide. Sometimes, under the bridge, among dumped rubbish he might find bottles. Beer bottles could be sold at a penny each and lemonade bottles, if they were in good condition, could realise two pence each. So it was always worth having a look around.

He scrambled up the mound of rubbish and mud and searched under the bridge. It was mysterious there, gloomy and often smelly. But sometimes, bits of debris became jammed there, and among the rejected flotsam and jetsam there might be something of value. As he poked around, he found the frame of a derelict bicycle.

The frame had obviously been there for some time. It was covered by a creeping white lichen that almost concealed it. The lichen was formed of long ribbons, strung with rows of buds like white beads. He hurriedly pulled the strands off the rusted frame and brought it out onto the open bank.

The bike was in shocking condition. Many parts were missing entirely. As he rubbed the clay and the general muck off the frame, it revealed no identifiable colour beneath its rust. It had obviously been abandoned by its owner, and to most people it would have been rejected as complete rubbish.

The boy, however, was jubilant: to him, the bike was something that the river had thrown up, something that had no owner and now was his.

As far as he was concerned, anything that was part of the river was his to catch.

He placed the shambles of the frame over his shoulder and slowly trudged home. Eventually, his father returned from school, where he had been working even though it was a Saturday. The boy told his father how he had found the bike frame and said excitedly, 'Do you reckon we could get it to go?'

His father smiled and obviously enjoyed the happiness of his son. His son had never owned a bike. Not many in the community did have bikes and very few had cars. His father had a bike, which he used to ride to school, where he was a teacher. Sometimes he would double his son on the bar. The father did not want to do anything to destroy the happiness of the boy. The boy's eyes shone with pride, achievement and happiness, and this made the father happy. The father was happy because the son was happy, and the son was happy because he had found the derelict bike.

Together the two of them worked on and off for the next two weeks on the bike, cleaning it, rubbing off the rust with sandpaper, oiling it and generally trying to make it a functional bike again. It wasn't an easy process. Not only did the many missing parts remain to be found, but the frame in places had almost rusted through. However, at the end of those few weeks, it did start to look like a bicycle again.

They painted the bike. They painted it bright red because that was a happy colour and this was a happy bike belonging to a happy boy who looked forward to an enchanted time when he would proudly ride this bike to school.

All was well with the boy's world and with his family. They lived in a rental house, where the mother gave great love and warmth and the father gave leadership and taught at a local school. He shared a small bedroom with his brother. Those were the days when money was not quite so important, and most people lived frugally. Only one person in their street had a car, and that was a stock agent whose firm had supplied him with a Chevrolet so that he could drive around his farmer clients.

Now, looking at the freshly painted bike, the father said to his son, 'There are a few things about it that we can't fix and there are some parts we need to buy. We will have to take it to the bike shop and see if they can complete the repair. And then, son, you will be able to ride the red bike. We are all looking forward to seeing you do just that.'

And so the two of them walked the mile or two into town, to a little shop that repaired bikes, and they left it with the owner of the shop, who said that he would fix it and supply the tyres and other parts that were missing.

A night or two later, the boy was in bed. He had gone to bed early, which was not unusual, but he was not asleep. Because it was a small house, he could hear most of the things that were going on, although his parents weren't always aware that he was listening.

There was an abrupt knock at the front door. He heard his mother open the door, and then with a tone of astonishment she said, 'What's going on? What do you want?'

At the door were three policemen, all dressed in uniform. They told the mother that they wanted to see her husband about a very serious matter.

The police were invited in. They went into the humble lounge where the floor was covered with a worn carpet and the furniture was slightly shabby. It was, however, a warm and homely sitting room, clean and well kept. In the corner was the family piano, a bookcase was full of books, and several framed prints of famous paintings adorned the walls.

The police declined the invitation to be seated and one of them said to the father, 'We are investigating a serious matter and I am afraid that you are the main suspect.'

The father couldn't believe his ears. He was completely shocked. He was a good man and always led a good life. He had always respected law and order and was a regular churchgoer, indeed he sang in the church choir. On Saturday mornings his pupils would come around and he would give extra tutelage without cost. He was well regarded by his neighbours and all who knew him. However, here now were three police officers, in full uniform, accusing him of a crime.

He said, stuttering with the confusion, 'W-w-what are you getting at?'

One of the officers, a sturdy Irish gentleman with a perpetual frown, piercing blue eyes and receding red hair, said, 'Well, to cut it short, you are suspected of stealing a bicycle. We have information from the local bicycle shop that you and your son brought in a bicycle to be repaired a few days ago.

'We have checked out the complaint and, sure enough, the bicycle is a stolen bicycle. We believe you knew it was stolen when you received it, and unless you give us a satisfactory explanation, we are going to charge you with either theft or receiving stolen goods.'

The boy, lying in his bed in the next room, overheard most of this and his heart began to pound. He was so worried about his father. The boy knew how much integrity meant to him, and he hated these police officers for their accusations. Filled with a tremendous love for his father, the boy was desperate to do something to help him. But he just did not know anything he could do. So he lay there in his bed with his heart thumping until his head started to ache.

In the lounge the discussion went on. The Irish police officer said, 'Why did you paint the bike bright red? It's obvious to us you did that to conceal the true colour so it would not be identified!'

The father replied, 'There was no paint on the bike to begin with. It was covered in rust and was derelict. It was rubbish. We just salvaged it.'

The officer said, 'Well, why didn't you report it to the police station? You are a schoolteacher, you should know the rules. Finding is not keeping. You should've reported it to the local police station and checked out whether it was stolen or not. Why didn't you do that?'

The father felt a great weariness coming over him – a tiredness that was almost a depression, a cloud of hopelessness.

There was a long silence, and then one of the other police officers said to the father, 'This could finish you. They won't employ you as a schoolteacher if you have an offence for dishonesty against your name. This could be your ruin. We are just doing our duty. We have a duty to arrest people like you who commit these offences. It's obvious to us that you knew the bike was stolen right from the start.'

The police officer went on and on: 'Anyway, where did you get the bike from? How much did you pay for it? We want all this information and then we will decide whether you should be brought down to the station and charged. We are only doing our job. You should know that.'

The boy heard these voices in the lounge. He felt a terrible desire to rush out and punch those police officers, but he knew how ridiculous that would be. So he remained there with his heart thumping, listening as well as he could to the interrogation that seemed to go on endlessly.

Eventually, the father broke down, almost crying but refraining from doing so. He had too much dignity for that. He had flaming blue eyes, and they were blazing that night, and he certainly was not going to give in without a fight. He thought about his wife, listening in the kitchen. He thought about his children in their beds. He thought about his class at school and the pupils he was helping there. And now all this could be ruined over this damned bike.

His father told the whole story to the police about how his son had found this wreck of a bike under the bridge in a shockingly deteriorated condition. And how the boy had brought it home, and the two had laboured on it, restored it, painted it, taken it into the bike shop for repairs and new parts they couldn't provide themselves.

At the end of all this, the police posse seemed to have lost some vigour. It was clear to them that this man was a genuine, honest and honourable person. They realised now that they were pushing the matter too severely.

'I'll tell you what,' said the Irish policeman, 'to cut it all short, we've got to get someone for this. But I can see …' and he stared with those bulging eyes of his at the schoolteacher. 'I can see your side of it. This doesn't mean we are going to let you go, but I can see your side of it. I'll tell you what, we just want to get one conviction for this. It's necessary for us, for our files and for our reports. We've got to tie it all up. I'll tell you what, I've had a thought.'

'What's that?' asked the father.

'Well, we could charge your son in the Children's Court with theft of this bike or receiving the bike. He would get no penalty in the Children's Court. There would be no publicity there, either. No one would know that he was charged. This would get you off the hook.'

The father lowered his head; his face showed deep concern. He loved his son, and he was worried about what damage might be done to the boy by a simple conviction in the Children's Court. He knew about the Children's Court. He had had pupils who had been there and he knew that basically what the police officers were saying was correct.

He also knew, on the other hand, that if he himself were charged, he would have to hire a lawyer from his meagre savings. It would all be reported in the local newspaper. The gossip would soon get around in the staff room at school where he worked. He would probably lose his job and other jobs would be hard to get.

Finally, he said to the police, 'Okay, we will do it that way.'

When the police left, his wife rushed into the lounge and threw her arms around her husband.

'The bastards,' she said, 'the bastards, the bastards, the bastards!'

She kissed him a great number of kisses on his face. She hugged him with all her might and the two of them inclined their heads together, as if they had physically become one to share the grief and unfairness of the situation.

The boy lay in his bed. He heard it all. It was beyond him, though, and gradually he went to sleep.

The police came again sometime later to deliver a summons for the boy to appear in the Children's Court. This included a summons for the mother and father, too, who both had to be present. The police then took the bike away, saying that it had to be returned to the owner when they could find him, and that the boy and the father would never see it again.

A few weeks later, the father, the mother and the boy appeared in the Children's Court at the local Magistrates Courthouse. When they arrived, the place appeared to be in great disorder. Children were running everywhere, parents were yelling at their offspring, and the place seemed completely out of control.

They sat on a hard bench in the waiting room and stared at other people who also stared at them. The children, who were allegedly the culprits of various crimes, didn't seem to care less, notwithstanding the growls and threats from the parents. They kept on playing endless games of cowboys and Indians and hide-and-seek, and showing general disobedience.

At last, the boy's name was called. An usher came out and gravely told the boy and his parents to follow him, and so the three were conducted into the courtroom, where they were told to be seated. Opposite, a steely little man with dark, penetrating eyes awaited them. He seemed to conduct the whole programme and asked the boy whether he had committed the offence. The boy looked at his father, who nodded his head, and the boy nodded his head then, too.

'A plea of guilty will be entered,' said the little long-faced figure behind a large table.

The boy sat there, dressed in his best school clothes. His parents sat there in their church clothes – the father in a suit and tie, the mother wearing her Sunday hat and best dress. And they all looked very worried.

The police officer read out the charge and the details. The atmosphere in the room was absolutely electric. The little mean-eyed man opposite began to talk again. This was the magistrate, the boy realised. But all his comments seemed to be directed at the father. He almost seemed unaware that the boy was there, even though it was the boy who had allegedly committed the offence. It was as if the magistrate had hated the father for a long time, even though he had never met him previously.

The magistrate started by telling the father how a schoolteacher should have known better. He told the father how he should have known to report the bike to the police. 'Why wasn't that done? Why did you paint the bike? Obviously to suppress the bike's identity! Why didn't you tell your boy when he brought the bike home that finding is not keeping? That was your duty. You, as a schoolteacher, should have known better.'

This was a strange monologue. It wasn't a dialogue because the father said nothing. The magistrate kept going over and over the same facts again, as if somehow he was thinking with his mouth, just pouring scorn and derision to humiliate the father.

Eventually, this soliloquy came to an end and it was only then that the magistrate turned to the boy and said, 'As for you, you are convicted and discharged. The bike is to be returned to the owner. Court adjourned.'

The family left the courtroom in silence with their heads bowed. They simply didn't know why all this had occurred. Why had all this humiliation been brought to bear on the father? The mother took his hand in hers as they walked down the street, back the mile or two to their humble little rented house, with the boy trailing behind, somehow trying to make sense of this very peculiar behaviour by the adults around him.

It took a while for all this to dissipate. The father was worried that rumours would get back to the school. He believed, in fact, that some did get back to the school. The headmaster, however, was a good man and totally sympathetic towards the father, who was his first assistant and a very good teacher, highly admired by everyone who worked there.

The boy slowly regained his confidence and went back to his boyish ways – the river, schoolwork, kicking a football around, and doing all the things that boys do. So the years went by and all this seemed to disappear into the past.

Quite some years later, the boy had grown up to be an adult who had done well at school and had gone on to take a degree at university. At the end of his studies, the young man applied to a tribunal to be registered in his chosen profession. He had worked hard to obtain his degree and his employers backed him to the hilt.

A few days before the registration application was to be heard, however, he received a letter in the mail. The letter informed him that the police had advised the registration board that the young man had a conviction in the Children's Court for theft of a bike and that his application for registration should be deferred until the matter of his conviction was investigated and the repercussions of it assessed.

The young man sat back with the letter in his hand and could not believe his eyes. His young wife came in, spick and span, blooming with the beauty of youth. She could immediately see how upset her husband was and ran over to him, crying out, 'What's the matter, what's the matter? What's in that letter?' And when he showed her the letter, she said, 'How could they? It's so long ago.'

'I have got only vague memories of this now,' he told her. 'I was only a kid! I found this abandoned wreck of a bike and took it home. The old man and I fixed it up and we took it to the bicycle shop – the next thing the bloody police were around and were going to charge my old man. Imagine that! It would have ruined him in those days, you know? Ruined him!'

'And now they want to ruin you,' said his wife. 'It's unbelievable. It's absolutely unbelievable!'

Next day, the young man took the letter to the head partner of the firm where he worked. The elderly man, who was about to retire and who had been a lawyer for about fifty years, said, 'Look, son, we will fix all this up – it's really bullshit.' He was a man for all seasons, this head partner. He grasped the facts very quickly and placed his hand on the young man's shoulder, assuring him, 'Young fella, don't you worry.'

What the old lawyer did was use his influence and the young man became a registered legal practitioner, one who went on to successfully practise for many years.

And the boy, of course, was me.

The Bloodbath

I don't believe I was ever particularly sophisticated, but I hope that mainly my heart was in the right place. I was fortunate in having two wonderful parents, and was brought up to consider moral issues at a young age. Like most New Zealand youths, rugby played a great part in my life, and I also excelled in athletics and tennis.

I was advised by the vocation officer at my secondary school not to take up law, because, he said, I had not sufficient contacts, and it would be better if I became a teacher like my father. All my schooling was at a country town named Feilding.

When I left secondary school, I had never met a lawyer personally, but had heard my father talk about them quite a bit. He said that the law was in my blood. One of our ancestors had been a lawyer in Wanganui, but had gone deaf, cutting short his career. Another had been a solicitor practising in Hokitika in the gold rush days. He had been a member of the Legislative Council, and was apparently quite eminent. His clients usually paid him in gold dust and it was said that when his office building was eventually demolished, the workers found gold dust in the foundations – it had trickled through the floorboards. Anyway, for reasons that are somewhat obscure,

I was determined to be a lawyer, and studied Latin at school, which was then a necessary component of a law degree.

From about the age of fifteen, I worked during each summer in the local freezing works – a large slaughterhouse where the animal carcasses were then frozen in preparation for transport. It was dirty, monotonous work, but the pay was good. The money enabled me to go to Victoria University, where, after a somewhat diffident start, I began passing my units.

At this stage, I lived at home during the summer vacation. My mother would often get up at four in the morning to pack my lunch, which I would take with me on my bicycle to the freezing works. On those early morning starts, I'd be loading frozen carcasses from the freezing chambers out into waiting railway vans. That was very heavy work.

After several summers – that is, from November till about May – I had a reluctance to go back to the freezing works. It was unhealthy work; the place had a terrible stench, particularly the fellmongery, where the wool was rotted off the hides of recently killed sheep. I didn't like the slaughter of animals, either, and hated the almost-human cries of the doomed pigs, which seemed to know what was ahead for them.

I was determined, that year, to do something different, and noticed an advertisement in the local paper for scrub-cutters. At that time, the government was giving a generous subsidy to farmers who employed them to clear land. The rationale was that pastures would be extended and the national product of farm exports increased.

I rang up the farmer who had put the ad in the paper, and he told me his farm was way out in the hill country, near a small hamlet called Halcombe. The farmer seemed a very reticent person, but he told me the job was available, and quoted me a reasonable hourly rate.

I later mentioned this to a mate of mine, who was keen for work too, and so together we told the farmer we accepted his terms.

We both rode out to the farm on our bicycles, and eventually found the homestead set in an idyllic gully between two massive hills. It was a large farm, and had a conservative but very prosperous atmosphere about it.

The farmhouse itself was a sprawling building, surrounded by overhanging verandas. The back entrance had a large outdoor roofed area, with shelves for boots and pegs for oilskins.

The farmer never invited us into the house, but merely said, nonchalantly, 'You've arrived, have you? Just wait there.'

With the back door open, we could see inside the house, and saw a woman bending over a stove. I thought to myself that she was probably the farmer's sister. In those days, quite a few of these farmer's daughters never married because their fathers would never approve a suitor unless he either owned a farm or was an heir to one.

The farmer emerged from the house, sat on the step and put on his boots. We then all walked down towards his tractor. He never spoke a word: there was practically no communication. We helped him hitch a trailer up to the tractor, and then he went into a refrigerated shed and brought out a whole sheep carcass. This was placed on the tractor, along with a sack of onions, a sack of potatoes, and a large bag of rolled oats. A few other bits were added, but not much.

He hitched up two horses to the back of the trailer, threw some cutting gear on it, including axes, sharpening files and slashers. Then we hopped onto the trailer and off we went. It was a jolty, rugged ride over rough and steep terrain, and after what seemed like eternity, we came to a small fertiliser hut.

We alighted from the trailer, and walked into the place. One end of the building was filled with sacks of fertiliser, but the other end had a chimney, fireplace, and a camp oven. The farmer said, 'You should cut the sheep up with an axe, throw the bits in that big pot, and boil them for a while. They'll last longer that way, and it may keep the blowflies away.'

Outside the hut, he turned to an adjacent hillside and said, 'That's where you'll work. Just cut all the scrub off that hillside and come back and see me when you're finished.'

We loaded the gear and provisions from the trailer into the hut, and without saying much more, the farmer left.

My mate said to me, 'That's how they are, these back-country farmers. They get very introverted and they don't say much.'

'I suppose they talk a bit more when they're pissed,' I replied, and we both laughed.

We tethered the horses near a trough by the hut, and inspected our new home.

It was pretty rough. The bags of fertiliser filled about a third of the space, but along two of the sides were homemade bunks of scrim and boards, and on the remaining side there was a stainless-steel basin that produced water from an outside tank.

'Ah well,' I said, 'we'd better get organised.'

So we collected firewood, cut up the sheep, put it on to boil, placed our sleeping bags on the bunks, and generally tried to make the place as pleasant as possible.

We stacked our cutting gear in one corner, and then, as we commenced chopping up some vegetables to add to our boiled sheep for a stew for our dinner, my mate remarked, 'Looks as if we're going to live on this stuff for the next month or so.'

'Ah well, it could be worse,' I said. And it was.

That night, in our respective bunks, we found we couldn't sleep because the place was infested with rats. We both got out of bed and thought out a scheme to get rid of them. Eventually, we devised a trap. Using meat as bait, the rats would be seduced into walking across a piece of cardboard set across a bucket of water. The weight of the rat would cause a slit in the cardboard to open, causing the rat to fall into the bucket of water below and be drowned.

The next morning was a beautiful day, and we set off on our horses to the chosen hill, with our cutting gear and water bottles, to start clearing scrub. Some of the scrub was really quite large, more like trees than scrub – they were 'tea'-tree shrubs, otherwise known as manuka – and had probably replaced the kauri and totara forests of the very early days of European settlement. But there was something beautiful about the manuka, with its distinctive small bright green leaves, tiny white flowers and delicious smell.

We devised a plan where we would first cut paths through the scrub, then cut small blocks at a time. And so that's what we did for several weeks, with the sun beating down on our backs, sweat pouring out and drenching our khaki shorts. We had to wear boots, but at times it was so hot that we would sit down and take them off to cool down our feet. The biggest of the manuka trees had to be felled by axe. I told my mate that my grandfather, Barney Pearce, had been a bushman in Okahune. I only had a very vague memory of him, because he died after being crushed by a falling tree when I was about four or five years of age. He had been a foreman at the local mill, and a local tree-chopping champion. Somehow, when I was hacking down the manuka, I felt the spirit of my grandfather running through my veins.

We laughed and joked, belting into the scrub, sometimes even with fury. Every hour or so, we'd stop for a break and drink cold tea. In the middle of the day, we would eat huge slices of mutton on stale bread.

And that's how it was. We lived in the hut, and became more and more attached to the horses as the days passed, too. After a while, we even raced each other on our horses every morning, from the hut to the hill, just for the sheer joy of it.

After we'd been going for a few weeks, maybe a bit longer, my partner fell off his horse. He was knocked around a bit by the fall, but at any rate he'd decided to give it all up – he said he'd had enough. He left on his horse to ride to the homestead and pick up his pay, leaving me on my own out there.

It was lonely. Only once did I see the farmer pass by on his tractor, just half a mile away or so, but he never waved or came over to see me.

Finally, I finished felling the scrub on the hillside, and it was time for me to pack up and ride to the homestead. The farmer came to the door, and I told him I'd finished, handing him a note of my hours. He never changed expression, but after looking at my hour sheet, he grumbled and said, 'You must've worked all night.' I smiled at the remark, but he didn't. There was no fuss, however. He went indoors, and after a few minutes, came out and gave me a cheque for the full amount. There was no handshake or anything like that. I got onto my bike and rode off.

As I cycled back home to Feilding, I was happy. I'd got my money, and was ready for another year at university. Someone later said to me once, 'After you've done scrub-cutting, you wouldn't want to talk to anybody. Scrub-cutters come to town, sit in a corner of the pub, and drink their beer, just like hermits.' I laughed and said I wouldn't be like that. I loved good company too much. Talking was one of my great pleasures.

That year, I transferred to Canterbury University at Christchurch because my family had shifted to Sumner, where my father had been appointed headmaster of the local primary school.

The law school at Canterbury University was not highly regarded on a national scale: the lecturers were mainly legal practitioners, and the pass rate in the external exams was comparatively pretty poor. However, one lecturer, Ben Drake, really impressed me. He was a practising criminal lawyer, and really loved to talk. He was easily sidetracked into telling the class about his own cases, and the law students loved him. He was a well-known criminal lawyer in the Canterbury District, a big man with a huge belly and a loud laugh.

I found Canterbury University a very friendly campus. I hitched up with an Indian student from Fiji there, named Sam Chauhan. The two of us made a workplace for ourselves in the basement under the library, where it was warm because there was a furnace down there that heated the library above. I also teamed up with a man called Des Boyle, who had spent six years in a Catholic seminary, training to be a priest. He had become disenchanted with the hypocrisy he found there. We called him 'the Mad Monk'. He was a great mate of mine, and later became a Crown Prosecutor.

At Canterbury University, I also joined a boxing club. I'd done a bit of boxing in Feilding, and again at Victoria University, but had never fought in a tournament. At Victoria University, I had trained in a town gym with the local boys. The local boys didn't like the students from the university much, and the training sessions often degenerated into all-out fights. After a training session, I would visit a milk bar and drink several pints of milk, then go back to Weir House, where I was lodging, to nurse my injuries. Things were a bit different, however, at Canterbury University. The boxing lessons were at the university gym, and were well controlled. I even learnt how to box a bit: how to keep my elbows in to protect my gut, and to hold my gloves up to protect my head. I learnt how to jab with a straight left, and to bring my right across as a king hit. I practised combinations of blows on the heavy punching bag. I really felt good in those days. The scrub-cutting had toughened up my muscles. I was young and had plenty of vitality. Sometimes we would fight in local contests on a Saturday night. These would often be sponsored by the Rotary organisation. At the end of each fight, coins would be thrown into the ring. With a bit of luck, you might pick up five pounds in tips. It was all a bit hilarious.

I loved boxing. I loved the smell of it, the liniment and the sweat, and the physical thing. A trainer said to me at the time, 'You'll go a long way if you really trained.' But deep down, I did not want to be a professional boxer. I wanted to be a lawyer, whatever that meant.

But one day, to my surprise, the boxing coach said to me, 'Peter, we've decided to select you as part of the Canterbury University boxing team, and we'll pay your expenses to travel to Auckland for the New Zealand Champs.' He added, 'It's nothing flash, however. You'll go in the ferry across the Cook Strait, then ride second class in the train up to Auckland, where you'll be billeted with some student's family.'

'You think I'm good enough?' I asked him.

And the coach replied, 'Well, quite frankly, you're not much of a boxer. But you're strong, and you never know your luck.'

The other members of the team were great guys, and we travelled to Auckland with a lot of good humour. I had never been to Auckland before, and it was all an exciting adventure.

The trip across the Cook Strait in the old ferry was pretty horrible, though. I shared the cabin with a jockey who vomited all night. The stench was terrible. I got up as soon as possible the next morning, and walked down the corridor to the communal shower. I stayed under that shower a long time, enjoying it. When I came out, however, there was a queue of angry, towel-toting people waiting their turn. They shook their fists at me, and I nearly had an early altercation.

The second-class train trip to Auckland wasn't all that comfortable, either. We had a few beers in Wellington, which made the trip slightly more bearable than it might have been. As we travelled second class, we had to sit up all night on hard seats, and at times the smoke from the engine found its way into our carriage.

When I got to Auckland, I was pretty exhausted, and all I really wanted was a good sleep. My host took me back to his home, and his parents made me feel welcome. I didn't see much of my host, though, since he was one of the organisers of the university tournament. When I had rested, I took the bus up to the town hall, and had a look at the place where we were going to fight.

The Auckland scene seemed to me to be a bit overwhelming. There were social things going on with beer and girls, but somehow I felt like a country hick, and they all seemed a bit sophisticated for me.

On the night of the fight, I arrived early at the town hall and met with our coach and the other boys in the team. My father had given me an old dressing gown to wear, and apart from that, I had my khaki shorts and a worn pair of tennis shoes. I waited in the dressing room for the fight ahead of me to finish.

Finally, I heard the applause and the yelling, and knew that my time had come.

My opponent was from Massey College, near Palmerston North. He was Russian and had a reputation for being a very good boxer – indeed, he had won a championship in one of those Russian satellite states.

In the ring, we stared at each other. The Russian was short and thick and looked pretty strong. I stood in my corner, wearing the red dressing gown. The faces outside the ring all seemed a bit of a blur. I can't remember what the ref said to us, but we touched gloves, and were told to come out fighting. I shot out of my corner like a jack-in-the-box. I couldn't restrain myself. I rushed at the Russian, forgetting all my boxing training, the straight left and the right cross, just hammering him with a flurry of blows. I never stopped punching, but the crowd loved it – they roared and yelled. I fought like a maniac. The Russian covered up well, but had to retreat under such a continuous barrage of punches.

Between rounds, the second said to me, 'For God's sake, slow down a bit.' But I bounded out for the second round just the same. It was like cutting the scrub, and I just belted into that Russian. By the third and final round, I was so tired I couldn't keep my gloves up. They felt like lumps of lead. The Russian was now hitting me, mainly in the face. I felt blood gushing down from my nose, and the front of my khaki shorts was crimson.

At the end of the round, it was clear who had won – it was the Russian. But it had been a great fight, and the crowd gave us a standing ovation. The next day, the *New Zealand Herald* said it was the 'Fight of the Night'. I'd had to go off to the casualty department after the fight, to have my nose cauterised to stop it bleeding. I never boxed again.

I did continue, however, with my law studies, to prepare for the many contests of words ahead.

Isabelle

Feilding is a small country town situated about twelve miles from the provincial city of Palmerston North. I had completed my secondary education at Feilding Agricultural College and had worked for two seasons in that local freezing works about a mile from Feilding. At seventeen years of age I was still an adolescent but the world was opening for me at an amazing pace.

As I've already mentioned, my job at the freezing works was sheer drudgery. Early on there, I worked in the wool room adjacent to where the pullers (who worked under contract) would push the wool off treated hides. These hides had been fermenting in the fellmongery for some time and, as I've also mentioned, the smell was unimaginable. The wool was taken from the pullers by cart into the drying area. First, it was placed in large circular spinners, where it was spun at a fast rate so that by centrifugal force most of the moisture was squeezed out of the wool. The wool was then placed in a large dryer, which was about the size of a railway engine. After the wool had passed through the dryer, it went via a chute to the room above, where it was baled and made ready for sale.

One of my tasks was to stand by that chute and make sure it didn't block. If it did block, in a matter of minutes half the room would be full of wool and the dryer would have to be stopped while things were sorted out. It was hot work – unhealthy and smelly – but the pay was good, and as it allowed me to go to university, it was essential.

University was a whole new world for me. I had never been to Wellington before and had thought male university students would wear shorts, like schoolboys. I had projected university as an extension of high school and expected lecturers to take an interest in me and exert a certain amount of discipline.

On the contrary, I found that no one took an interest in me and there seemed to be no discipline whatsoever. During term, I stayed in a boarding house called Weir House situated in Kelburn, just above the cable car that took people down to the city. Within a very short time I began to immerse myself in the joys of this unfettered freedom, living away from home. This led to much convivial drinking at the hotels in Lambton Quay with fellow students and other people I'd met. My father had warned me about certain dance halls I should not attend because they were of ill repute, and I made a bee-line for these places.

At the end of the first university year, I passed one unit by one mark, and failed all the rest.

When I returned home to Feilding, the displeasure of my father was very real. Long discussions were held as to whether I should choose another occupation, either as a teacher like my father, or perhaps as a journalist. I indeed applied for a job with the *Manawatu Times* but was rejected.

I went back to the freezing works again that summer in the expectation that I would go back to university and try again in the new year. This time I worked in the freezer department.

The freezer department was where the meat was railed in from the cooler floor and left to freeze. The sides of beef were stacked up right to the ceiling and the work was heavy and, at times, dangerous. These large freezer apartments were the size of several warehouses and were cooled by ammonia pipes. On one occasion I had a fight in the freezer.

My opponent was a union delegate opposed to student labour being used in the freezing works. He argued we were taking jobs from true working men, and further that many of us were 'smart arses'. I had accidentally sent a frozen sheep carcass too quickly down a wooden shute, causing his hand to be jammed. These chutes were made icy and slippery by buckets of water being poured on them. As a result, the frozen lambs travelled like lethal projectiles from the upper to lower floors.

The injured delegate screamed and immediately attacked me. Fortunately, he fell over backwards on the frozen floor, and I sat on him until he quietened down.

The floor was icy and if an ammonia pipe had been broken in the scuffle, dangerous gases would have been immediately emitted – right at us.

Every hour the team of workers would come out of the freezer into the smoko room for ten minutes to thaw out. During this time I would hastily down hot mugs of tea and drink condensed milk direct from the tin. Amazingly, the card-players among us were able to get one or two hands of euchre in during those ten minutes.

It was not the greatest way of spending a summer, working in a freezer. No time for playing sport.

Saturday night was always fun, though – my big night out. I had a great friend, Ted, who was, like me, about seventeen or eighteen. Ted had also enrolled as a law student and already was doing very well. He was academically very bright but also an excellent sportsperson and a great companion. Ted mainly worked for his father, who was a builder, during the so-called summer vacation.

On Saturday nights we would journey from Feilding to Palmerston North to attend the ANA Dance Hall. To get there, sometimes we would go to the Feilding railway station and jump a freight train just as it was moving. This meant that we would stand between the carriages for the twelve-mile trip. If one of us had slipped into the connecting mechanisms, he would at the very least have lost a foot. At other times Ted was able to borrow his father's truck. It was a Ford with a V8 engine and we would time ourselves to see how quickly we could get from Feilding to Palmerston North. On the route was a one-way bridge with a ramp on either side and, as Ted was an expert driver, we would hit the initial ramp at high speed so that the truck would sail up into the air and then crash down onto the ramp on the other side. We found this feat of aerial truck-driving hugely enjoyable.

At Palmerston North we would first go to an after-hours pub and at the back entrance buy a bottle of cheap wine each. With the wine stuffed into our jackets we would then walk to the war memorial in the centre of the city. While seated on well-inscribed park seats we glugged down the wine. Well fortified, we then attended the ANA Dance Hall in George Street.

In our eyes at least, the ANA Dance Hall was a wonderful place. It seemed to be a huge building and was always well patronised on a Saturday night. On the platform stage at one end of the room, a large, mainly brass band called the Commandos played all the modern hits with great energy and fortissimo. There was a star vocalist out in front singing the latest tunes of the day. The atmosphere was wonderful.

On one side of the dance hall sat all the girls and on the other side, milling around, were all the young fellows. When the MC announced each dance over the microphone, the boys would rush across the dance floor to secure the consent of their selected female to be their next dance partners.

This often led to fights. The young men in the Manawatu were generally a healthy lot and accustomed to manual work. Fighting was just a part of their lifestyle. The manager of the ANA, however, did not allow fights inside the dance hall, of course – that was strictly prohibited. The procedure then would be for the combatants to go outside to a designated place where the spectators would form a ring and the fight would be carried out in a rough and unruly manner. I had been in several of these fights and afterwards, provided there was not too much blood, would return to the dance hall, wash my face in the hand basin in the toilet and continue my pursuit of a suitable partner.

These fights would often originate from a trivial incident, such as refusing to give up a partner during an 'excuse me foxtrot', or allegations of deliberate barging during the Gay Gordons or other similar revolving partners' dances.

The climax of the evening was the last dance. There was almost an implied agreement that if a girl danced with you for the last dance you would be able to escort her to her home.

Sometimes, however, girls could be deceptive and slip away on the pretext that they had to go to the cloakroom, and then would not be seen again that night by their eager, waiting, last dance partner.

It was at the ANA Dance Hall that I met Isabelle. She was about sixteen or seventeen years old and, in my mind at least, absolutely beautiful. She was a part-Maori girl with fine features and alluring looks and I was obsessed with her.

Isabelle's response was somewhat more reserved. She was obviously aware that I was an immature adolescent and really had little to offer. I had no car, not even a motorbike, or a place to take her, but on the other hand, I sensed she did feel a certain attraction to me.

And so one night, at last, after having the last dance with me, Isabelle agreed that I could escort her home.

I was in a fever. There were strong instinctive drives boiling inside me and my desire for Isabelle was almost uncontrollable.

I had managed to secrete some bottles of beer outside the dance hall and stuffed these down into my bomber jacket as we left. The two of us then took a bus to the suburb where Isabelle lived.

There was no question of her taking me into her home, so our romance had to take place in the bus shelter. Like most bus shelters, it was a pretty bare and desolate place with a fairly strong smell of stale urine. Outside was a typical Manawatu night with the rain pouring down and the wind whistling.

I produced the beer from my jacket and opened the bottle tops against the bus shelter seat. We both drank our beers holding tightly onto each other.

My lovemaking was clumsy and inexperienced. She obviously knew far more than I did, and she wasn't going to let me go too far. But I was in heaven. I loved the feel of her body and her delicious scent. The awkward fumbling went on for quite a while, until eventually Isabelle said she had to go home.

There seemed to be no more buses, so I walked back to the central bus station at Palmerston North, only to find I had missed the last bus to Feilding. In those days there weren't so many cars travelling around, least of all at one or two in the morning, so I had to walk the twelve miles. I reached home at about five o'clock in the morning, tired out.

In my family home, there were two bedrooms in the house – one occupied by my parents and the other by me and my older brother, James. When I turned the light on to get undressed, my father appeared in the room in his pyjamas. He asked me why I was so late home, and I said I'd missed the bus and had to walk. But he seemed to know everything. He said, 'You've been fooling around with a girl, haven't you?'

I didn't much like the expression 'fooling around' and told him I had found a proper girlfriend. He just sneered at me and said, 'What's her name?' I said, 'Isabelle,' and he repeated the name sarcastically several times: 'Isabelle. Isabelle. Isabelle.'

My father was not impressed. He said, 'You're just a disgrace. Last year you failed all of your units bar one. You've been turned down as a reporter and now you're fooling around with Isabelle. You're a no-hoper! You're a disgrace! I don't know what's going to happen to you.'

I was so angry that I felt like punching him, but managed to restrain myself.

The romance with Isabelle didn't last long. I couldn't compete with older and more worldly young men.

I continued to work in the freezer chamber, though, and, with my accumulated capital, went back to Victoria University for a second year.

That second year, by chance I met another student called Dutch, whose surname was Chateau. Dutch's father was a prominent advertising agent in Wellington and very successful. Dutch, however, had failed his units the previous year – to the dismay of his own father – and so the two of us found a common bond. We both were determined to pass our examinations this year, though. He was a delightful companion, always warm, and would drop his books to enthusiastically shake hands whenever we met. Together we made the Wellington Town Library our workplace and applied ourselves diligently to our studies.

At the end of the year we passed all our exams and never looked back. But I never heard from Isabelle again.

The Boarding House Years

After I had completed my training in the air force at Hobsonville under the compulsory military training scheme, I decided to stay on in Auckland rather than return to my home in Sumner, Christchurch.

The training at the air force base was just what I needed after having spent ten days in jail for riding a motorbike while intoxicated. The officers at Hobsonville gave me no quarter and referred to me as 'jailbird'. But eventually I was accepted, and, by the end of my three-month stay, was elected dormitory leader and offered an officer's course. I enjoyed the air force – the food was great, there was plenty of sport, and when I got to know the officers, they were not bad at all.

I had never been to Auckland City before, and driving through Newmarket on my two-stroke motorbike, I thought I had found the centre of Auckland, and had to be redirected by a chance acquaintance. I was lucky to obtain a job in the Justice Department, considering I had a conviction for riding a motorbike while intoxicated.

This had occurred while I was travelling from home at Christchurch to Hobsonville in order to carry out my CMT, or compulsory military training, in the air force. I had stopped at

Feilding to see an old friend. We had a few beers at the Denby Hotel and I was arrested afterwards, riding in the town square while waiting for my friend.

The belligerent magistrate sentenced me to ten days imprisonment. He was known as 'Whisky Bill', and had been a judge at the Nuremburg war trials. It was said at those trials he would always accept, as evidence, a prisoner's written confession, provided it was not so bloodstained as to be illegible.

Nonetheless, the job in the Magistrates Court gave me a living wage and a feeling of financial security.

In those days there was only one University of New Zealand and Auckland University was a mere college. The same applied to Canterbury University College. All students in New Zealand took the same external examination, regardless of their geographical location. I resumed my legal studies at the University College of Auckland.

My life was kept busy mainly by work at the courts, where I was a clerk, and attending the lectures at the university, which were held early in the morning, before the working day commenced, and then afterwards from 5pm onwards. I soon found my employment in the courts was fascinating, and eventually I was transferred to the Supreme Court (now the High Court), where I worked with a happy and dedicated staff. The registrar at the Supreme Court was a man called Mason. He was a short, stumpy, gruffly spoken man in his sixties who demanded attention to detail and absolute courtesy, particularly to the lawyers who came to the office to file documents. He was very kind to me, however, and when he knew that I was a keen debater, he would take me to Courtroom No. 1 and give me lessons in elocution. He would stand at one end of the courtroom and I at the other and he would advise me on improving my oratory. I may say that under his tuition I won the Joint Scroll medal for oratory at Auckland University College and also represented New Zealand University in its debating team against the Australian universities. At this stage I had almost completed my law degree.

I found among the court staff men who were experts on legal documentation. Eric Morsley was one of these. He was an elderly man with a limp, and his knowledge of the drafting of court documents was prodigious. Practising lawyers in Auckland would often pay him to draft difficult documents. Lawyers like Jimmy Dickson, renowned for his courage and quick wit, were invariably bright and cheery with such court staff and more than willing to give a clerk a financial inducement for help in this regard.

The Supreme Court staff tearoom was also frequented by practising barristers, who would drop in for a cup of tea. The conversations were brilliant and the anecdotes about trials and judges were colourful and usually humorous.

One of our jobs was to file disused court files in the basement beneath Courtroom No. 1. This was a dark and gloomy place but certain old files protruded out slightly from the rest. These files recounted dark stories of infamous old court cases back many years ago. We would take some respite from our filing duties and read extracts from these well-worn files, much to our horror and amazement.

Death by hanging was then still relatively recent in the memories of New Zealanders, as was punishment by flogging. Some of the senior court staff could recount attending on some of these occasions. The registrar of the Supreme Court also acted as the Sheriff of Auckland and it was mandatory that he attend all hangings and floggings in the Auckland jurisdiction. It was said that the acting sheriff would be granted six weeks leave to recover from the shock of being a spectator to these gory events.

We seldom saw the High Court judges. They were like gods, and if in fact we did meet a High Court judge by chance in a corridor or somewhere, we would modestly bow our heads and only speak if spoken to first.

A well-known filer of documents was Frank Haigh, a prominent civil rights lawyer. He acted for most of the unions in Auckland. In those days, injured workers could sue their employers for damages and every week bundles of writs would be filed by the Haigh office.

I was later to learn that the various union officials were treated every Friday night at his office with generous supplies of liquor and food. Union secretaries were paid generously to photograph scenes where accidents had occurred, too. At Christmas time a van would arrive at the Supreme Court courthouse and every member of the staff would receive a present from the Frank Haigh law firm. The presents were graded in value according to the status of the recipient in the office. Lowly clerks like myself would receive, say, a tie or a pair of socks. Naturally we all gave preference to files where Frank Haigh was acting.

At this time, I resided in various boarding houses in Auckland. One of the first of these boarding houses was in Jervois Road and my room was adjacent to the footpath. The drawback was that a neon light outside flashed all night right into my room, which was irritating. I remember the winter being very cold. I bought cheaply an ex-army overcoat, which I would wear while studying, sitting beside a sideboard (a make-do desk), poring over my textbooks. This boarding house provided an evening meal, which was usually cabbage and stew. We boarders were a mixed lot, to say the least, mainly invalids, ex-prisoners, or women fallen upon hard times.

I soon purchased a table for ten shillings at an auction, and when I changed boarding houses from time to time, I would usually walk to the next boarding house with a mate in the early hours of the morning carrying my bags and my table.

Another boarding house that I stayed in was off Queen Street, somewhere near the old town hall. This was a bed-and-tray place, which meant that at about half past six each morning there would be a thud on the door of one's room to signal that a tray had arrived with a pot of tea and plate of sliced toast saturated with melted butter.

This place had very small rooms, but a boarder was allowed to have a small stove. My girlfriend at the time, who will be mentioned later, would sometimes come over in the evening and we would cook a simple meal together in the room.

There was a fair amount of promiscuity going on and some of the housemaids were almost predatory, though the management did their best to make the place 'decent'. Illicit affairs had to be conducted quickly and furtively. The boarding house was, however, conveniently located. I could easily walk to the university and the courthouse. There were several good Chinese restaurants in the vicinity, and for two shillings and sixpence, one could purchase a huge bowl of either chow mein or chop suey. I have never again been able to find such excellent meals in any Chinese restaurant. It did not matter if the health inspector had found a skinned cat in one of these restaurant's refrigerators, it did not stop me from eating there. Chinese opium was also available in this area, namely Greys Avenue, but I never even entertained going to such places. Frankly, in those days, from my experience at least, very few people took an interest in illicit drugs. We were content with alcohol and tobacco, although, apart from the odd cigar, I was a non-smoker.

It was during this period that I made my first visit to Mount Eden Prison. My girlfriend's mother had been charged with murder. The alleged offence occurred in Christchurch but she was remanded to the women's division at Mount Eden Prison without bail. My girlfriend insisted that I accompany her to visit her mother.

The allegation against her mother was that she had deliberately run her boyfriend over, and had in fact reversed the car and run over him a second time. This boyfriend was a well-known high society figure in Christchurch.

We entered the main prison gate and turned to the left where there was a prison within a prison, namely the Women's Prison, then we sat in the visiting room with a group of other women prisoners and their visitors. The atmosphere was quite tense. My girlfriend's mother kept questioning me concerning legal aspects of her case. She thought because I was a law student that I was knowledgeable about these matters, when in fact I knew very little.

It was on one of these occasions that the infamous teenage killer Juliet Hulme entered the visiting room. She had been convicted of the murder of her friend Pauline Parker's mother and the case was already very notorious – it would many years later be immortalised in the film *Heavenly Creatures*. I never spoke to Juliet but she looked, even in prison uniform, quite serene and, I thought, quite beautiful. All this increased my ambition to one day become a trial lawyer.

I later transferred myself to a boarding house in Princes Street next to the imposing and brewery-owned Grand Hotel. This boarding house was called 'Le Grand' and was nowhere near so imposing. It was a large establishment, though, with many rooms. The back rooms were quite dilapidated, with the wallpaper peeling off the walls in many places, and the landlady did her best to get rid of permanent boarders at Christmas time because she said she could make more money with tourists staying in her hotel.

Several of the other boarders were commercial travellers who were mainly a seedy lot often striving to keep up appearances with limited budgets. The food was not too bad there, but the servings were very small. If one asked for a second serving he or she was treated like an Oliver Twist.

Fortunately the door to my room had an internal lock, as almost invariably people seemed to be walking around the corridors at night. One night, I was awoken at about 2am by a furious knocking on my door. I called out, 'Who is that? Who is that?' And a frightened female voice replied, 'Let me in, let me in – he is going to kill me.' I begrudgingly opened the door and a young female scantily dressed in night attire shot into my room. She said, 'Quickly, lock the door, he is after me – he is going to kill me.' Sure enough, I could hear heavy footsteps in the corridor and an angry voice shouting, 'Where are you? You bitch! I'll get you! I'll get you!' She was in a shocking panic, asking me, 'Can I hide under your bed?' And I let her.

Finally, I put the light out and got back into bed, knowing that the girl was underneath. The shouting outside the room eventually went away and soon I realised that the girl had come out from under the bed and was in the bed with me.

Actually, the night turned out to be pleasant in more ways than one and in the morning she left me with a kiss and I never saw her again.

The last boarding house that I stayed in was in Valley Road, Epsom. I had replied to an advertisement in the paper and when I arrived at the boarding house I was interviewed by a young and very attractive woman. I learnt later that the boarding house was owned by her grandmother, who was part Jewish and part Maori, and owned several other boarding houses around Auckland. By this time, I had qualified as a solicitor and was working at Russell McVeagh, a well-known law firm who treated me very well. Within a couple of weeks I had fallen in love with and married my young landlady Zelda. Within a year or so, and at her instigation, I had resigned from Russell McVeagh and begun to practise on my own account at the Commercial Union building near the Kitchener Street courthouse. Zelda was my typist and managing clerk. It was just the two of us.

My fledging law office was without clients and very little furniture. Each morning, I would stroll over to the Magistrates Court, which was very close by, and, without making it too obvious, I would make myself available to prospective clients.

Generally speaking, criminal work was looked down on by the profession, so there was no shortage of work. I found, however, that if an accused person did have access to substantial funds, lawyers would soon appear from the most conservative law firms.

Legal aid rates were so low that for lower court cases the money was hardly worth applying for. However, in the absence of credit cards, many of the so-called 'criminal fraternity' carried a roll of cash currency. Bookmakers, sly groggers and fraudsters usually came within this category.

Zelda and I also established a debt-collecting company, and I practised in a great variety of jurisdictions, including matrimonial, company formation, conveyancing and negligence claims. Soon my fledgling firm was to expand.

The Farmer Who Detested Scientology

I once acted for a shearer who had been cited as a co-respondent in a divorce case. The petitioner was a farmer who was not only seeking a divorce on the grounds of his wife's adultery, but was also seeking damages from the co-respondent. This case was heard at the Supreme Court at Auckland (now the High Court) before a judge and jury, about forty years ago.

In those days, it was open to the court to award the petitioner substantial damages to compensate him for the value of the wife that he had lost because of the adulterous conduct of the third party. Although there was no legal formula to assess the value of the wife lost, a series of headings were usually addressed by the petitioner's counsel. These would include such items as: 'She was a good housekeeper!', 'She was a good mother to the children', 'She was affectionate and lovable', 'She was good-looking and a woman that you would be proud to have on your arm when entering a social gathering', and 'She was well educated and a devotee of the arts'. The list could go on and on but generally it was laudatory of the woman who had deceived him.

In the case of the shearer, the farmer petitioner was represented by Michael Robinson, who was a celebrated divorce lawyer. Mick Robinson was a legend in his time and appeared frequently in all of Her Majesty's courts, showing not only brilliance as an advocate but also an amazing amount of energy.

I can remember going to see him on behalf of a client, visiting him at his office on the tenth floor of a city building at 2am. His clients were queued to see him in the corridor, with many sleeping on the floor. Because I was a lawyer, I received preferential treatment and was able to consult with him immediately. He sat behind a huge desk, puffing at a cigar, virtually hidden by the immense pile of files on his desk. He operated a finance company that granted immediate loans to his clients, which were then transferred to him as fees. His knowledge of the real estate market in Auckland was also without equal. He exuded vitality and warmth and was immensely likable.

At the divorce trial, however, his case rested solely on the evidence of a housemaid. She had allegedly entered a room at a city hotel, where she had seen the respondent and the third party (my client) in bed together. But under cross-examination, she expressed uncertainty as to the identification of the third party and she was unable to say, in particular, whether the man only had one arm.

The shearer for whom I acted had lost an arm in his younger days and was renowned in his circles for being able to hold his own with two-armed shearers and regularly sheared his standard quota of sheep. He was a handsome young man with a vibrant personality and was well liked in the community. The jury, reflecting the housemaid's uncertainty as to the identity of the alleged adulterer, failed to reach a verdict and the case concluded with the petitioner unable to obtain his divorce and the damages sought.

A new trial was ordered, but subsequently, prior to this new trial taking place, an arrangement was agreed upon whereby the divorce went through undefended and the shearer was relieved of any financial responsibility. Then, sometime after this, suddenly and sadly, Mick Robinson died. He was still a young man, probably in his early sixties, but he was overweight and addicted to his work. He died of a heart attack. Some months later again, the petitioner appeared at my office with an unusual request.

He was rather a taciturn and quietly spoken man, this farmer. If anything, he was slightly introverted. He was, however, a hardworking man and, I believe, completely honest. He said, 'I have come to see you because, as you know, Mick's dead.' I said to him that I did not think I could act for him because there could still be a conflict of interest. He replied that he had not come to see me for legal advice but had come to see me to take up a cause against Scientology.

'I believe that Scientology caused the rift in my marriage and I want to stop it from breaking up other families!' he said. He asked if he could tell me his story and whether I had time to listen.

'Sure!' I replied. But I told him I would be listening as a friend, not as a legal advisor, and he agreed.

He told me that, years ago, he was happily married but that he had reason to believe his wife had, behind his back, joined the Scientologists. And it was from that point that their marriage had begun to deteriorate.

'On one occasion I went into town and was involved in an accident where I broke my back. Following that, I had a long convalescence and during that time I sensed that my wife no longer loved me and I suspected that she was carrying on with a one-armed shearer, who worked occasionally on my farm,' he said.

The man broached the matter with his wife a few times but she became very angry. The next thing he knew, a couple of doctors arrived at his place and said that they had been directed by the court to examine him psychiatrically. When he told the doctors in answer to their questions that his wife was carrying on with a one-armed shearer, the doctors looked knowingly at each other and finally agreed that he was paranoid and suffering from delusions. As a result, he was committed into Oakley Hospital as a psychiatric patient.

'I found life at the hospital unbearable and all I wanted to do was to get out of the place,' the man remarked. He was also scared that he would be given electric shock treatment, having quickly discovered that such treatment was dispensed not only as a therapy but also as punishment for those who did not toe the line. The place was a real bedlam and at times he feared for his safety, due to the aggression of some of the patients, and indeed he could barely trust some of the staff.

After some months the man realised that the only way to get himself out was to tell the doctors that he had made a mistake about the one-armed shearer and his wife, and that he now knew that it was all nonsense. Finally, because the doctors thought the man was healed and that he had abandoned all allegations of adultery, he was released from Oakley Hospital.

'I did not go straight back to my farm but stayed in Auckland and consulted Mick Robinson about my situation. I was really impressed with Mick, who summed up the situation very quickly and hired a private investigator named Alan Brownlie,' the farmer explained. By chance, the man's wife and the one-armed shearer were staying in a city hotel and the investigator was able to obtain the evidence of which I was aware from the divorce case. 'But this is all history now,' the farmer said to me. 'I want you to stop these Scientologists from damaging other people's lives!'

I asked him what he proposed. He told me about a Royal Commission into Scientology that was presently going on in Melbourne, and he advised me that I should go there as an observer. He said that I should then form a committee in New Zealand with a view to convincing the New Zealand government to set up a commission of inquiry here. I had little time for Scientology myself, and I told the farmer that. One of their chiefs practised medicine in the same building in which my office was located, and I could not understand how the ethics of the medical profession could be consistently followed if one is a believer in all the rubbish that Scientology promoted.

The upshot of all this was that I did travel to Melbourne and sat in as an observer at the Commission, which had already heard a substantial amount of evidence by the time I got there. Some of the witnesses had stated that the Scientologists had taken money from people suffering from cancer under the pretext that they could be cured. This evidence had obviously been very damaging to the organisation. There was also a submission that the Scientologists were using a form of hypnotism to seduce new followers, and the Commission was very interested in whether there was any validity in that allegation.

I was told anecdotally that the Commission had approached a very eminent doctor in Sydney to give evidence in relation to hypnotism generally. This doctor was a world authority on hypnotism and had given relief to many patients suffering from psychosomatic illnesses. Hypnotism had also been used on many occasions to alleviate pain during operations. The doctor had, however, told the Commission that it was his policy not to give evidence in the courts and he graciously refused to be a witness. The anecdotal evidence I heard was that he had in fact been subpoenaed to give evidence at the Melbourne inquiry, and that he had attended the inquiry very reluctantly but still entered the witness box in a dignified and professional manner. From the witness box, this doctor supposedly turned to the three commissioners, who were seated on a bench adjacent, and had within a few minutes hypnotised all of them, placing them into trances. He told them that they would awake from their trances at 5pm and that he was now leaving them as he had given them a good example of the effectiveness of hypnotism. The doctor then returned to Sydney. I was told that the commissioners did indeed remain entranced and all duly awoke at 5pm.

In any event, the Commission in Melbourne found against the Scientologists and recommended laws abolishing Scientology in the state of Victoria. Back in Auckland, I formed a committee of anti-Scientologists, which included my friend Kevin Ryan QC and others. We collected evidence to show how families had been broken up by Scientology and prepared a petition to the New Zealand Parliament asking for a Royal Commission into Scientology in New Zealand, with a view to it being abolished.

Some weeks later, in 1969, we were allocated a date to appear before a parliamentary committee in Wellington to present our case. We were told that the Scientologists would be given an

THE FARMER WHO DETESTED SCIENTOLOGY

equal opportunity to be heard. On the day of the hearing, we went to the Beehive, New Zealand's house of parliament, and were directed to a room where the parliamentary committee would sit. We were told to be seated in a corridor outside and to await our names being called. It was a rather strange situation as we sat on one side of the corridor and the Scientologists sat opposite. Although there was no explicit animosity, the looks that were exchanged were far from friendly.

The parliamentary committee was chaired by the Honourable Whetu Tirikatene-Sullivan MP, and when I gave my evidence I had the distinct impression that she was favourably inclined towards us. Acting on the recommendations of the parliamentary committee, a commission of inquiry into Scientology was then established in Auckland. At the inquiry, the Scientologists were represented by the inimitable Frank Haigh, who was, as I have mentioned elsewhere, a well-known civil rights and union lawyer, and Robert Adams-Smith, who was then regarded as one of the up-and-coming barristers.

Their argument was that it would be an affront to democracy if Scientology were to be abolished. We called evidence from parents whose children had been turned against their family after becoming adherents of Scientology. Eventually, however, while the inquiry concluded with some heavy criticism of the practices of Scientology, it held the view that it should not be compulsorily abolished.

It is somewhat disappointing that, with all its weird beliefs and grotesque representations, Scientology is apparently still flourishing, particularly in America. Its late founder, L Ron Hubbard, reputedly left behind a $400 million fortune, yet his organisation has been given the status of a church, which relieves it of its taxation obligations.

Sometime later, the Scientologists brought out a newspaper which published the names of people who should be 'suppressed'. My name was top of the list. I considered suing them for defamation but because of the difficulties in serving documents and identifying the legal entity of the organisation, the idea was abandoned.

The newspaper article recited a list of untrue statements concerning myself, which brought home to me what a ruthless organisation Scientology is. The subsequent growth of this so-called 'church' reflects the gullibility of so many people who have been converts to Scientology.

My personal crusade against this pseudo-heretical movement is over, but my detestation remains.

The Fist Through the Judas Hole

At the time, I had an office in the old Lister Building in Victoria Street. This was in the 1960s when life was pretty exciting. We had the Vietnam War and its opposition. New Zealand was starting to distrust its mother country England.

My office was quite a small one, but we seemed to get through a fair amount of business. Jim McLay worked for me, and he later became Deputy Prime Minister. Mick Brown worked for me, too, and he later became a famous District Court judge. Later, Eb Leary worked for me, and he gave the office a bit of elegance and swank. Karen Soich was also employed, and she kept things very tidy and orderly.

Looking back, I reckon we were a great team, and we handled virtually every branch of the law. Jack Wiseman was our conveyancing guru. Jim McLay took the matrimonial work. His brilliance, which brought him to the top in politics as Deputy Prime Minister, was already evident. We acted for several unions and carried out their negligence cases against employers. We drafted wills, formed companies, and generally were like many small law firms that existed in Auckland in those days: a jack of all trades. We treated our clients like family members, and enjoyed a beer after work at the Central Hotel opposite. We were never short of clients, either. They flocked in, although many were not great payers. It was our practice in those days, too, to dictate documents while the client was in the office, so if he or she wanted a writ issued, it would be done there and then, and similarly with most other pieces of legal work. We were on the ball.

It was in this environment that an elderly man was ushered into my office one day. He was a rather frumpy individual, a bit overweight and weather-beaten. He brought with him a battered suitcase. I was always wary of clients with suitcases. It usually meant piles of well-fingered and soiled documents – a lawyer's nightmare. However, I greeted him cheerfully and courteously, and he told me he had been to several other lawyers, all of whom had refused to take his case. I had then been recommended to him by someone, virtually as a lawyer of last resort.

I turned on the desk tape recorder, and said, 'Well, tell me what it's all about.'

He looked at me with an almost timid expression, and said, 'Well, you might not believe it, but this is what has happened to me, and, Mr Williams, I want justice.' Then he began his story: 'You see, a couple of weeks ago, I was drinking in the local hotel. This was a pub that I had frequented for some time, and I knew the six o'clock procedure.'

'What do you mean by the six o'clock procedure?' I asked him.

'Well, you know,' he said, 'under our present law, hotels are not allowed to serve liquor after 6pm.'

I nodded. 'Yes, I know that.'

He said, 'Well, they give you a certain time to finish your jug of beer, and then you're supposed to leave.'

I said, 'Fair enough.'

Then he explained: 'Well, I knew that in this hotel, the clocks were fast. I knew they were deliberately set like that so that the hotel employees would have additional time to get the drinkers out of the pub. I was on my last jug and the police came in and told us to get out. I said it was only six o'clock, and we were allowed five minutes to finish our drink.

'The sergeant then said to me, "No, look at the clock. It's fifteen minutes past six – you've had your five minutes and more."

'So I said, "No, the clock's fast – it's actually only six o'clock. Give me another five minutes to finish my jug."

'The sergeant replied, "Unless you get out right away, I'm going to arrest you for drinking after hours."

'I said to the sergeant, "I'm going to finish my drink, and then I'll leave."

'Then the sergeant said, "You're under arrest."

'The next thing I knew I was seized by a couple of constables, dragged out of the pub, and thrown in the back of a paddy wagon. I was then driven, with a number of other drinkers, to the Auckland Central Police Station, where, after going through the routine of fingerprinting and other formalities, I was locked in a cell.

'After I had been there an hour or two, a police officer came in with a piece of paper. He said, "Look, buddy, we don't want to hold you all night. Sign this, and you can leave. If you sign it, the case will be called in the morning at the Magistrates Court, but you won't need to attend. You'll be fined five pounds and costs in your absence. There's enough money in your property here at the police station to cover that. So sign this paper here, and bugger off. I hope we don't see you again."

'I read the paper. It was very brief, and stated that I admitted to drinking after hours, and that I authorised the police to pay any fine from the money held on my behalf at the police station.

'I looked at the police officer and said, "I'm not signing this."

'The officer said, "What's wrong with you? Don't you want to go home? You want to stay here all bloody night?"

'I said, "I'm not signing it because I'm not guilty. I bought my drink before six o'clock, and I'm allowed reasonable time to finish it. The clocks in the hotel were fast. I know that."

'The policemen got quite angry with me, and started to call me names. They virtually pushed me back into the cell, and said, "You can bloody well stay there all night then, you stupid arsehole."

'I want to tell you, Mr Williams,' he then said to me, 'that I am an obstinate man, but I am also an honest person, and I knew I was right.'

He continued his story: 'So I took off my boots, and lay down on the bunk, which smelt of urine and vomit.

'During the night, sleep was impossible. The police brought in various people, usually intoxicated. There was much shouting and screaming, but I was determined not to give in, and lay wide awake, waiting for the morning.

'Around about 2am, I heard shrieking and yelling, which was far worse than anything I'd heard during the night. I went to the door of my cell and looked through the Judas hole.

'I could see a small man, lying on the floor, being kicked and beaten by three or four police officers.

THE FIST THROUGH THE JUDAS HOLE

'I yelled out, "Stop that! Don't hit that man! You've got no right to beat that man!"

'One of the police officers turned around and yelled at me, "Shut up, you old bastard! It's got nothing to do with you!"

'They continued to beat the small fellow, who was screaming with pain, and I yelled out again, "Stop it! Or I'll report you in the morning!"

'One of the police officers came over to my cell. He looked at me through the Judas hole. He said, "It looks as if you need a bit of treatment yourself." And the next thing I knew, his big fist came through the Judas hole, and bashed me in the middle of my face. I fell back with the force of the blow, and crashed to the floor of my cell. My teeth were broken, and so was my nose. Blood flowed out from my face, pouring down all over my clothing. I was unconscious for a while, dazed and disorientated, but eventually I managed to crawl back to my bunk and stayed there till morning.

'Next morning, I washed myself as well as I could in the basin, and was transported by a paddy wagon to the Magistrates Court at Kitchener Street. I was held in a holding cell until my case was called, and then taken to the dock where I stood before the magistrate. The registrar of the court read out my charge. I turned to the magistrate, who seemed to be quite a bad-tempered little fellow, and said, "Before I answer the charge, I want to tell you what happened last night. I'm still covered in blood. I was assaulted in the cells."

'The magistrate did not seem even slightly interested in what I had to say. In a bored manner, he drawled, "Just get on with it – answer the charge."

'I said, "I'm not guilty, of course."

'"Well," said the magistrate, "I'm giving you bail, and you can appear here next week when the charge will be heard. Mr Registrar, call the next case."

'I signed some bail documents at the court office, and then made my way home. I felt physically and mentally sick.

'I rang my family lawyer and told him what had happened. He said that it wasn't worth making a fuss about, and that I would never win against those people – I should just plead guilty, and accept the fine.

'After phoning my lawyer, I thought for a while and said to myself, "If they get away with it, they'll do the same to someone else, and I'm buggered if I'm going to let them off the hook."

'So, as I told you, I went to see a couple of other lawyers and nobody seems to be interested in the case. I have all the exhibits here in my suitcase, though, including my bloodstained clothing, my broken dental plate, and a report from my local doctor that my nose was broken. I've got it all here.

'I haven't got much money, but I'm prepared to pay you if you take the case. It's a matter of principle with me now – I'm not going to let it go.'

I said to the man when he'd finished his story, 'Well, the first thing you'd have to do is to successfully defend the present case against your drinking after hours. The law is quite plain that you can't sue for malicious prosecution unless you've been found not guilty on the actual prosecution, so before you think about compensation and damages, we would have to defend the present charge against you. And if we fail, that would be the end of the matter.'

He just looked at me, a bit like an old owl. I felt genuinely sorry for him, and I knew in my heart that he was right, and that he had been badly treated by the police, and indeed by the magistrate, who had dealt with him so abruptly.

So I assured him: 'Yes, we'll fight the case.'

The following week, I appeared for him, to defend the charge of drinking after hours.

We subpoenaed the proprietor of the hotel, and he admitted that his clocks were fast. He said that he deliberately did this as it was sometimes difficult to get rid of patrons who didn't want to leave the hotel promptly. The police, in their evidence, denied any violence, and said that the defendant was intoxicated and he could not be believed. However, this time we had a different magistrate, who seemed to be very fair and judicial.

At the end of the case, the magistrate said, 'I've got a reasonable doubt about this charge, and I find you not guilty.'

My client and I walked back to my office, which was close to the courthouse. When we got there, he said to me, 'Thank you, Mr Williams, for that. But I haven't finished with these people yet. I want you to sue them for damages.'

In those days we had to give written notice when suing a government department under the Crown Proceedings Act, so while my client was still there with me at the office, I dictated into my tape recorder an official notice, giving the police department one month to settle.

The letter from the Attorney-General, in reply, denied all liability.

At the end of the month, the old man again appeared at my office, and I dictated a writ claiming damages for assault and malicious prosecution.

In due course, we received a statement of defence denying all allegations.

We chose trial by jury, and eventually the case was set down for hearing at the then Supreme Court in Auckland.

The Crown Prosecutor, Graham Speight, appeared for the police department, and a judge and jury were assembled. Graham Speight was known as a brilliant advocate and was very confident that we would lose our claim.

Halfway through the case, Mr Speight made an application in chambers for the jury to inspect the police cell where the plaintiff had been held. In support of this application, Mr Speight said that he had information the case was a fabrication. He was instructed that the door to the cell does have a Judas hole, but it is far too small to enable a man to be punched through it. He submitted that the case could be shortened by the jury inspecting, for themselves, the cell door.

The judge granted the application, and the jury were taken to the Auckland Central Police Station at Princes Street to take a view of the cell door where the assault had allegedly occurred.

The judge also attended the view, and so did Mr Speight, myself and my client.

We stood apart from the jury, who entered into their task with great enthusiasm, and even merriment. Mr Speight's information had been totally incorrect. The Judas hole was well large enough to allow a fist to pass through it, and indeed the jury were taking turns at pushing their fists through the Judas hole, mimicking the allegation.

The rest of the trial was a formality. The jury retired, and returned with substantial damages in favour of the old man. Justice had been done.

The Boy Who was Tortured

As a young lawyer who frequently visited clients at Mount Eden Prison, I formed a friendship with a welfare officer named Graham. He was an interesting character. At about six feet, four inches tall, he had recently migrated from England where, he told me, he had been involved in an incident where a person had been killed. He was never charged with any offence but decided to start a new life in New Zealand.

The first job he had in New Zealand was as a herd tester. This entailed driving around the farms and ensuring that they complied with the health regulations. In those days tuberculosis was quite common in New Zealand and some doctors thought that our milk might be contaminated with this disease. Finally, though, he became a welfare officer at Mount Eden Prison.

He was popular with the inmates there, taking an active interest in their problems, and one day I received a telephone call from him asking me to come to the prison to speak to a young inmate whom we shall call Joseph.

'There are some unusual features about this case,' Graham said. 'Joseph is a very shy boy and there is something not quite right about the manner of his arrest – I think his case might require some careful investigation.'

Next day, I drove out there. This was the old Mount Eden Prison, built like a medieval castle, and as I climbed the spiral staircase leading up to the visiting room, I couldn't help but notice what an appalling place it was. Mount Eden Prison was built in 1856 by prison labour and had a bloody history of many floggings and hangings.

I waited while Joseph was brought out of the main prison to the interview room. This room was mostly comprised of a large area with tables and chairs where prisoners could meet with their family members; small children ran around noisily, while mothers sat at tables opposite their partners holding hands and conversing in a whisper.

Wardens were walking around trying to be inconspicuous and making sure that no contraband was being transferred. There was, however, much more freedom in prison in those days, and I believe most of the wardens were quite sympathetic to the sad and awkward attempts by the inmates and their visitors to, at times, express their intimate feelings for each other.

Later, I would visit several prisons in Holland with the cooperation of the Dutch government and was shown family visiting rooms where people could be accorded privacy and even stay overnight. Imagine the shrieks of disapproval from Sensible Sentencing, the right wing anti-prisoner organisation in New Zealand, if family rooms were suggested for New Zealand jails.

Anyway, when Joseph arrived, we both climbed some steps off the main visiting area that took us up to some small, partitioned interview rooms.

Joseph immediately impressed me as inordinately shy, and as the interview progressed, it soon became patent that for some years he had been treated virtually as a slave on a large farm in the back country of Rotorua. Joseph was an orphan who had spent his early life in various institutions, and when he became old enough to work he had been placed under the Maori welfare scheme as a worker on this farm. He was paid a pittance, accommodated in a rough shack well away from the farmhouse, and generally treated as a person of very low status. The farm was owned by a wealthy Maori family who were highly regarded in the district.

Slowly, I managed to earn Joseph's confidence, and in a somewhat reluctant manner this is the story he told me. On the night that this young man's present troubles began, his employer, the farmer, had gone out on a nocturnal fishing expedition. Maybe he went to catch eels or some other fish in the nearby lakes, some of which were controlled by the Maori tribes. The farmer's wife, meanwhile, was left alone in the farmhouse and no doubt she was busy attending to chores. While the farmer was still out fishing the boy knocked on the door of the farmhouse and asked the farmer's wife for a pillow. She apparently found this request somewhat cheeky but supplied him with the pillow, and then he went back to his room in the hut.

When the farmer returned from his fishing expedition in the early hours of the morning, his wife told him about the boy knocking on the door and requesting the pillow.

Whether the farmer had been drinking during the fishing expedition is not clear, but what is plain is that he became enraged by what he termed the arrogance of Joseph in approaching his wife during his absence. The farmer concluded, quite illogically, that the boy had intended to rape his wife and therefore deserved punishment.

The farmer went outside and dragged Joseph out of his room and into the farmhouse.

He then angrily interrogated Joseph, demanding that he admit that he had attempted to rape the farmer's wife.

The more the farmer yelled and shouted, the less Joseph said in reply, merely denying the allegations. The farmer became incensed by Joseph's irresponsiveness, and his range of allegations now included a litany of sexual misbehaviour, including indecency with animals and a history of all manner of sexual perversions. The farmer's wife was present during this inquisition and cooperated with her husband throughout. They stripped Joseph of his clothing and, after tying him up, applied a heated soldering iron to his private parts, including both his posterior and genital region.

Joseph, yelling and screaming, tried to avoid being burnt, but was extensively injured with the hot soldering iron. When Joseph could bear the pain no longer, he 'confessed' to all these crimes that he had not committed. The farmer and his wife were still not satisfied. Joseph was ordered to dress himself and the local police officer was summoned – a police officer the farmer happened to know on a personal basis.

In a remarkable sequence that is hard to understand, the local police officer came out to the residence and, in the presence of the farmer and his wife, took a written statement from Joseph. In the statement, Joseph allegedly admitted that he had intended to rape the farmer's wife. The local police then charged Joseph with attempted rape, bail was denied, and he was eventually sent to Mount Eden Prison on remand awaiting his trial.

I was absolutely furious at what I had heard. In the next day or two I arranged for a photographer to go to the prison with a doctor so that the scars could be photographed and the doctor could prepare a medical report. The doctor whose services I had obtained was Morris Johnson, whom I knew personally. In due course, the photographs and medical report proved conclusively that Joseph had been tortured.

Joseph's trial for attempted rape was held at the Supreme Court in Hamilton before judge and jury.

Both the farmer and his wife gave evidence and said that Joseph's injuries were self-inflicted. For the defence, the photographer and Dr Johnson gave evidence, the latter quite adamant that the injuries could not have been self-inflicted.

The jury brought back quite a remarkable verdict. They decided that not only was Joseph not guilty on all charges, but that in a rider to the verdict, the jury held that the farmer and his wife should be charged criminally for wounding and torturing Joseph.

Soon after the trial, I issued civil proceedings for damages against the farmer and his wife on the basis that they had committed a civil wrong in torturing Joseph.

As a result of the jury's rider, the police were then compelled to bring criminal charges against the farmer and his wife. They were defended by a Wellington lawyer, Roy Stacey, and his defence was not only that the boy had self-inflicted his wounds, but that I had helped him invent his defence so that damages could be obtained in the civil suit.

The trial of the farmer and his wife was also held at the Hamilton Supreme Court, presided over by Justice Clifford Perry and a jury of twelve members. The main witness against the farmer and his wife was Joseph and he was vigorously cross-examined by Mr Stacey. During this long and exhaustive cross-examination, the boy became confused and wrongly agreed that his lawyer may have helped with his evidence.

At the conclusion of the criminal case, the farmer and his wife were convicted by the jury but were sentenced to remarkably lenient sentences by Justice Perry. I was not present during the couple's trial.

Then, a few days after the farmer and his wife had been convicted, I was in my office in Auckland when suddenly a posse of police officers arrived and demanded to search my office for Joseph's file.

I took legal advice from Stuart Ennor, a senior lawyer who acted for the Law Society, who told me that my future as a lawyer was at stake. Mr Ennor and I approached Dr Johnson, the doctor who had examined Joseph's injuries at the prison, and he said he was in a strong position to help me because he had been with me at the Hamilton Supreme Court when I last interviewed Joseph in the cells, before he gave evidence. The doctor was adamant in his affidavit that I had emphatically told Joseph to tell the truth and nothing but the truth.

A copy of Dr Johnson's affidavit was sent to the Solicitor-General, who eventually made a pronouncement that he was not prepared to give his consent to a charge of procuring perjury.

I continued then with the civil action against the farmer and his wife, and eventually the lawsuit was settled, with Joseph being paid a large sum of money. I believe that Joseph later used this money to obtain a home for himself and a newly acquired wife.

And so in the end justice was achieved in more ways than one.

The Schoolgirl Who Lied to the Court

Early in my career, an old friend of mine, Roger McLaren, rang me one day and said, 'Peter, are you interested in defending a chap on a rape charge?'

I was a little surprised at the query. 'Well, Roger,' I replied, 'there must be something odd about it if you're not defending him yourself.'

'Quite frankly,' he said, 'I don't seem to be able to communicate with the man – he's a difficult fellow. And the case against him is pretty overwhelming.'

I asked him what the evidence was.

First, there was the girl herself. She was a schoolgirl, and the police believed her story was convincing. She had come home from playing hockey one afternoon in a dreadful mess, with mud and leaves all over her. Asked by her mother for an explanation, she said the accused had been on the same bus as her and had got off when she did.

'She said that he followed her,' Roger told me, 'and when they were passing by the trees in a small park, had grabbed her, pulling her under the trees, and raped her.'

I asked if there were any forensics.

'Yes, they found her hair on his clothing. But there's a bit more to it than that. The girl pointed him out in an identification parade, and the chap lied about being on the bus. There's independent evidence from the bus driver that he was on the bus. I believe he should plead guilty, otherwise he'll get a long stretch. He keeps on telling me he's innocent. He admits he lied about not being on the bus, but I can't get an explanation from him for that.'

I told Roger I'd have a preliminary interview with his client, to see if I'd fare any better with him.

A few days later, the fellow, whom we shall call Bruce, was in my office, and he was very tense. He said, quite angrily, 'No one believes me, but I can tell you now, I did not rape that girl. In fact, I have no memory of ever having seen her.'

There was something about him that impressed me, and I agreed to take the case.

The trial took place in an upstairs courtroom at the Auckland Supreme Court. The presiding judge was Justice Terrence Gresson, for whom I had the utmost respect. We had an all-male jury, and they gave me that enigmatic but undeniable impression that unless the defence came up with something pretty drastic, a verdict of guilty was a foregone conclusion.

The girl's parents sat in a prominent position in the courtroom, and the mother rose to give evidence first. In a hostile and emotional manner, she told how her daughter had returned home, muddied and with her clothes covered in leaves and debris. She said her daughter was very distressed, and when asked for an explanation, said she had been raped in the park by a man off the bus. The mother said she then rang the police immediately, and luckily they were able to trace the man. Before she could be stopped, she said, 'And there's the fellow over there, the rotten bastard,' pointing to Bruce in the dock.

We had a few things up our sleeve. The hair from Bruce's clothing had been independently analysed and found to be artificial hair, which could not possibly have come from the complainant. It obviously had come from some other woman he had had contact with. Furthermore, Bruce had admitted to me that he had lied about not having been on the bus only because he didn't want his present wife to know that he had been in the area where his previous wife lived. He told me there was great jealousy between his present and previous wives.

As the trial unfolded, the girl gave her evidence well. She wore her school clothes, and looked even younger than her actual age of fourteen. She described the event dramatically, and told how she had picked out Bruce at an identification parade, and that she was absolutely certain he was the assailant.

Her clothes were produced, and there was no doubt that they were muddied and soiled. An expert from the Crown gave evidence that the debris on the clothes was consistent with that coming from the park.

I could feel the case slipping away from me, and some of my cross-examination became repetitive. At the 5pm adjournment, I had not completed my cross-examination, and was ready to resume at 10am the next morning. The judge, however, called the prosecutor and myself into his chambers after the jury had left.

Justice Gresson was renowned for his courtesy, even temperament and great judicial bearing, and as I sat down with the registrar and the prosecutor, from behind his desk the judge said to me, with a smile, 'Peter, you're not getting anywhere with this witness. I think there's even a danger that you're overdoing it, and it could well be that you are annoying the jury.' The prosecutor did not comment, but it was plain from his demeanour that he agreed.

When the case resumed in the open court, I really felt quite desperate. I believed the girl was lying, but also that no one in the courtroom agreed with me, except my client in the dock. I felt a rush of blood to the head but knew I had to continue if we were to get a breakthrough. The atmosphere in the courtroom had become quite tense, and when I resumed the cross-examination, the jurors would not look at me.

Then suddenly, without provocation or any obvious reason, the girl began to cry. I knew now that any residual sympathy the defence might have enjoyed was lost forever. Justice Gresson, in his kindness, said to her, 'Would you like an adjournment? We all understand the strain you're under, and there's no hurry. Would you like half an hour to settle yourself?'

But, between sobs, she called out, 'No! I can't stand it anymore. I've got to tell the truth. He's not the man at all. I did see him on the bus, but he never raped me!'

The mood in the courtroom reached fever pitch. Justice Gresson took over the cross-examination. He said, very gently and quietly to her, 'Well, tell us what really happened.'

And so she explained: 'Well, after I got off the bus, I met my boyfriend. He knew that I was coming home at that time, and he met me near the park. We both went into the park together, and he started to kiss me. After a while, we both lay down on the ground and, really, things got out of control. I don't want to talk about it anymore, but when I got home, my mother was so angry to see the state of my clothes that I had to make up a story. I remembered the man on the bus, and I described him to the police. I never thought they would find him, but they did, and he was in the identification parade. I got deeper and deeper into this. Everybody was so kind to me, including my parents and the police. I just felt I couldn't go back on the lies I had told. I can't keep going. The strain is just too much.'

She pointed to the accused. 'I know that man over there is completely innocent.'

I sank back in my chair at the bar table. I could not believe my ears. The judge directed an acquittal and Bruce walked free.

Looking back at this case, I must now compliment the girl on her great courage in making her important retraction, albeit belated.

Natural Justice at Te Awamutu

When I was a young lawyer, I was prepared to take on virtually any case, provided it had some merits and the possibility of payment. That's the great thing about being a young lawyer – with energy and enterprise one can tackle a huge variety of cases. The older, successful lawyer will probably be pinned down to a certain extent in the allocation of his or her energy and skills. He or she will probably have built up a reputation in some field of law, and people wanting services in that area will more than adequately supply the advocate with briefs. This sort of specialisation, although it has the advantages of making the lawyer more knowledgeable and skilled in that area of law, does also have the drawback, from the lawyer's point of view, that he or she may miss out on the broad experience of helping people, including the impoverished.

They were the good old days; days of personal freedom, with the profession of law providing a great adventure. I was robust and healthy, and eagerly explored every new case. Every day I would look forward to some new experience, some new challenge, some way of helping the underdog, and the possibility of making a few dollars.

In those days I drove a yellow six-cylinder Zephyr, of which I was very fond. Thanks to Henry Ford, I enjoyed great mobility. There was nowhere in the North Island that I wouldn't go for a court case. I enjoyed the travel and meeting new people as much as the work itself.

One morning, I received a telephone call from a Salvation Army officer. This was not out of the ordinary, as we often had instructions to act for underprivileged people who were receiving help from the 'Sallies'. This usually involved some person who had fallen through the cracks of society and needed urgent support.

The law has never been very good at assisting people at the bottom of the heap: those with alcohol, drug or money problems. In fact, in many cases, the courts are not really accessible to people with no money or status, unless they are charged with criminal offences. Justice, to them, is just a dream that they may read about in some novel.

Anyway, in this instance, the Salvation Army officer at the other end of the telephone said to me, 'We have a woman staying here, and she has four young children, most of them under the age of five, and they are entirely destitute. They have nothing. No clothes, no toys, no blankets. Nothing. And the husband is in Mount Eden Prison.'

It sounded like a very sad case, and I asked him why she was in such a bad way.

'Well, the husband was a labourer,' he told me, 'working on a dairy farm in Te Awamutu. Some weeks ago he was arrested by the police and taken to Mount Eden Prison, where he is still locked up. When he was arrested, he and his wife and children were living in a farm worker's cottage on the property, but now the farmer is saying his former worker owes him money for rent, which of course he can't pay because he's in prison, and so the farmer is refusing the wife access to the shack – he won't even allow her to take out her few possessions, even the blankets and clothing for the children.'

I said he sounded like a mean bugger.

The Sallies officer laughed and asked me, 'Have you had much to do with Te Awamutu farmers?'

I chuckled. 'I have had a bit to do with farmers. I was brought up in the Manawatu and I know how tight-arsed some of them are.'

'Well, this fellow is real mean,' the Sallies officer said. 'He claims he has a lien over her clothing for unpaid rent, and he won't budge.'

A short time later, the woman concerned came to my office. She impressed me as an honest, stable sort of person: hardworking, caring for her children, and worried about her husband. I wrote a letter on her behalf to the farmer, claiming the woman's chattels.

I soon received a blistering reply from the farmer's lawyer in return, stating that the farmer had a lien over the chattels in question, and unless the arrears of rent were paid they would be sold, and the proceeds set off against the debt.

After reading the letter, I was shaking with anger. I wondered how low human nature could get. What explains such a pathetic lack of humanity? I immediately issued proceedings in the local Magistrates Court in Te Awamutu for the return of the woman's possessions.

Eventually, the court notified a date for a special fixture, so I drove down to Te Awamutu on the morning of the hearing. I took the claimant with me, expecting she would give evidence.

At the courthouse, my client sat in the back with a couple of her children, and I sat at the bar, waiting for the case to be heard. I waited and waited, but the case was never called. The few local lawyers there eyed me with curiosity, and I suspected the registrar had a wry grin on his face when he looked in my direction.

At one o'clock, the court was adjourned, and our case had still not been called. I went up to the registrar and asked him what had happened to the case, only to have him tell me it had been adjourned earlier.

'How could it have been adjourned earlier?' I asked him. 'I've been here all morning, since ten. As you know, I've been sitting in front of you.'

'Well, you'll have to take that up with the judge,' he replied nonchalantly. 'Nothing to do with me. As far as I'm concerned, it's adjourned. You'd better apply for another fixture.'

I left the courthouse extremely annoyed. I knew there had been a little conspiracy behind my back, and the local lawyers, in my imagination at least, were tittering among themselves at my discomfort.

I returned to the courthouse early from lunch and went into the court office. The court itself had not formally begun, but there were several members of the court staff eating their lunch in the office. Some of them looked up at me in surprise, and one said, 'Oh, the court's not open yet.'

'Well, I'm very irate,' I said. 'I had a special fixture today. I've come all the way from Auckland, bringing my witness with me. I'm now told that the case has been adjourned behind my back. What right,' I then asked, 'has anyone got to adjourn a special fixture without at least notifying the other party? I want to see the judge, in his chambers, and I want to see him now.'

The little fellow I was talking to looked at me slightly nervously, and replied, 'I am the judge.'

Only then did I realise that he was, in fact, the judge who had been presiding over the court. He looked very different off the bench, though.

'Yes,' he said, 'and you'd better be careful, young fellow, about what you have to say. If you get too insolent, I'll make a complaint about you to the Law Society.'

I could see immediately I was getting nowhere and that I was, in fact, on dangerous ground. It was clear the case would not be heard that day, and that I would need to apply for a further fixture.

I left the courthouse, with the woman and her children trailing behind me. We all climbed into my Zephyr, where she looked at me despairingly and asked, 'What now?'

I asked her where the farm she'd been living on was. She told me that it was only a few miles away.

'Let's go then. We're going to your farm cottage.'

She was a little hesitant. 'You're not going to get us into trouble are you, Mr Williams?'

'You just do what I say,' I replied stiffly. 'We'll get that stuff of yours back. Now let's go.'

So we drove to the farm, through the front gate, down the track, past the main farmhouse, and she directed me to the cottage. It turned out to be a small, poorly maintained shack. I parked the Zephyr and told her to go inside, get her gear, and put it in the boot.

'Are you sure that's all right?' she asked.

'Of course it's all right. You own these things. They have no legal lien over them. Hurry up before someone arrives.'

She pushed on the door and luckily it opened. Within a matter of minutes, she was loading up the car boot with piles of clothing, blankets, toys and miscellaneous household items. Before she had finished, however, a loud, angry voice began yelling. It was the farmer's wife, a gaunt, hard-looking woman, grey with anger.

'What are you doing here?' she screamed. 'You're trespassing! You've got no right to be stealing this stuff! I've already rung up my husband, and he'll be here very soon. I've also rung my lawyer. He's said you're in real trouble. Now you return all that stuff! Otherwise I'll call the police as well.'

'Lady,' I said to her, 'what you are doing is so mean and so pathetic that I can hardly believe that people could be so low. This clothing belongs to this woman and her children, she's entitled to it, and she's going to get it. I take full responsibility for her actions here, and she's taking her own property under my advice. There is no such thing as a lien over clothing for alleged unpaid rent. What you and your husband are doing is not only inhumane, it is quite illegal. You're the one who's trespassing, not this poor woman.'

The wife began to shout abuse at me, yelling that my client's husband was a jailbird and that he wasn't any good, and repeating that she would get the police.

'You go ahead and ring the police – they have no grounds to act anyway,' I told her.

She eventually went away, still yelling, though: 'I'll get the police! I'll get the police!'

I asked my client if she'd collected everything, and she had, so we drove off. When we reached the Salvation Army hostel in Auckland, she unloaded all her belongings, and finally said to me, 'Peter, I'm eternally grateful for your assistance, but I hope I haven't got you into any trouble.'

'I am not the slightest bit concerned,' I assured her. 'I'm just happy that you've got all your property back, and that your children have their toys and bedding.'

And that was that. I never heard another word from the court, the farmer, the farmer's wife, the country lawyers, or the local police. I've always thought this was a prime example of natural justice – though some of the law professors might disagree.

A Chance Encounter

As I've mentioned, my first office as a sole practitioner was in the Commercial Union building on Chancery Street, near the Kitchener Street courthouse, in Auckland. Opposite me was a bespoke tailor, who carried out his work seated in the lotus position on a large oak table. He loved to talk, and frequently took a break so he could nip across the road to DeBrett's Hotel for a stiff whisky. He was also an excellent musician, and played the double bass in the National Orchestra – I often heard him practising. He and I were great mates.

Upstairs on the fourth floor of my building, two elderly practitioners had their office. They were very much 'old school', and drafted their documents in copybook longhand. They both worked standing up, facing a raised table, which was the practice in earlier times. They specialised in Maori land work, and I gained the impression that this was difficult and slow. I loved visiting them and being regaled with stories of the old days.

Maori land work included transferring tribal land to purchasers. All the members had to agree, and the consent of the Maori Land Court had to be obtained. It was a long and tedious process.

THE DWARF WHO MOVED

My practice, at that stage, was mainly in the Magistrates Court, where I acted for a great variety of people, mostly on charges that would be regarded today as quite petty. The great – some would say the greatest – American lawyer, Clarence Darrow, once described the miscreants who appeared in the lower courts of America as follows:

> *From the beginning, a procession of the poor, the weak, the unfit have gone through our jails and prisons and to their deaths. They have been victims. Crime and poverty and ignorance have gone hand-in-hand. When our law-makers realise this, they will stop legislating more punishment and go after causes.*

I, by no means, would classify myself as a Clarence Darrow, but similarly, I found most of the people who appeared in the Magistrates Court (in those days, at least) had a background in poverty, illness, mental disability, sorrow, helplessness and an inability to cope generally with life.

In those days, drunkenness in public places was a criminal offence, and each day a drove of mainly elderly alcoholics appeared singularly in the dock, after having spent a night in the cells. These people had been dredged up by the police from under bridges and from public parks, and other places known to the police. They would be solemnly lectured by the presiding magistrate on their obvious deficiencies. Some of these people had literally vomited up their liver during the night, many drank methylated spirits, and most of these desperately ill men could in no way understand what they were being lectured about so pompously by the erudite magistrates. They all needed help and kindness – some indeed did receive that at the Salvation Army hostel on Rotoroa Island in the Hauraki Gulf – but most were reduced further into their depressive worlds by the police and court intervention.

Attempted suicide was then also a crime. From time to time, often a young adolescent would appear in the dock, still bearing the lacerations around his or her throat resulting from an abortive attempt to die by hanging. Again, these desolate young men and women, crying out for help, would receive a firm lecture about the sanctity of life and the evils of self-destruction. Some magistrates would even add to their soliloquies quotations from the Bible. I knew somehow, in my gut, that all this was so wrong, and that to bring these people into the glare of publicity and the court process was negative and non-rehabilitative.

Abortion was a criminal offence then, too. I remember one case in particular, where a young woman had attempted to abort the child herself, and developed septicaemia. The hospital reported her case to the police and, when she was well enough, she was brought before the court and sentenced to imprisonment. I could hardly suppress my anger at this harsh and merciless treatment.

There are so many stories that could be told about the ordinary lives and sad circumstances I found in the courts – the bookmakers, the shoplifters and many that were, in fact, falsely accused. I soon found this work completely absorbing.

But the story I would like to tell here involves a rather odd encounter that almost tempted me to change the course of my professional life. I was tempted to deal in stock and shares, and to mix with the moneyed class of society. Back in the day, those offices at the Commercial Union building, at least on the third floor where I had my office, were each equipped with a large, walk-in safe. We didn't have credit cards then, and most transactions involved either cash or cheques. These valuables would be placed in a cash box, which each night would be taken, usually by myself, to the large walk-in safe at the end of the corridor. They were a handy place for keeping old files and other records, too, and there were at least half a dozen of these large safes on each floor.

On this evening, around about six o'clock, I had finished for the day. My last client had left the office, and I was packing up, getting ready to go home. My then wife Zelda, who was in those days also my secretary and typist, was tidying up and putting the cover over our typewriter.

We didn't have much furniture in the office. When I first rented it, I borrowed £30 from the bank, which my schoolmaster father had to guarantee, and purchased the bare essentials, including a typewriter from the City Mission. I was given a second-hand desk by my friend Julian Firth, who was then a city councillor.

My income from the law was pitiably low, but because I had never enjoyed a high income previously, I was young, healthy and happy. Each morning before work I ran around the Auckland Domain twice, and was fit as a proverbial rabbit.

After clearing away a few last odds and ends into the various trays on my desk, I took the small cash box and walked down the corridor, with the key in my hand, to open the large walk-in safe. These safes could not be opened or shut from the inside, and I often thought how gloomy it would be to be locked in one for the night. This night, as I went to the safe, which I thought was mine, I noticed that the door was slightly ajar and unlocked. What I didn't realise was that this was not my safe at all, but belonged to the stockbroker in the office next door.

I gave the door a push, and it slowly swung open. What I saw gave me an immense surprise: there, on the floor of the safe, was the stockbroker's assistant, an elderly gentleman, and highly regarded, with his pants down, involved in lovemaking with his elderly secretary.

They both sat up, pulling at their clothes furiously; I think they got just as much of a shock as I did. I immediately closed the door. I did not even stay to deposit my cash box, which probably didn't have much in it at any rate, and hurriedly went back to my office.

I laughed to myself about the incident, and really didn't think much about it after the initial surprise had worn off.

The next morning, however, much to my astonishment, the stockbroker's assistant appeared at my office. He was, as usual, impeccably dressed, and his expression was deadpan. No reference was made to the incident at the walk-in safe, and he addressed me courteously, and with a certain element of seriousness. I believe he had given considerable thought to what he was about to say.

'Have you ever invested on the stock exchange?' he asked me.

'No, no, not at all,' I replied. 'Quite frankly, I don't have any spare capital.' And I didn't, although, on the other hand, I wasn't short of cash, and I had no debts, either.

The stockbroker's assistant went on: 'Peter, to be quite frank with you, there is good money to be made on the stock exchange, if you know what you're doing.' And he explained: 'We have what is known as "first issues" – that's when private companies become public companies and place their shares on the stock exchange at par. They almost invariably immediately increase in price, and the shares can be immediately resold at a considerable profit. But you've got to know what you're doing.'

'I find that very interesting,' I told him, 'but I must reiterate, I have no spare capital.'

He looked at me again with a solemn expression, and said, 'Peter, you don't need any capital. I can apply for the shares for you, and sell them immediately, and send you the cheque for the profit. These shares in selected companies are hard to get. In fact, they're rationed, and it's only a carefully chosen few in the city who are able to get them. I would like to see you get involved in the share market. You'll have to, of course, join the Northern Club, and perhaps even the Auckland Racing Club. Membership of those organisations would certainly help.'

'Well, that's very kind of you,' I said. 'I'll think about it.'

'In the meantime,' he continued, 'I'm going to get you an allocation of Allen's Printing Company's shares. This is a blue-chip company that's just become public. I guarantee I'll get you a good profit – and you won't even have to touch your pocket.'

'Well, I can't see any objection to that,' I told him.

In due course, I did receive the cheque. I considered the advantages of joining the Northern Club and the Auckland Racing Club, becoming an active investor on the Auckland Stock Exchange with access to inside information, and that afternoon, I went upstairs to discuss this possible new venture with the two old lawyers on the fourth floor.

They made me a cup of tea, as they had no secretary. We sat down, and I told them the whole story. And indeed showed them the cheque.

What the old fellows then said to me was something like this: 'Peter, you've got to make a choice. If you start investing on the stock exchange, and get involved in business generally, you might as well give up being a criminal lawyer. Your pattern of life will be totally different. You will spend your evenings at the Northern Club, discussing the pros and cons of share investment. You will receive large quantities of mail from the various public companies, including brochures, prospectuses and balance sheets, and you will soon be inundated with documentation.

'On the other hand,' they said, 'being a criminal lawyer has its drawbacks, too. You will come across some very tricky clients. Some members of the public, no doubt inspired by friends in the police, will say that there isn't much difference between criminals and criminal lawyers. Very few prominent criminal lawyers ever become judges, if that's what you want to be.'

I told them that there was no doubt that there were some judges I highly respected, and that I realised the advantages of being a member of the judiciary – they had security, status, respect and, with a bit of luck, a knighthood at the end of their term. Not many criminal lawyers had those advantages. However, by that time, I'd seen enough criminal trials to be sure that some of the people I respected most were counsel for the defence.

'Furthermore,' I admitted to the old lawyers, 'I am somewhat obsessed with the psychology of human nature, with such concepts as rehabilitation and the improvement of penal conditions and the judicial process. I suppose you could call me an idealist.'

Both the old lawyers laughed – not scornfully, though, but in a respectful manner. They said to me, 'It's a hard world out there, Peter. You'll take plenty of knocks, and your views may well substantially change with the passage of time. But in the meantime, God bless you. Keep your idealism. Continue what you're doing, acting for the rogues and vagabonds. Forget about judgeships and making money on the stock exchange. Be true unto yourself, and be what you are. And we both wish you all the best.'

I finished my cup of tea and walked slowly back to my office. I never bought a share again, and continued to act for alleged villains – prostitutes, sly groggers, conmen and, eventually, in the higher courts, murderers and rapists.

I'm eighty now, and I have no regrets.

The 'Lost' Hotel Register

Back in the 1960s, I was regarded as a 'middle band' criminal lawyer. Often when an accused person's funds had been depleted by paying a top flight lawyer, I would be briefed as a more economical alternative. The case of Bull Jr is an example of this.

Bull Jr was extradited from Australia to face charges in Auckland of knowingly receiving four stolen fifty-pound notes. He was a domiciled New Zealander, but had broken bail in New Zealand and fled to Australia to evade trial. Extradition from Australia, in these circumstances, was generally a fairly simple procedure. A senior police officer would obtain an extradition warrant, signed by a New Zealand judge, and fly to Australia to give evidence at the extradition hearing. The main task of the New Zealand police officer was to identify the accused and to deliver the warrant to the Australian judge.

After extradition back to Auckland, Bull Jr was then duly lodged in Mount Eden Prison. He hated being locked up. He was strongly built, and ebullient by nature. Being incarcerated was contrary to all his natural instincts, and he paced around the remand yard like an entrapped wild animal.

In view of his history, though, there was no way he would be granted bail. Before being captured in Australia, he had spent a year or two there as an escapee, but had found himself a decent job and had been living there quite happily with his rather glamorous wife. She was blonde, immaculately manicured, and a woman who dressed well. They were both young, and had only been married for a few years. The difficulty was that her father was a senior police sergeant in New Zealand, and he absolutely detested his son-in-law. Bull Jr had a few other convictions, too, mainly for petty offences like fighting and unruly behaviour, but he was well spoken, and reasonably successful as a salesman. He had not, however, accumulated much money.

He was represented at the preliminary hearing in Auckland by Paul Temm QC, who later became a High Court judge. Temm was regarded as one of the top barristers in Auckland, and was known for his strong cross-examination, his powerful forensic addresses, and for being somewhat autocratic.

The preliminary hearing, or depositions, as it was known, culminated in Bull Jr being committed for trial, and he was, as expected, refused bail and dispatched back to Mount Eden Prison to wait in custody for his case to be heard in the then Supreme Court. One of the difficulties that he now faced was that the briefing solicitors for Mr Temm had relieved him of all his cash in payment of legal fees. He now faced the somewhat daunting task of getting legal representation without funds.

His wife, however, kept battling for him. She was a formidable woman, and not at all the archetypal blonde. As a result of a visit by her to my office, I agreed to represent him at the trial, with the promise of fees eventually coming from Australia.

I found him a somewhat difficult client. His hatred of being trapped in prison had made him very emotional and tense. He, however, again and again emphasised his innocence, and told me that when he had possession of those fifty-pound notes, he was totally unaware that they had been dishonestly obtained.

The gist of the prosecution case was that he had deliberately booked into a hotel at Whangarei under a false name, so that he could cash the relatively unusual fifty-pound notes at the local races, and then leave with his true identity having been concealed the whole time.

The trial was heard before a judge and jury. The prosecution was represented by a tall, stern, bespectacled man with grey hair, Stan Cleal. This barrister was regarded as very urbane: he was a member of several clubs, including the Auckland Racing Club, and was a popular tennis player. It was said of him that he knew virtually everybody. His cross-examination technique was to avoid looking at the accused, but to look at the jury instead, and put the Crown case to the accused with an apparent indifference to what answers he received. It was as if he regarded the accused person as having no credibility whatsoever. He was a formidable opponent.

The jury lists in those days were selected by police officers going door-to-door, collecting the names of potential jurors. It was well known that if anyone was believed to be anti-police, he would not be on the jury. Women were not eligible for jury service, and it was very seldom that a Maori person appeared on a jury, either. The first jury gave no hint of sympathy for the accused.

The first trial ran like clockwork. The receptionist from the hotel in question gave evidence of how the accused had booked in under a false name. She fortified her evidence by producing a slip of paper with a name on it that was not that of the accused, but saying that that was what Bull Jr had written when he booked in, and that the signature confirmed that he had tried to conceal his true identity.

It was a robust trial, particularly when the accused gave evidence. He stoutly declared his innocence and replied to Mr Cleal's cynical cross-examination with anger and brimstone. The jury were out for several hours deliberating. Finally, they returned with the foreman stating that they were unable to agree, and had reached an impasse. The jury were dismissed, a new trial was ordered, and the accused was returned to Mount Eden Prison again on remand.

When I went to visit Bull Jr at the prison after that first trial, he was very upset, and he said: 'They put it over us, you know. I did sign my correct name in the register. They cut someone else's name out deliberately.'

'Well,' I explained to him, 'I demanded the register, and wrote letters requiring its production. But I received the same reply each time: that, with the passage of time, the register has either been destroyed or lost. The prosecution has told me that they cut the piece out of the register in the first place because it was necessary by law for the register itself to be kept on the premises. But because of the lengthy delay in this case being brought to trial, obviously the register has been filled and replaced by a new one.'

'Well, they're bloody liars,' Bull Jr said. 'I don't believe they've replaced the register at all. They're just putting it over us. Why don't you get some person to go to Whangarei and pretend that he needs to look at the register, around about that time, to get information for his tax returns? You never know, they might still have that register – I bet they bloody well do.'

THE 'LOST' HOTEL REGISTER

There was something about his outrage that impressed he was telling the truth.

So I sent an agent to the hotel, posing as a commercial traveller who wanted to get information from the register for tax purposes. The response I got was that the register containing the dates around that time did exist, and was in fact still being used in this Whangarei hotel.

The second trial was duly heard at the Supreme Court in the upstairs jury room, which was known as Judge Gresson's courtroom. The judge liked that courtroom because it was airy, and in summer, the sun beamed through the windows. It was not as morbid as the more formal courtrooms below. As I have mentioned, Terrence Gresson was widely regarded as one of the best of Her Majesty's judges, renowned for his courtesy and judicial manner. He was also renowned for his beautiful prose, and as a cultured man, he was well known in musical and artistic circles. As I have also mentioned, I liked him very much, and as a young lawyer, he often gave me words of encouragement and sound advice; one such memorable piece of advice being, 'Never be rude or offensive to a witness – you will be far more effective if you act with restraint and politeness.'

Before the second trial commenced, Stan Cleal spoke to me confidentially. 'Look, Peter,' he said, 'we're not going to use that evidence about him booking in under the wrong name in this trial, and provided you don't ask questions about it, I won't be adducing any evidence on that point.'

'I'm sorry,' I said. 'I'm not prepared to be party to that deal. Let the trial proceed.'

In due course, the hotel receptionist was called as a witness. She, however, made no mention at this second trial of

Bull Jr booking in under a false name. In particular, she did not produce the slip of paper cut out of the register.

I knew I had to take a risk. I asked her, 'Didn't you give evidence at the first trial that the accused booked in under a wrong name?'

She looked at Stan Cleal. He lowered his head. She paused and said quietly, 'Yes, I did.'

Then I asked, 'Didn't you give evidence that the accused failed to write his true name in the register?'

Again she reluctantly said, 'Yes.'

'Didn't you in fact produce a slip of paper that you said had been cut out of the register to prove that he had deliberately registered himself with a false name?' I asked.

Again she reluctantly said, 'I did.'

I then said to the court crier, 'Will you show the witness the piece of paper that was exhibited at the last trial?'

He did so, and I asked the receptionist now, 'Is this the piece of paper that you say was cut out from the register?'

Again she reluctantly said, 'Yes.'

'Did you give evidence at the last trial that the register had been lost or misplaced?' I asked.

Again she lowered her head and said, 'Yes.'

I asked her, 'Where is the register now?'

She pointed to the police officer in charge of the case, sitting at the back of the court. 'He's got it,' she said.

I said to the court crier: 'Will you get that register and show it to the witness?'

The crier walked to the officer in charge, who, with a stormy expression on his face, handed over the register. The crier then passed the register to the witness.

I then said to her, 'Now show the jury the page from which the slip of paper was cut out. That is, the piece of paper that you produced at the first trial.'

Slowly, she turned the pages until, sure enough, she came to the page which bore the relevant date.

I said, 'Show the jury the place where the name has been cut out.'

She did that.

'Now, read to the jury the name above the space left by the paper that was cut out.'

Almost crying, she read out the name. It was the correct and full name of the accused, which he had inscribed in copybook writing with absolute clarity.

You could hear a pin drop in the courtroom.

Judge Gresson was not a man to be trifled with. He immediately halted the trial, directing both an acquittal and a formal inquiry.

When the accused was released, I have never seen a defendant so exuberant to be free. He raced around the courtroom in almost a frenzy of excitement. He strenuously embraced his wife, and eventually the two of them left together, stepping off into the outside world.

I never saw Bull Jr again. Nor did I ever see my fee.

The Exotic Stripper Whom the Judge Found Appealing

In 1967, New Zealand finally abolished six o'clock closing for licensed premises. This had been the law for about fifty years.

As a result of this infamous law, we had what was known as a 'six o'clock swill', where men and women jostled in bars to ensure they could obtain enough liquor to satisfy their thirsts before closing time.

In all this barging, copious amounts of beer were spilt on the bar room floor. The spectacle of these people drinking furiously and treading through pools of beer was not only disgraceful, but damning to any dignified culture that might be associated with the imbibing of liquor.

Consequential to six o'clock closing was the proliferation of after-hours drinking places, both legal and illegal. Licensed restaurants mushroomed. The now ACT New Zealand party politician John Banks established a chain of steakhouses where liquor could be obtained and his restaurants became very popular.

There was also an increase in unlicensed supper clubs, where patrons could hide their liquor under the table and musical entertainment was provided. These nightclubs were usually to be found in the upper floors of old buildings, and patrons would surreptitiously bring with them a bottle of wine. The door would be opened by the proprietor with a knowing smile and the patron encouraged to keep the wine out of sight, just in case the police arrived.

There were also rougher places, known as the 'beer houses'. Many were in Freemans Bay and Grey Lynn, which were then the proletarian areas of Auckland. Alcohol was available in these places until the early hours of the morning, and they attracted a great cross-section of people, including prostitutes, burglars, business people, undercover policemen, lawyers and more. The goings-on in these unlicensed premises could fill many volumes of books, but if one wanted a night out and one was young and strong enough to take care of oneself, these were exciting places to be.

The police really rejoiced in these illegal liquor outlets, because, as they said, if they wanted a fugitive criminal, they knew where to go.

However, the backdrop of this narrative is not one of the notorious beer houses, but the more sophisticated city nightclubs, where live music and professional dancing were presented, often of a surprisingly high standard. There would be a band, consisting of, say, a double bass, lead guitar, percussion instruments or even a trombone, with a singer out in front, taking the limelight. Generally speaking, the atmosphere was warm and delicious, and personally, I loved these places.

One of the entertainers in these nightclubs was the celebrated Sante Collins. She was an exotic dancer. Not only superbly talented at her art, she was also a very sexually attractive and beautiful young woman. In those days, she was the icon of nightclub patrons, in great demand, and invariably well appreciated by her audiences.

Before she came on stage, the band would play sensuous music, and then she would appear, glamorously attired, and slowly start to dance. When her routine reached its climax, to the great joy of her audience, she would seductively undress. Everything she did was artistic. There was nothing garish, nothing bawdy, and nothing uncouth about her performances. Every movement was sublime – her whole act was pure poetry.

Sante Collins was New Zealand's Gypsy Rose Lee. Lee was the American burlesque entertainer famous for her striptease act who rose to prominence in the first half of the last century. In 1960s Auckland, though, the police had the notorious Vice Squad, headed by a devout Roman Catholic police officer, adamant that he would root out evil in the city. This wickedness, according to him, included any artist who stripped off her clothes. The Vice Squad also relished smashing up beer houses and generally saw themselves as the equivalent of the American police inspector Eliot Ness and his team, who became renowned during the Prohibition period in America.

This Vice Squad was the same team who later charged the Auckland producers of the international hit musical *Hair* with indecency – because, in the course of the performance and in accordance with the script, some of the actors stripped naked. Auckland's *Hair* was a sophisticated, professional production, well-attended by the public, and played for a season at the town hall. But members of the Vice Squad, after attending several of the performances, gave evidence at the trial against the producers stating that they were all disgusted at the depravity of the show. Other witnesses were called, including Pat Booth, editor of the *Auckland Star*, who, incidentally, later became a crusader for the wronged Arthur Allan Thomas, a case I will detail later in 'The Police-planted Shell-case' story. Pat was a well-known Catholic, who in this instance said he was shocked and appalled by the performance of *Hair*. The jury brought back verdicts of not guilty on all counts, however, and that night the defence lawyers danced on stage with the performers.

But to come back to Sante, the darling of the nightclub scene: it was not long before the Vice Squad became determined that she should be prosecuted, too. Indeed they were determined that she be imprisoned.

I was sitting in my office when my secretary came in and said, 'There's a young lady to see you. Shall I bring her in?'

When Sante sat down opposite me, I couldn't help but notice that she was very attractive, distractingly so.

Sante told me that she had been dancing at a well-known nightclub when, suddenly, a few men and women rose from the audience, yelling out, 'Police! Police!' There was general pandemonium. She was arrested by women police officers, taken backstage and told to get dressed. At the police station, she was charged with indecency and refused police bail. She told me she'd never had such a terrible night in all her life as the one she spent in the police cells and was relying on me to help her.

I must say that I remained very conscious of her beauty throughout, but somehow maintained my professionalism; I called in my secretary and took a statement.

What Sante told me essentially was that she had been performing her usual dance routine and at the high point of her performance she had shed her clothes. She said that she was not completely naked, however, because she had been still wearing a small piece of black, triangular-shaped cloth that she had glued across her private parts. She said this was always her practice in case anyone accused her of indecency.

We elected trial by jury and, in due course, the case was heard in the Auckland Supreme Court before an all-male jury and Justice Reginald Hardie Boys, a short, bespectacled man, who was renowned as being pretty tough on crime. Justice Hardie Boys had conducted, when at the bar, many high-profile trials, and was regarded as a highly skilled and very confident judge.

I was greatly assisted in the preparation of this case by a university lecturer, Bernie Brown, who later became an Associate Professor at the University of Auckland Law School. Bernie and I had worked together on many cases. In those days, he was something of a night owl and I would often call at his home at breakfast time to pick up his written opinions. These documents sometimes showed evidence that they were prepared in some late-night supper club. Bernie was one of the great lawyers of Auckland: modest, poetic and always a gentleman – and he still is, as one might guess from his generous foreword to this book.

Juries in those days were often unpredictable, though. I suppose they still are. There had been a sensational case in England, where celebrity osteopath Stephen Ward had been charged with living on the earnings of prostitutes. He was something of a hippie and an eccentric, but had eminent clients in London, including Lord Astor. One of his alleged prostitutes was Christine Keeler, who was the mistress of a

Soviet diplomat; and as well, most famously, her relationship with John Profumo, then Secretary of State for War in the Harold McMillan government, had caused his resignation. The evidence against Stephen Ward included that he was sometimes seen walking around Soho with two or three of his young bimbo girlfriends, each wearing dog collars attached to leads. This trial caused enormous publicity around the world.

The trial judge was very conservative, and did the extraordinary and unforgivable by allowing the jury to bring back a verdict after he knew that Ward had attempted suicide. To his everlasting ignominy, the judge, on learning Ward had attempted suicide and was in a coma, refused to adjourn the trial to see whether Ward was well enough to attend. Ward's bail was withdrawn, and he was put under police surveillance in a hospital. The judge, in Ward's absence, continued his summing-up, and sent the jury out to consider their verdict. The jury had been informed of Ward's suicide bid. However, they returned with a verdict of guilty. Geoffrey Robertson QC, in his book *Stephen Ward was Innocent, OK*, described the judge's actions to be 'a final act of unfairness, to try a dying man'.

There were similar dangers of sanctimonious prejudice in the trial of Sante Collins. There was a possibility that some of the jurors might be conservative bigots and therefore the defence had to be conducted carefully and sensitively.

At the trial, Sante Collins appeared in the dock primly dressed. It could not be denied, however, that she exuded her Delilah-like charm.

The prosecutor, in his address to the jury, warned them about being sympathetic towards Sante. He said that the public must be protected from performances that could well corrupt the morals of our nation.

Regardless of the fact that the nightclub had been poorly lit, all the Vice Squad witnesses uniformly deposed that Sante Collins had been completely naked, and that they could see, during the performance her pubic hair.

I tried to conduct the defence with dignity and restraint. The prosecutor, however, seemed to be obsessed with obtaining a guilty verdict and, in my opinion, went well beyond the constraints of prosecutorial conduct with his histrionics and emotional pleas for a conviction.

However, before the jury retired, a crucial development occurred during the trial. The judge said that he wished to see counsel in his chambers, in the absence of the defendant. That was not uncommon in those days, and so we all trooped into his private room. After we had been seated, the judge lit up a cigarette and asked whether any of us wanted to smoke. He seemed very relaxed and not at all indifferent to the defence; indeed he seemed in a somewhat humorous mood, with a kindly expression on his face.

Then the judge said to the prosecutor, 'Do you find the accused an attractive woman?' The prosecutor was taken aback by this question, and obviously became very uncomfortable. The judge then added, 'To be perfectly frank, gentlemen, I find the accused to be a beautiful young lady and, quite truthfully, I can't imagine her doing anything during an artistic dance that a reasonable person would consider indecent.'

The prosecutor had become pale and started to stammer some sort of protestation which was virtually incomprehensible. The judge then started laughing and, knowing the rule was that it was always safe to laugh when the judge laughs, I began to chuckle myself.

The judge by now had lit a pipe, and was sitting back, obviously enjoying the prosecutor's discomfort, while puffing blue smoke into the air. I enjoyed the aroma.

We stood up and bowed, leaving the room and walking back to the courtroom.

The Vice Squad members rushed to confer with the prosecutor and their chagrin was obvious.

The jury were reassembled and the judge gave them a quiet, unassuming summing up. Later he ordered Sante to come up for sentence if called upon. This was, in effect, an acquittal.

Her many supporters in the back of the court could not restrain their approval and the Vice Squad members were left muttering and very dissatisfied. I believe that justice was well served, and that the boundaries of freedom of expression were extended that day. Today, hopefully, no prosecution would ever be entertained in similar circumstances.

I might add that before we left the judge's chambers, the prosecutor had informed the judge that if he directed an acquittal, the prosecution would take the case to the Court of Appeal.

The judge had sat back and laughed at this, saying, 'Well, Mr Prosecutor, would you allow Sante to dance before the Court of Appeal? They might appreciate that.' And he laughed even more loudly.

The Dwarf Who Moved

Jasper the Gypsy was a dwarf, his body small, but his head of regular size, and his limbs remarkably short. This didn't seem to inhibit him in any way, however. He was a gregarious person. He loved to talk, to have a good yarn, and he was an expert on many subjects. For instance, he was very knowledgeable concerning the value of jewellery and gold. People came to him for his opinion on many different kinds of matters requiring expertise. He was also something of an inventor: he devised a type of spray unit for painting the roofs of factories, quickly and efficiently. He was one of the more interesting persons that you would ever meet.

When I knew him, he was a mature man and had spent most of his life in circuses, both here and in Europe. Indeed, at a later point, he showed me a scrapbook of newspaper cuttings relating to his performances in circuses in Russia and other parts of the Continent. In the circus, he had performed many roles, including lion tamer, high-wire walker, clown and strongman, lifting trucks and other weights.

When I first met him, he had been performing at the Easter Show in Auckland, where he would climb a hundred-foot pole and stand on his head at the top for a considerable period of time. He and his wife had a booth at the Easter Show, where they put on demonstrations of sharpshooting. Jasper would stand with a cigarette in his mouth and, from a distance, his wife would shoot the cigarette out of his mouth with a .22 calibre rifle. This was a very dangerous type of exhibition, obviously. It entirely relied on Jasper being absolutely motionless and cool, and his wife concentrating and being accurate with her shooting. But they had apparently been conducting this sharpshooting sideshow for some time, and were both confident and skilled at it. Nobody really was concerned about potential danger.

One night, however, during this exhibition of sharpshooting, Jasper's wife shot him in the head. This immediately caused great distress to all who witnessed it. An ambulance was called, police were brought in and, for a while, confusion reigned, until Jasper, now unconscious, was taken away to hospital.

The police carried out an investigation, and in the course of it they found that Jasper's wife had a lover in the circus, and that this affair had been going on for some time behind Jasper's back.

As a result of all this, a charge of attempted murder was brought against Jasper's wife, and the case was heard in the then Supreme Court in Auckland. Jasper's family, including his adult daughters, attended the trial, as did other people from the Easter Show and also a retinue of personal friends. Jasper had, by this time, recovered from the injury to his head, but since the shooting, he had not spoken to his wife.

His wife was a good-looking woman, of ordinary stature, and the circus people had little sympathy for her. She had been carrying on this performance, shooting a cigarette out of her husband's mouth, for quite a while now, and many thought she had made a deliberate attempt to kill Jasper.

The case was heard in Courtroom No. 1, which was a beautiful courtroom, lined with exquisitely carved and varnished kauri, and after the jury had been empanelled and the prosecution had made a short opening address, Jasper was called as the first prosecution witness.

Here, Jasper's shortness was patent, as his head hardly came above the top of the witness stand. He looked well, however. He was a handsome man, very intent, and all eyes in the courtroom were on him, waiting for his testimony.

His wife sat in the dock with her eyes downcast. She looked sad and demure. The body of the court was filled with spectators.

The prosecutor started to question Jasper: 'Is the defendant your wife?'

Jasper answered, 'Yes.'

'You've been together for quite a few years and have a family?'

'Yes.'

'And both you and your wife have been performing this sharpshooting routine for some time?'

'Yes.'

'You've never had a problem before?'

'No, never.'

'Coming now to the occurrence itself,' the prosecutor continued, 'you were standing in the usual place with a cigarette in your mouth, waiting for the cigarette to be shot out of your mouth by your wife. Is that correct?'

'Yes.'

'And of course, you didn't move.'

There was a long, pregnant silence in response. Everybody in the court was watching Jasper.

And then suddenly he broke the silence, saying, 'No, I did move.'

The prosecutor was astounded, almost in a state of shock. 'Did you say that you moved?'

'Yes,' said Jasper. 'It was my mistake, I moved.'

Now the judge joined the interrogation. This is quite normal when things get tense in a courtroom. The judge asked Jasper, 'You realise what you are saying?'

'Yes, sir,' Jasper replied.

'But you never said that in your statement,' said the judge. 'Why are you saying it now?'

There was another long silence before Jasper finally said, 'I'm saying it because it's the truth.'

The prosecutor then addressed the judge, and applied to see him in chambers.

In chambers, in the absence of the jury and the spectators, the prosecutor admitted that the Crown had no hope of gaining a conviction and the judge gave leave for the prosecutor to withdraw the charge.

Jasper's wife was discharged and she was taken down to the prisoners' cells to obtain her belongings and to be released.

At the back of Courtroom No. 1, there is a large entrance foyer between the front door of the building and the door of the courtroom, and Jasper's family waited here for Jasper's wife to appear.

After a delay of a few minutes, his wife hurried out from the cells below, and ran across the foyer towards Jasper and her family, crying out, 'Oh thank you, thank you, thank you!'

Jasper, however, did not return her overtures of reconciliation; he said, 'Get away from me, you bitch. I will never speak to you again, nor will any member of your family.'

Everyone was astonished, but no one commented. Jasper and his daughters went on their way, and the acquitted wife separately disappeared into the evening.

It was some years later that I received an invitation to visit Jasper. He had bought a catamaran, which he had moored at Leigh, a small inlet opposite Kawau Island. I accepted his invitation, and a few days later, I was sitting in the catamaran, enjoying a very delicious meal. Jasper was an expert fisherman, among his many talents, and a competent rabbit hunter, too.

It was during that night that Jasper showed me his scrapbook of all the cuttings that revealed the amazing history of this man, who had performed in so many roles in the circus world. He was quite elderly by now, and his family treated him like royalty. He had also acquired a young female companion, who lavished affection upon him.

Jasper died not long afterwards, but his memory will always live with me. He was one of the most remarkable people I ever came across in the law.

He Laughed with the Wind and the Sky

In 1963, I was holidaying at Lake Taupo in a small bay called Hatipi, during Christmas time. In a bach nearby, incidentally, was the young Kiri Te Kanawa, later to become one of the greatest opera singers in the world. While I was out on the lake trawling for trout in a small clinker dinghy, I received a message that Ron Jorgensen – a New Zealand crime figure – had been arrested for murder.

I returned to Auckland and appeared in the Magistrates Court for Ron. When I stood up and introduced myself to the court, the magistrate, Fred McCarthy SM, answered with a broad smile, 'Yes, and I see you've brought your friend.'

Turning around, I saw that my dachshund Ambrose had followed me into the courtroom and was standing there, wagging his tail vigorously.

Right from the start, the heat was on. The basic facts alleged by the Crown were that Ronald John Jorgensen and John Frederick Gillies had been operating a beer house in Auckland and that a feud had developed with the hosts of another beer house carrying on business at Bassett Road,

Remuera. The two other operators – and murder victims – were George Frederick Walker and Kevin James Speight. The two victims were well known in the criminal underworld of Auckland as spivs, small-time cheats and gamblers. But it was not so much their deaths that rocked the world of crime and police detection as the manner of their execution.

The Crown case was that a Reising machine gun had been smuggled into New Zealand in the petrol tank of an imported car. Gillies had obtained this weapon, together with ammunition, and allegedly practised firing it on a remote West Coast beach, in the company of Jorgensen. The prosecution claimed that Jorgensen and Gillies had taken a taxi to Bassett Road in the early hours of the morning. They had held Speight and Walker in their beer house at gunpoint, and then, after making them both kneel, Gillies had pumped bullets into them using the machine gun on single shot.

The allegation against Jorgensen was that he was an accessory to these murders, and that he had tried to arrange a false alibi.

The newspapers went into a frenzy when the police released details of these killings. It had all the hallmarks of a Mafia-style execution, and the police soon assembled a high-profile investigation team, including Bob Walton, who later became Commissioner of Police, Graeme Perry, later Superintendent of the Auckland Police, and John Rex Hughes, who would become the most notorious of Auckland detectives.

On the forensic side, Dr Donald Nelson of the DSIR, the forensic scientific laboratory, was engaged; he would later become disgraced in the infamous case of wrongful conviction that was the Arthur Allan Thomas saga. Together with Nelson, Dr Frank Cairns, renowned for his honesty and objectivity, acted as police pathologist in this case against Jorgensen.

The public were aghast when the details of this homicide were made known and, right from the start, we defence lawyers knew we faced an almost insurmountable wall of prejudice.

Gillies had allegedly made full confessions to various persons and the case against him seemed watertight. He was represented by Ken Richardson, who would become a greatly admired District Court judge. His second counsel was Colin Meade, a popular Auckland lawyer.

The inimitable Kevin Ryan agreed to assist me on the case and, as usual, his services were invaluable. The Crown was represented by Graham Speight and Colin Nicholson (both of whom became High Court judges), and the prosecution wasted no time laying a few traps for us.

Jorgensen had made clumsy endeavours to arrange a false alibi, citing a woman named Heather Hutchinson, and when I interviewed her, the police had covertly placed microphones in the room; but to their chagrin, I emphatically told Heather to tell me the truth and nothing but the truth.

The next prosecution trick was to send one of their witnesses to my office, again hoping, no doubt, that I would give improper advice. I remember quite vividly when this witness, Mere Veronica Rapira, was ushered into my office at the old Commercial Union building – it took me a minute or two to realise that she was, in fact, a prosecution witness. I think she was just as embarrassed as I was, and I immediately rang Graham Speight and complained about their weak attempt to discredit me, but received the usual stonewall denial, of course.

Ron Jorgensen himself was strongly built; he had been a seaman earlier in his life, and was regarded as pretty formidable throughout the underworld. He was a tough customer, and had come up the hard way through the borstal system, later having served a seven-year sentence for robbery. In those days, a young offender sentenced to borstal for a period of three years, the usual sentence, received a thorough education in criminality. The borstals provided an apprenticeship for these young men, preparing them to become serious adult offenders. The borstals also created a criminal fraternity, which for many, like Ron Jorgensen, provided lifelong friends with common bonds.

The police investigated this case with amazing ferocity. A material witness for the Crown, Bryan Peterson, testified that before he made his statement to Bob Walton, he had been taken out to the Waitakere by four detectives, who gave him a savage beating. Peterson said in his evidence that he was assured by a police lawyer that he would not be beaten up again if he cooperated, and as a result he made his so-called 'voluntary' statement to Senior Inspector Bob Walton.

The names of virtually all of the prosecution witnesses were suppressed at the preliminary hearing, on the grounds that they would be interfered with by the defence if their names were revealed. Accordingly, they were referred to, by a magisterial ruling, as witness A, witness B, etc. The courtroom was heavily guarded, and the whole atmosphere deliberately created by the prosecution exacerbated the tidal wave of prejudice against the defence.

Kevin and I analysed every aspect of the case to try to find a way through for the defence. For example, we scrutinised one of the lynchpin witnesses for the prosecution, a woman named Lola Fleming, who had been with Gillies and Jorgensen earlier in the night of the killings and gave evidence of their preparation for the crime. On researching her background as closely as we could with our limited resources, we were able to obtain substantial material to damage her credibility as a prosecution witness. It became clear to us that she had made five differing statements to the police in regard to her evidence, but although the defence applied repeatedly for copies of these statements, they were never handed over.

The trial was heard before Justice Gresson and jury. Although the defence later appealed his rulings and summings-up robustly, in fact he did accord a fair trial to both prosecution and defence.

Both men were found guilty of murder. That night, the police and the prosecution held a great party to celebrate at the Station Hotel in Auckland, which is fairly near the Supreme Court. The Station Hotel was well known as a second police headquarters. In fact, one bar upstairs was specifically reserved for police officers. There were many anecdotes about this hotel. In those days, it was generally believed to be the centre of an abortion racket and a place for the sale and distribution of stolen property. Just how closely the police were involved in all this is not clear, but rumours were rife.

We took the case to the Court of Appeal but failed. We petitioned the Governor-General for an exercise of the royal prerogative through the Privy Council, but to no avail. Again we appealed to the Privy Council on the basis that the trial judge had erred in failing to regard Lola Fleming, a material Crown witness, as a possible accomplice. This meant that the trial judge would have been obligated to warn the jury that her evidence needed corroboration. But once more, we were unsuccessful.

The publicity generated by all these legal proceedings was quite substantial, and as a result, Ron Jorgensen, to many members of the public, became something of a folk hero. For a long time he was kept in the so-called Separates, a high-security part of Mount Eden Prison, where the conditions were absolutely disgusting. Any man of lesser courage would have had a complete mental breakdown in those conditions. The Separates was really just a row of cells where the prisoners spent twenty-three hours of the day with absolutely no provision to do anything whatsoever, and during the other hour, they were individually allowed into a steel cage where they could exercise.

Ron Jorgensen had an artistic side to his personality. His paintings appeared in art galleries and were sought after. Many of the writers and artists of Auckland eventually went to see him in prison and to encourage him in his artistic pursuits. Eric McCormick, who held a doctorate of literature from the University of New Zealand and also a Master of literature from Cambridge University, visited Ron and said of his illustrated children's stories, 'My immediate impression of these stories was their beauty, their sensitivity, their script, their illustrations, and particularly the general depth of feeling.' McCormick was not alone in his praise. Painters such as Garth Tapper and writers such as Maurice Shadbolt and others made sure that Ron Jorgensen was encouraged in his art and, after some difficulties with the authorities, managed to procure for him paints and brushes.

Ron Jorgensen wrote to me frequently, and I visited him in prison whenever I could. It was necessary for his survival that there always be a ray of hope that one day he would be released. To a certain extent, I provided that ray of hope.

The police naturally revelled in the success of the prosecution and loved to portray Ron Jorgensen as the most notorious criminal in New Zealand. I, however, found another side to Ron and believed that if this could be properly kindled, not only could he be rehabilitated, but he could make a major artistic contribution to society.

He studied and mastered Braille while in prison so that he could write books for the blind. His paintings, on the other hand, became in great demand by the public. He had much depth to his character, too. During the Mount Eden Prison riots of 1965, it was Ron Jorgensen who led the prisoners to a peaceful settlement with the authorities. But again and again his overtures seeking parole received a bleak and negative response from the Justice Department.

After Mount Eden Prison had been virtually demolished by the riots, the department announced that it was transferring twenty of the so-called 'top hardened criminals' to a new high-security wing at Waikeria Prison near Te Awamutu. It was incredible that Ron Jorgensen, who had been instrumental in peacefully resolving the riots, was selected as one of those criminals and taken away in handcuffs to this new series of indoor cages inside Waikeria.

When I visited Ron there, I was appalled by the conditions and immediately began a campaign of complaint to the government. What the authorities had done was build a series of steel cages within the prison, in which, for almost twenty-four hours a day, each prisoner was separately incarcerated. The conditions were worse than in the Separates at Mount Eden Prison in Auckland. The prisoners were allowed no privileges whatsoever and had access to no recreational facilities. Food was given through a slot, pushed to the prisoner with a long wooden rake. The food was always cold, badly prepared and of little nutritional value. The SPCA would never have condoned animals being housed in such atrocious conditions.

During the first few months of this unconscionable treatment, most of the so-called top criminals became mentally ill and were transferred to psychiatric institutions. I was concerned about Ron's mental and physical health during this period, but our complaints to the Minister of Justice received the usual bland and negative replies.

Eventually, Ron Jorgensen was given temporary release as a prelude to being paroled. He had been in prison over twelve years. I knew how difficult it was going to be for him to readjust to the outside world. Ron now had become not just a client, but a close friend; a deep bond had been forged between us.

Some say a lawyer should never be close to his client emotionally and perhaps there is some wisdom in that. But there's another side to the ledger, and that is, we are all human beings passing through this strange experience called life. No one has a right to create a wall between people who find truth and worthiness in their relationship.

When Jorgensen was released, albeit only for a short period of time, in August 1976, I invited him to come for a cruise on my yacht *Fidelis*. This was a 63-foot racing sloop and Ron, while in prison, had followed *Fidelis*'s successes through the sports reports in the newspaper, always expressing a keen desire to become a crew member. I arranged for another friend, John Dunne, to take his launch as a companion boat, and we took crews representing a cross-section of the community.

I'll never forget Ron's joy at being at sea. I've never seen a man so happy on a boat. His energy seemed to be boundless and he had no fear whatsoever. He literally swung from the shrouds and laughed with the wind and the sky and the sea.

We sailed to the Great Barrier Island and cruised its coastline for a few days. While aboard, Ron Jorgensen proved he was a great cook, too, with a large repertoire of dishes. Some nights, we would eat Chinese food, other nights Spanish or Italian, and the conversation was always animated. With classical music playing in the background, we would usually talk into the early hours of the morning.

I learnt later that there was a posse of policemen surveying our progress. Their attention was unwarranted, though; I was convinced that Ron would never offend again.

While we were anchored at Port Fitzroy, Link Cartier, a carpenter and fisherman who had joined the crew, went ashore and brought back plant material that he said was taro. After peeling and cutting the material into pieces, he boiled it in a pot, but nobody was keen to taste it.

Link was an alcoholic and later that night, while intoxicated, we heard him urinating in the scuppers. I yelled out and told him not to be a filthy bastard. Link came down the steps into the saloon, raising a knife above my head saying, 'You arsehole, I'm going to kill you!'

I was in my sleeping bag and an easy target. I realised that this man was completely out of his mind with alcoholic rage. Ron, however, was lying in an adjoining bunk, and grabbed Link's arm by the wrist, shaking the knife from his hand. Link was lucky he did not receive a battering from Ron that night.

The next day, I gave Link some money and ordered him to leave the boat, there at Fitzroy Harbour.

We then decided to sail to Smokehouse Bay to anchor for the night. However, on the way, one of the other crew members noticed that Ron was vomiting from the stern of the boat. It soon became apparent that Ron was extremely ill. Thick saliva was flowing from his mouth. He was in agony and unable to speak coherently.

We gave him pencil and paper and he wrote that he had been poisoned by eating a small portion of the so-called 'taro' that Link had left in the galley.

I decided to return urgently to Port Fitzroy to get help but found that the steering wheel had become locked and could not manipulate the rudder. We were forced to drop the anchor again and found that, for some inexplicable reason, the wires around the pulleys that operated the rudder had jumped. To save time, we inserted the tiller into the rudder stock and motored back to Port Fitzroy.

By this time Ron was in great pain. He was choking on his saliva and wrote that his mouth and throat seemed to be on fire. We gave him a mug of salt water in an attempt to make him vomit, but this only seemed to aggravate his symptoms. We tried fresh water, but this only seemed to increase the saliva flow. We now realised that Ron's situation was very serious and might possibly even be fatal.

Ron was crouched at the stern of the boat with his head in his hands, trying unsuccessfully to vomit. With paper towels, he would frequently wipe long strands of white, almost jelly-like saliva from his mouth.

By the time *Fidelis* arrived at Port Fitzroy, Ron was having difficulty breathing and we immediately took him ashore to the district nurse's office. She was not home, so we went to the storekeeper's house. It was now about 6pm.

The storekeeper and his family were most cooperative and a telephone call was made to the New Zealand Poisons

Bureau (now known as the National Toxicology Group) in Dunedin. They said they would ring us back and hopefully find an antidote.

Eventually, the district nurse was contacted and she said she would come immediately. We also contacted a doctor who was holidaying on the island, and he said that he would come as soon as possible, too. By this stage, Ron was lying on the bathroom floor with white saliva still pouring from his mouth. He was in a state of collapse; he had developed a high temperature and his pulse was becoming weak.

When the nurse arrived, we gave her samples of the plant that Ron had eaten, which were eventually sent to the Poisons Bureau. She tried to feed Ron milk, but this only seemed to make the saliva flow worse. Eventually, a telephone call was received from Dunedin to say that they had identified the plant as the lily-taro which is very dangerous and has often killed cattle. By now, it was impossible to get a pulse from Ron, who was semi-conscious. When the doctor arrived, Ron was placed on the operating table and given an injection of morphine because he was now suffering from shock.

Ron thought he was dying and, just able to scratch out the request with a pencil, he asked me to phone his wife to tell her that he loved her. I phoned her, but did not say he was dying.

At this stage, several police officers appeared, including a Detective Sergeant Kemp, all of whom gave great assistance, and a plane was arranged to fly Ron out at daybreak.

In the meantime, the crew and I returned to the *Fidelis*, which was now bumping violently against the wharf. The wind had risen to about 30 knots and the high hills around the harbour had a funnelling effect, which at times increased the gusts to about 50 knots. The rise and fall of the tide also meant that we had to adjust the ropes every hour. Little sleep was had that night.

At first light, we returned to the nurse's surgery, where she and her husband were preparing to send Ron back to Auckland. We were all impressed by the nurse's dedication to duty. She had sat up all night with Ron, in case the swelling in his throat might cause him to suffocate or choke on his own saliva. She said that the danger period was now over, but he was still a very sick man. Throughout, Ron had acted with courage and had done all he could to cooperate, through all the many attempts to make him vomit, and all to no avail. His mouth and throat had been burning furiously the whole time, and the nurse said that his oesophagus and intestinal tract would no doubt have been burnt as well, adding to his pain.

The nurse and her husband drove us to the airport in their Land Rover and Ron was taken away in a small aircraft. Because of the high winds, the plane was rocking wildly and at one stage we thought it might tip right over.

Ron recovered in the Auckland hospital, thankfully, and later, his poisoning was described in detail in the 1976 annual report of the National Toxicology Group, which explained that the lily-taro plant he had eaten is one that contains needle-like crystals of oxalic acid – and that's what had caused the terrible reaction.

When Ron had recovered sufficiently, at my request he addressed the Criminal Bar Association, of which I was then president. Ron spoke to a packed meeting of lawyers, and the address he gave on his experiences of the justice and penal system was one of the best ever heard at such a gathering. However, once back at my home, where he was staying for that weekend, still on temporary release from prison, he privately confided to me that he was suffering from deep depression. It is hard for the public to understand how difficult it is for a person who has served a long sentence in prison to adjust to the outside world.

While Ron was in prison, I prosecuted several libel actions on his behalf. One of these against the *Auckland Star* was successful. This action was based on an article, dated 29 April 1972, headed 'The Stench of Prison – Part of the Life and Bad Times of Muhali Bede'. The gist of this was that Bede accused Ron of being a nark in the prison and receiving advantages from the prison authorities as a result. The presiding judge was Justice Clifford Perry, who held that Ron could recover damages for his reputation in prison and evidence was called by the defence to the effect that Ron was not a nark and that he was highly regarded by both the prison population and the prison officers. The jury found in Ron's favour and awarded substantial damages.

The senior counsel for the defendant (*Auckland Star*), Lloyd Brown QC, was magnanimous in defeat. He subsequently wrote a letter stating he had been so impressed by Ron in the witness box that he was prepared to write a favourable letter to the Parole Board urging Ron's permanent release.

When the popular prison psychiatrist, Donald F. McKenzie, wrote his book on prison life in New Zealand entitled *While We Have Prisons*, it was Ron Jorgensen's painting of a prisoner sitting on a bench in a prison yard that was chosen for the cover. Ron's painting encapsulates the misery, despair and loneliness of a typical inmate.

Ron Jorgensen was no angel – he was at least on the perimeter of culpability in regard to the Bassett Road murders and there's no doubt that he deserved a period of imprisonment as a result – but the system over-punished him and eventually crushed his spirit.

Even when, on 3 February 1983, he was finally given parole by Jim McLay, who was then the Minister of Justice, the terms were so onerous that they really didn't give Ron a chance to rehabilitate, to resume any kind of 'normal' life. He had to live in Kaikoura with his elderly father, who was in his eighties and almost senile, and Ron was not allowed to work. He was virtually under house arrest. Then, in about December 1984, Ron disappeared from his Kaikoura home and committed suicide by driving his car over a cliff.

Some say he feigned his own death and is still alive, living incognito in Australia. But the fact that he has never communicated with me is clear evidence that he is dead.

Ron Jorgensen was an extraordinary man. He had exceptional artistic ability, combining masculinity with sensitivity and cultural expression. He was neither black nor white, but he was without doubt a man of great courage, spirit and loyalty.

He was my friend.

The Most Courageous Man

Sometime in 1969 I received a telephone call that went something like this:

'Is that you, Peter?'

'Yes.'

'It's Peta Awatere here.'

'Good to hear from you, Peta.'

'Well, it's not so good, really. I'm at the police station and charged with murder.'

'Christ Almighty, I don't believe you! You're having me on!'

'No, Peter, I wish I were. I'd like you to come to the station as soon as you can, if you don't mind.'

I had known Peta for a number of years. He had been commander of the Maori Battalion during World War II and was highly regarded as an expert on Maori language and culture. After his return to civilian life, Peta first travelled around the maraes, and gave his respect to the war dead and their loved ones. But, from then on, he refused to talk about his war experiences. He burnt his many medals and uniforms, and dedicated his life's work to improving the welfare of Maori people.

At the Bar

Counsel at the Bar!
Vigilant poised meticulous
devastating debater
exquisite in expression
precise in presentation!

Lion in the jungle!
Vigilant poised majestic
Cunning prowling predator
serene in meditation
fierce in concentration!

Lightning speed in action
Brain and brawn reflexed..
locked mortal combat!..
licks his wounds..is gone!

NOTES

Dedicated to my friend Peter.A.Williams, barrister, whom I had observed on several occasions in action at the bar.

A poem in English and Maori given to me by Peta Awatere, who was allowed a typewriter in his cell.

I te Whakawaa.

He rooia kei te Kooti!
Mataara matapopore matahii
tohunga waananga
maarama ki te koorero
pokarere taana takikoorero!

He raiona toona rite!
Mataara matapopore matahii
kararehe papatu muurere
rere ana te ihi
rere ana te wehi!

Me he uira toona nakawhiti
Oona wheeue oona rei
kua ngangau kua mate te hoariri!..
kua miti i oona taotuu..kua haere!

WHAKAMAARAMA

I tuhia he mihi nooku ki tooku hoa ki a Pita
Wiremu he rooia. He maha ooku kitenga i a ia
i te Kooti Whakawaa Hara.

Peta went on to be elected to the Auckland City Council with the largest majority of any member, and he became totally immersed in helping the underprivileged and assisting various academics with Maori cultural studies.

When I had represented Roy Rau, who was charged with murder, it was Peta Awatere whom I turned to for help in applying for an all-Maori jury. When the defence wished to challenge for cause, on the grounds that some jurors might be from the tribe of the deceased, it was Peta Awatere who gave evidence that tribal enmities still existed in New Zealand. Peta was severely cross-examined by the prosecutor, Graham Speight, who was to become the judge presiding over the trial of Peta Awatere himself when he was charged with murder.

The Roy Rau trial was in 1961, and was the first major murder trial of my career. The first trial concluded in a verdict of guilty, but the Court of Appeal quashed this conviction on the grounds of bias by the trial judge. In the second trial, the defence was granted an all-Maori jury, which probably was the last all-Maori jury in New Zealand's legal history. It was at this second trial that we challenged for cause.

A challenge for cause is distinct from a pre-emptory challenge, because the former is not as of right, and leave must be obtained from the trial judge. In the Roy Rau trial, this leave was obtained by calling Peta Awatere as an expert witness, as mentioned above. The all-Maori jury finally returned a verdict of not guilty on the grounds of insanity.

I may say that the controversy stirred up by this latter verdict was probably causative for the then government to pass legislation abolishing future Maori juries, and that remains the law today.

Roy Rau himself, as a result of the verdict, was placed in Oakley Hospital as a patient. However, because the then superintendent, Dr Savage, had given evidence at the trial on behalf of the prosecution that Roy was sane, the hospital refused to treat him. For some years, the hospital, in their annual report, would record so many insane patients, and one sane patient, namely Roy Rau. Roy was kept busy assisting the nurses at the hospital in treating the other patients.

The trial of Peta Awatere caused a sensation, particularly among the Maori community, where Peta was revered as a great warrior, teacher and follower of the Ringatu religion. There were those, however, who held a grudge against Peta on the alleged basis that the Maori Battalion, under his command, had been too savage against the Germans during the war and had killed prisoners. Some in the RSA argued that a number of New Zealander prisoners of war had been shot by the Germans in retaliation for the actions of the Maori Battalion.

Peta denied these rumours, believing they had a foundation in German propaganda, and maintaining that they were invented to justify the German brutality against Allied prisoners of war.

The Maori Battalion, in World War II, was widely regarded as the greatest fighting group among Britain and its allies. The result of this was that the Maori Battalion suffered the highest number of casualties.

The facts of the case against Peta Awatere were relatively simple. Peta was a married man, living with his wife and family in Grey Lynn, Auckland. He, however, had a mistress, whom he regarded as his de facto wife. Her name was Mrs Hakaraia.

Peta himself, at this stage, was in poor health, and suffered badly from diabetes. He complained to me that the many huis he attended had served sugar-sweetened cordials and overly generous desserts that aggravated his diabetes.

Each Maori iwi in New Zealand has its own *marae*, where tribal members meet, mainly for formal occasions such as burial ceremonies, known as *tangi*. After these ceremonies, a rather sumptuous meal is held, and because alcohol is prohibited at a marae, large quantities of cordial and soft drink are consumed.

Mrs Hakaraia lived with her children at Glen Innes and was regarded as an energetic worker behind the scenes at Maori functions. She would be in the kitchen preparing the food and always remained afterwards to help tidy up.

Peta's belief in his Ringatu religion ran very deep, and he experienced vivid spiritual premonitions. He told me once that before each battle during the war, the faces of those who would be killed would pass before him. He knew that these men would die. Peta himself knew no fear. On one occasion, he led a platoon of Maori soldiers with fixed bayonets, and attacked and defeated a German machine-gun post. Peta led from the front, and when badly wounded by enemy fire during another incident, he continued to supervise his men, moving by crawling over the ground on his belly, as his legs had been immobilised due to his injuries. It was only when he became unconscious because of loss of blood that his men were able to carry him away on a stretcher. His bravery was renowned and commended.

On the night before the homicide, while sitting in the main hall, next to a church, he experienced one of his strong, spiritual reveries, a clairvoyance of sorts. In this premonition, he had seen Mrs Hakaraia, whom he called Tuini, weeping and lying on her side, possibly dying. This type of premonition is called by ancient Maori a *rehu*, or a *matakite*.

Then, the following morning, on that fatal Sunday, he had been sleeping at his own home with his wife, when, at about 2am, he woke and felt unsettled. Eventually, at about 3am, he got dressed and told his wife that he was going for a long walk. He walked to the bottom of Frances Street, Grey Lynn, where his home was and it suddenly came to him that his restlessness was caused by the premonition he'd had the night before. Prior to the presage, he had written a letter to Tuini, declaring his love for her, and he took this letter with him.

He walked back to his house and considered what he should do. In view of his interpretation of the spiritual warning, which was that Tuini was in danger, he took a bread knife for his own protection. He believed, because he had had a stroke some months before, and his knees were weak, that he needed the knife to protect himself if he were attacked by a third person. He wrapped the knife in a cloth and put it in his coat pocket.

He caught a taxi to 3 Rowan Terrace, where Tuini, Mrs Hakaraia, lived.

He took off his shoes, according to Maori custom, and entered the house. He pushed the bedroom door open and entered the room, holding the letter.

In the darkness, he did not immediately realise that a man was also in the double bed with Mrs Hakaraia. The man, who Peta would only later discover was a Dutchman called Joe, sprang up, yelling out, 'Leave her alone!'

Peta shouted in reply, 'Keep out of this! She's my woman!'

In self-protection, Peta took the knife out of his right-hand pocket, warning Joe not to approach.

Unfortunately, however, Joe rushed at Peta, impaling himself on the knife, which pierced his heart, killing him instantly. There was only one wound.

Peta Awatere immediately rang the police, but was later charged and convicted of murder.

After the trial, it was ascertained that a workmate of the deceased had been on the jury. As well, while Mrs Hakaraia had given evidence against Peta, denying that the Dutchman had risen from the bed, after the trial she swore an affidavit stating the true situation was that the Dutchman had rushed at Peta. This evidence, however, was rejected by the Court of Appeal.

The trial itself was, as I mentioned, conducted by Justice Graham Speight, who made a serious error in his summing-up: he told the jury that if they rejected self-defence, then they should not go on to consider provocation, as that rejection implied they did not believe the Dutchman had rushed at Peta, and therefore provocation was out of the question. This was manifestly a serious misdirection.

While the jury were out considering their verdict, I could hear Peta and some of his friends singing hymns in the Maori language from the holding cell below. It was tragically beautiful.

After the trial, the Court of Appeal simply seemed prejudiced against Peta. On the question of provocation, Justice Alfred North commented, 'How could Peta have been in love with Mrs Hakaraia, when he already had a wife?'

Justice North was a Baptist, who was known, at the Court of Appeal, as an aggressive interrogator of defence counsel, whom he would often derail by asking trenchant questions.

Peta was sent to Mount Eden Prison, where he was revered by the other prisoners. I visited him frequently, and eventually Peta gave me a folder containing poems that he had written while in prison. He also presented me with a ceremonial walking stick, known in the Maori language as a *tokotoko*, that he had carved himself, as a token of his appreciation.

While incarcerated, Peta's heart condition worsened. After receiving many written requests for Peta's release, the Minister of Justice, Dr Martyn Finlay, finally gave the order. But for some administrative reason, the release was delayed and, to the discredit of our justice system, this courageous hero died in prison of a heart attack.

Peta Awatere, without doubt, was a great New Zealander who served his country, both in war and peace, with incomparable courage and devotion. He should never have been convicted of murder, but only manslaughter, and the government should never have allowed him to die in jail.

Peta was the most courageous man I have ever met.

The Jurors Who Used Sledgehammers on the Loghaulers

Frank the Tank and Toofat were what the police would call 'hardened criminals'. They had both been through the approved training course for young offenders in New Zealand. This course commenced with borstal training for three years in their adolescence, followed by corrective training in an adult prison for a further three years. The Corrections Department, however, did nothing whatsoever to correct them, and the majority would finally graduate to longer terms in Her Majesty's prison.

In the late 1960s, Frank and Toofat had spent time in a prison in the centre of the North Island known as Tongariro Prison, or, more colloquially, 'National Park'. Such places of detention in the centre of the North Island were sometimes referred to by the rednecks as comfortable hotels for prisoners, since the conditions were more open and freer than city prisons. The National Park prison was spacious, as the land was almost useless for farming, and therefore of a low value. This prison was covered in snow in the winter, and was referred to by some prisoners as 'New Zealand's Siberia'. The paddocks around the prison were striped with small creeks, thickly iced over in the winter, and here and there copses of native forest lent a sylvan beauty to the place.

The greatest advantage to the prisoners, however, was the degree of freedom available in these camps. During the day, the prisoners worked outdoors, and there was a cleanliness to the atmosphere that compared favourably to the pollution of the city prisons. At the National Park prison, each inmate had his own small hut, and most had his own keys. Indeed, inmates were so 'free' that at times they caught trout in the creeks or enjoyed midday siestas in the sun. The manager of the prison was a woman who was highly regarded for the liberal manner in which she conducted the place. I believe the recidivism rates for these farm prisons were substantially less than their oppressive city counterparts. Although the manual labour at times was tough and arduous, and although the prisoners worked outside, escapes were seldom. The main drawback to these detention centres was their remoteness. Visits by family members and loved ones were expensive, and therefore often caused financial hardship.

To come back to the narrative, though, while at National Park prison, Frank and Toofat formed a firm friendship. Frank the Tank was a big man, and even stronger than he looked. He had earlier killed a man in a fight, and had been sentenced to a harsh period of ten years imprisonment for manslaughter. Toofat was also a large man, but somewhat overweight. Highly intelligent, some said he was a leader in the underworld. His father had been a police sergeant in London, and he was fairly well educated.

Toofat and Frank were adventuresome and active men, who often walked around the prison farm together. In one of their tramping expeditions, they stumbled upon a disused timber mill. This mill had been closed down by its owners; its machinery, however, greased and partially covered in canvas, remained in place. Possibly the owners hoped to eventually reopen the mill.

Most of the machinery consisted of large loghaulers, which were designed to drag tree trunks out of the bush to the mill, where they would be sliced up for building material. These loghaulers were heavy machines: powerfully built of steel, and equipped with winches and thick cables. But these loghaulers were mobile, too, and could be shifted by tractor and trailer from one place in the bush to another.

The caretaker of the mill was a shepherd who lived on a farm nearby; he visited the mill from time to time to check that the covers were in place over the machinery, and that all remained reasonably tidy. The shepherd generally travelled the few miles from his farm to the mill by horseback, with his dogs trailing behind.

Time passed and both Frank and Toofat were released from prison, returning to civilian life in Auckland.

Then, some months later, the shepherd was approached by two men, whom he later identified as Frank and Toofat. The shepherd recounted that these two men said they were potential buyers of the mill, and had obtained the owner's consent to inspect the machinery. The shepherd, being a courteous person by nature, served them both tea at his homestead.

Frank and Toofat made frequent visits to the mill after that, and eventually told the shepherd that they had purchased

THE JURORS WHO USED SLEDGEHAMMERS ON THE LOGHAULERS

the mill, and intended to break up the machinery and sell it for scrap metal.

The shepherd was suspicious about this purchase, but unfortunately he was unable to locate the true owners of the mill. Finally, he was convinced by Frank and Toofat that they were genuine. To his everlasting regret, he was persuaded to help them break up the machinery and load it onto a truck to be transported to the nearest railhead, and he was paid for his services by cheque.

The machinery was, of course, made of solid steel, and breaking it up with sledgehammers was no easy task. But the three of them applied themselves vigorously and, ultimately, most of the loghaulers were smashed to pieces and taken away on the truck.

After some weeks, the true owners of the mill finally contacted the shepherd, and when he explained what had happened, the owners immediately contacted the police, making a complaint of theft and intentional damage.

The police made extensive inquiries, but were unable to locate the broken loghaulers. However, Toofat and Frank were arrested as a result of the farmer's descriptions of them, and brought to trial at the then Supreme Court at Hamilton.

Frank and Toofat denied their guilt, and said they had purchased the loghaulers from the shepherd, on the basis that it was only fit for scrap metal. They said the money they had paid him was part of the purchase price.

This defence was not very convincing, however, because the value of the machinery, as assessed by the prosecution, was by far disproportionate to the money paid to the shepherd.

But then, at trial, a second defence was developed: the defence of impossibility. It was submitted that the machinery could not have been broken up with sledgehammers as alleged by the shepherd. They said this was a fabrication, and an attempt by the shepherd to justify the payments he had received. The defence argued that, in reality, it would have been physically impossible to break up these machines with sledgehammers.

The trial proceeded before Chief Justice Harold Barrowclough and a jury of twelve. The Chief Justice had been a major-general during the war, and was known as a strict disciplinarian. At a law conference once, he had submitted that all prisoners in New Zealand jails should have to perform a series of press-ups in their cells before they were eligible to be fed in the morning. As head partner at Russell McVeagh, a large Auckland law firm, he'd been regarded as pragmatic and a straight talker.

At the onset of the trial, the Chief Justice informed counsel that he would not tolerate unnecessary delay. He said that civil cases were more important than criminal cases, and there were several of the latter to be disposed of, so we had better be efficient with the court's time.

The prosecution called expert evidence to establish that the stolen machinery was valuable, that it was still usable and certainly should not have been classified as scrap metal.

In due course, the defence called a rebuttal expert named Opie Rae. Opie qualified as an expert because he had been an Auckland dealer in scrap metal for many years, and much hinged on whether the jury would accept his evidence.

A tense moment arrived as Opie Rae was summoned to give evidence, however. Although the usher called out his name loudly, both inside and outside the courtroom, there was no response. Opie Rae did not appear. The Chief Justice became very restless and angry, demanding to know where the witness was. Not without some difficulty, the defence obtained a short adjournment so that Opie Rae could be found.

Opie Rae was regarded as a somewhat colourful character. An unusual feature of his face was that his nose had been so badly bent it sat at about a forty-five degree angle. It was said that he was popular in Auckland among his fellow scrap dealers, and had a great sense of humour. He was also addicted to alcohol.

Without much trouble, counsel found Opie at the Central Hotel in Hamilton, quite intoxicated. He was taken to the bathroom where his head was doused in the hand basin, which had been filled with water. This had a sobering effect, but resulted in his shirt being saturated.

It was necessary then to take him to a menswear shop and replace his shirt with a new one. When he appeared from the changing room, he said to the defence counsel, with a delighted grin, 'God, the sheilas will go me now!'

However, in the witness box back at the trial, he gave his evidence surprisingly well. He referred to old photographs of the mill, and said that the machinery appeared rusted and obsolete, and was therefore only valuable as scrap metal. The judge looked at him with absolute distaste, but the jury obviously enjoyed his appearance, and laughed spontaneously at his numerous jokes, which liberally sprinkled his evidence.

Before the final addresses, the defence made yet another risky move. Mysteriously, during the previous night, one of the loghaulers had arrived on the lawn of the Hamilton Supreme Court. No one knew where it had come from, or who had delivered it, but all parties agreed it was identical to one of the stolen loghaulers. The defence requested that the Chief Justice allow the jurors to be supplied with sledgehammers to see if the loghauler could be broken up in the manner described by the shepherd.

Legal precedent, by which judges are guided, frowns upon any type of forensic experiment being carried out by jurors. However, these did not deter the pragmatic Chief Justice from making an order that the jury should be allowed these sledgehammers in order to test whether the loghauler could be broken up.

Consequently, an unusual scene eventuated. Outside the court stood the Chief Justice and the court registrar, with the prosecutors nearby and, further away, the defence lawyers and their clients, as the jury, equipped with these sledgehammers, took turns attempting to break the loghauler with them.

As they bashed away at it, one of the defendants confidentially whispered to his counsel: 'I hope, Peter, these buggers don't break it.'

Fortunately for the defence, after a somewhat energetic few hours, the jury concluded it was impossible to break up the loghauler using sledgehammers.

Back in the courtroom, after final addresses and the summing-up, the jury retired but soon brought back verdicts of not guilty on all charges, and the Chief Justice, with obvious reluctance, discharged both Toofat and Frank the Tank.

It may well be that a certain amount of alcohol was later consumed by the defence team at a Hamilton hotel.

Dynamiting the Wall of the Wellington High Court

Sometimes a barrister has to make a decision very quickly and the correctness of that decision may seriously affect the future of that barrister's professional career on a somewhat permanent basis.

Unlike many other professionals, the criminal lawyer acts out in the open. His or her arena is the courtroom, where quite often the drama being carried out is subject to the full focus of public examination. Often the issues involved in the trial are controversial and extremely serious, but the criminal lawyer must always appear to be detached and in control.

I have known several occasions over the years where barristers have lost self-discipline in the court situation and have ultimately brought upon themselves severe condemnation for their histrionic and overemotional responses to difficult situations.

The barrister must keep his cool at all times. He should only laugh when the judge laughs first, and should never become, in the opinion of the jury, a conceited, arrogant, overpaid idiot. What I am about to relate is one of the most agonising decisions or dilemmas a barrister could experience in a trial situation.

In October 1978, Terry Clark, later to become known as 'Mr Asia', stood in the dock at the Wellington Supreme Court before Mr Justice Joseph Ongley and jury, and pleaded not guilty to a very serious charge of importing heroin into New Zealand.

Terry Clark had the somewhat dubious distinction of later becoming ranked among the top ten criminals in the world according to Interpol, and his notoriety is still remembered and chronicled in television documentaries and news media publications today.

In those days, Clark's shocking reputation as a criminal had not reached its zenith, as he was yet to go on to commit his most heinous crimes, including murders in Australia and in Britain. He was ultimately convicted of murder and drug dealing in England. He was sentenced to a long period in prison, where he would subsequently die by heart attack.

However, to come back to the trial in Wellington in 1978, he then stood before the jury as a relatively young man, someone thin and emaciated, with a receding hairline, and nothing about him to indicate his criminal potential.

The Crown case against him was marred because the defence had ascertained that the original evidence regarding the identification of the heroin, given by the DSIR, was flawed, and had not been appropriately briefed by the prosecution services in Auckland. It is an unfortunate fact for the prosecution that if it can be established that the prosecution itself has been guilty of some type of malpractice, particularly through their essential witnesses, such as the DSIR, then the edge is taken from their cases. In many trials, the contagion of their own neglect, to put it mildly, will deprive the prosecution of a reliable platform upon which a jury can hang a verdict of guilty.

Until a verdict is announced, however, it is usually quite impossible for the defence, and the prosecution, for that matter, to know what the verdict will be. This unknown factor hangs over the trial throughout like the sword of Damocles, especially during the period when the jury is deliberating.

I know of trials where the prosecution does know what the verdict will be. These are trials where the police have contacts on the jury. In the old days, when we were preparing a trial, we would often go through the electoral rolls to try to ascertain whether any potential juror was closely connected with a police officer. Often we found that there would be several wives of police officers on the list, and indeed sometimes we would find other close relations of police officers listed as potential jurors. That is not to say that these people will be corrupt, or that they will necessarily be partial towards the prosecution. However, there is a real danger in those circumstances that the jury will be informed of damaging information about a defendant which otherwise would be inadmissible, or that information might be filtered back to the police detailing what is happening in the jury room. The defence in the Clark trial, however, had no reason to suspect that anything like that was happening in October 1978.

The antecedents of the trial revealed a long history. Clark had been granted bail by Justice Graham Speight in somewhat unusual circumstances. The probable reason why he had been granted bail was so that he might be free to unwittingly lead the police to other accomplices. However, once on bail, he quite predictably broke the terms and spent some time in

Australia before he was again arrested and extradited back to New Zealand, where ultimately he faced this trial.

The trial was onerous and the cross-examination detailed. The focus of the defence's attack was, as I mentioned, on the faulty method of the identification of the heroin. Was the substance found on the cigarette packets, recovered by the police at the home of Clark in Auckland, indeed heroin?

Unfortunately for the prosecution, the DSIR had not carried out tests that were conclusive in this regard but had merely made screening tests. Initially, instead of being honest about this, the DSIR had given evidence at the depositions that the tests had been conclusive.

When the DSIR knew that the game was up, in the sense that the defence knew that their evidence had been tainted, new proofs of evidence from the DSIR were served by the Crown, admitting that they had made errors, and now conceding that their tests for heroin, although a basis for suspicion, were not conclusive.

There was other evidence in the case, but most of it was quite fragile. At the last moment, indeed the day before the trial was to commence, the prosecution filed a further proof from an Australian detective stating that he had obtained admissions from Clark, and that Clark had confessed his guilt to him. Mr Justice Ongley, the trial judge, was very sceptical regarding the credibility of this new evidence, though, because it had taken so long for the police to divulge it to the court. As a result, he excluded this evidence altogether, much to the chagrin of the prosecution. Justice Ongley was one of those old-fashioned judges who was renowned for his fairness and evenness of judgment – he had been a great cricketer in his day, and it was said of him that he was always prepared to give the accused the benefit of the doubt, as was normally done in LBW appeals.

There was no way of knowing which way the jury was leaning, however. Eventually, after a lengthy, hard-fought trial, when the jury had retired and had been out for six or seven hours, as senior counsel for the defence, I decided to go down and see Clark, who was in one of the courthouse cells, waiting for the verdict.

It's an unusual time for counsel when the jury is out, because suddenly the barrister has nothing to do. For many weeks or months, he or she has been working assiduously, preparing the case and striving for an acquittal. Once the jury is out, however, there is nothing more he or she can do. Sometimes counsel is permitted to leave the precincts of a court, on the promise that they will return immediately when telephoned by the registrar, and on many such occasions counsel repair to a nearby hostelry, where a certain amount of imbibing is carried out.

The cells where prisoners are held in the Wellington courthouse are underneath public areas, but have a wall adjacent to the outside street. I walked down the concrete steps alone to where these prison cells were to have a chat with Clark.

The lights over the steps going down to the cells were not bright and the atmosphere was grim and drab. The prison officer waiting down there in an adjoining room was having a cup of tea, and when he heard my footsteps coming down the stairs, he got up and said, 'I suppose you want to see Clark?'

'Yes,' I replied. 'I'll have a word with him and see how he's getting on.'

Without more ado, the officer led me, still attired in my gown and carrying a wig, to one of a row of cells and loudly opened the door with a large key.

Clark was sitting inside on a bench. There was another prisoner in there with him, being held for some unrelated reason, and Clark said as we arrived, 'Can I speak to my lawyer alone?' At which the warden grunted and took the other prisoner out.

I went into the cell and sat on the bench opposite Clark. The warden closed the door and turned the key in the lock. The time now was one or two o'clock in the morning. It was a cold night and the cell was icy and desolate. There was only one thing to talk about: the possible verdict.

'Well,' said Clark, 'what do you think? Are they going to find me guilty or not?'

I leant forward with my head resting on my hands. I was tired, but felt a duty to keep up morale and encourage my client to be positive.

'I think it'll be all right,' I told him. 'I think we'll get there. They buggered it up with all their false evidence from the start. I believe the jury can see that quite plainly. On the other hand, however, you never know.'

The two of us looked at each other quickly. There was a pause.

Then Clark said, 'Well, any rate, I'm not that worried.'

'What do you mean you're not worried?' I said. 'You could get a long term out of this if you are convicted.'

Clark laughed, a sort of a bored laugh, and said, 'Well, I'll tell you something. We've got this building dynamited. If the verdict goes against us, we're gonna blast this wall off. I've got an escape plan. They'll never get me. I'll get away.'

I was aghast. This was something I had never anticipated; nor had I encountered such a threat in any case previously. From an ordinary prisoner this would be merely a joke or fantasy. But the more I had got to know and learn about Clark, the more I realised that anything was possible with this man, who didn't seem to have any limits to his criminality. Indeed, he seemed to be obsessively drawn to the dangers of crime like a moth to a flame.

In my brain, already aching with fatigue and worry, there was now a new danger. What if this bugger was right? What if he were found guilty? What if his accomplices do blow the bloody back of the court building off, and he makes an escape, abortive or otherwise? There would surely be an inquiry. One of the first things they would ask would be whether the barrister knew. Did he know that this was going to happen? Had he been told that they were going to blow the back off the courthouse?

I looked at Clark and said, 'You must be bloody joking.'

Clark looked at me with his merciless, unblinking blue eyes and laughed: 'Well, believe what you bloody well like.'

The warden let me out, and slowly, stooping with weariness, and now with a new burden, I walked slowly back up those concrete steps to the court above.

What should I do? Should I tell the judge? It is usually the duty of counsel to report to the trial judge any irregularity that he or she becomes aware of in the course of a trial. This is done in chambers, in the presence of the prosecution and the clerk. The burden then shifts to the judge. He then must decide what should be done.

I pondered the absolute audaciousness of the idea that the courthouse might be dynamited. Would I make a fool of myself if I related my conversation with Clark to the judge? Would I become a laughing-stock? If nothing came of it, I would be derided for being duped by my client.

On the other hand, what if the verdict was guilty and the bloody wall was dynamited? What if my conversation with Clark was bugged, which was highly likely? Godammit! What should I do?

Then, mercifully, came the cry: 'A verdict, a verdict!'

The time-honoured procedure of transmitting verdicts begins with the jury knocking on the door of their room to alert the ushers outside that they have reached a decision. The usher then has a quick word with the foreman of the jury, which is usually restricted to the question, 'Do you have a unanimous verdict?' The usher then reports immediately to the judge that the verdict is available. The judge then makes an order that the court is to reassemble, and the various barristers and people connected with the case gather and take their places back in the courtroom.

The word gets around quickly. 'A verdict! A verdict!' Reporters, police officers, spectators, relations – for all those people who have some sort of interest in the trial, people who often have been waiting for weeks or months, now is the time of judgment. Will it be guilty or will it be not guilty?

The thought of an immediate verdict replaced my anxiety over the escape plan. At least now, things would be brought to a head. I pulled my robe over my shoulders, straightened my wig and entered the courtroom, taking my place at the bar next to my junior, Kevin Ryan.

When the court was ready, the last person to be brought in was the accused: Clark was placed in the dock, pale, but not showing any signs of emotion.

The foreman of the jury was asked to stand. The clerk of the court asked him whether they were unanimous, and the foreman replied that they were. The clerk then read out the charge, and asked him what their verdict was. The foreman answered slowly, but gravely: 'Not guilty, sir.'

I felt not only the jubilation of winning the case, but also the relief that now there would be no reason for Clark's mates to blow the back of the courtroom off. Clark was duly released and free to go. The trial was finally over.

I do not know, to this day, whether that court building was primed with dynamite or not. Maybe it was, and maybe it wasn't. It will forever remain a mystery to me.

Polling the Jury

In 1979, I travelled to Gisborne to look over the farm of Simon Dods, who had been charged with criminal offences relating to 38 large fertiliser sacks containing 161 kilograms of cannabis. The sacks had been found, together with $50,000 in cash, secreted under the concrete floor of an old, disused freezing works, situated on land leased by Simon, who lived on a property adjacent to the freezing works with his wife and family.

He was a very enterprising young farmer, who not only grew all sorts of crops, but bred eels, which he exported to China. A highly intelligent young man, his close-knit family helped him work the farm, which was a hive of industry. Simon was a successful farmer, and it was rumoured that other farmers in the district, who were jealous of his success, had 'dobbed' him in.

The first trial against him took place before Justice Lester Moller and jury in the Gisborne Supreme Court, where the prosecutor was Tom Thorpe, who later became a highly respected High Court judge. Before the judge summed up, I obtained his consent to allow a local lawyer to take my place at the bar, as I was required back in Auckland, so I was not present when Simon was found guilty and sentenced to six years imprisonment.

A perusal of the judge's summing-up, however, revealed that he had made a serious misdirection of fact to the jury. The judge had told them that the making of the large hole in the concrete floor of the freezing works, where the cannabis and the money were found hidden, must have caused a lot of noise, and surely Simon and his family would have heard the racket. The truth was, though, that the hole had been there for many years previously, and had been part of the drainage system of the now-disused freezing works when it had been operating.

Simon's case went to appeal, and at that hearing the judges of the Court of Appeal asked Tom Thorpe, who appeared on behalf of the Crown, why he didn't stand up and correct the trial judge.

Tom replied, 'Well, Your Honours, if you know Mr Justice Moller, he's not a judge that one attempts to correct lightly.'

This raised a judicial laugh among the appellate judges, who finally quashed the conviction and ordered a new trial.

The second trial was held at the Wellington Supreme Court, and this time I was assisted by Dick Kearney, who was a brilliant advocate; he later became a District Court judge. The prosecution case was tainted with police malpractice this time. One of the pieces of evidence against Simon were some cannabis reefers found in his car. But when defence scientists analysed this cannabis, they found that the active ingredient of cannabis had been extracted. The inference was that the cannabis had previously been subjected to DSIR analysis. In other words, the police had taken this cannabis from an exhibit belonging to some previous case, and deliberately planted it in Simon Dods's car. After a vigorous trial, the jury retired, and after some hours, returned with the foreman, only to announce that they had reached a unanimous verdict of guilty.

There was much tension in the courtroom. The detectives were riled because allegations of malpractice had been made against them, and now they were delighted with a guilty verdict. The defence, on the other hand, was very disappointed, as we had been confident that, this time, Simon would be cleared.

After this pronouncement of guilt on all counts by the foreman, the laughter and jeers of the detectives were quite audible. I could feel the anger rising in my head. Simon cried out from the dock that he was innocent, and the distress of his family in the public gallery was painfully obvious.

This trial was presided over by Mr Justice Ongley, who, as I've noted elsewhere, was renowned for his fairness, and so, acting on impulse and motivated by a desperate attempt to reverse the verdict, I rose to my feet, and applied to him now to poll the jury.

I had previously seen, on television, a fictitious portrayal of a jury being polled. The American actor Raymond Burr, in the role of Robert Ironside, had polled a jury from his wheelchair in the American courtroom drama *Ironside*. Robert Ironside never lost a case, and he didn't lose that one, either. His jury poll, however, was my only precedent – not that I mentioned any of this to the trial judge.

The judge, very calmly, asked me, 'Do you mean that the registrar should ask each juror whether he or she has a reasonable doubt?'

I replied, 'Yes, Your Honour.'

The judge spoke to the prosecutor and said, 'I can't see any harm in that.' The prosecutor seemed confused, and did not give a clear answer.

After a short sojourn to the judge's chambers, the judge then directed the registrar to poll the jury. He first asked the foreman, who appeared quite defensive as he loudly reaffirmed that he had no reasonable doubt that the accused was guilty. He further said that the jury had been unanimous and none of them had any doubts.

However, this was not the case for the next two jurors. Both women, seated adjacent to the foreman, said they had reasonable doubts about the verdict.

The courtroom became very quiet; a pin drop would have been heard. Again, the judge called all the lawyers into his chambers, and after legal discussion, the court was reassembled. His Honour then announced that the trial was to be aborted, and a new trial was ordered.

Back in the courtroom, the glee of the police officers turned to scowls and growls. This was the first and the last time a jury was ever polled in New Zealand. Soon after this trial, all judges received a direction from the Chief Justice that such a poll must never be granted again.

At his third trial, held in Wellington between 16 and 20 July 1979, Simon Dods was finally found not guilty on all counts.

That night, the defence, with their client Simon and his vivacious wife Sharon, celebrated the acquittal with gusto. After a few drinks, Dick Kearney, a great humorist, danced an Irish jig. At the same time, he recited a ballad that he composed on the spot, entitled 'The Ballad of the Trials of Simon Dods'. I can no longer recall the words, but it was a mightily impressive performance.

She Killed Her Baby

Many years ago, I attended the old Mount Eden Prison to interview a woman who had been charged with murder. The allegation against her was that she had suffocated her newborn child with a pillow.

I was met at the prison by the matron, who had expressed a wish to see me. She was a kindly woman but strict, and we sat down in her office while an inmate made us tea.

She said, 'I am very concerned about this inmate you are about to interview. She has been here for a couple of weeks on remand. She eats practically nothing and spends most of her time crying. She is deeply depressed and we have been keeping a special eye on her. I want to tell you that if we, the prison staff, can do anything to help her, we will. I do not understand why she has been charged with murder and not the lesser charge of infanticide. We believe that she is a good woman but a person who urgently needs help.'

As I drank my tea I thought to myself how generalisations are made about prison staff. Like the matron, so many of them strive to do their best to help the unfortunate people in their care.

When the woman was brought into the visiting room, I immediately saw how right the prison matron had been. The woman, whom I shall call Marie, was, as the matron had described, deeply depressed. She wore no makeup, her hair was not brushed, and in her prison clothes of grey she looked so pathetic and anguished.

She did not look at me but hung her head and started to cry: 'You have no idea how much I miss my children, what a dreadful thing I have done,' she said. 'They have taken away my other two children, I don't know where they are, I have never heard from them, my heart is absolutely broken. I really don't want to go on living.'

It was difficult for me to get a logical statement from her. She seemed to have no memory of the suffocation and did not have any enthusiasm for defending herself.

I had taken another lawyer with me that day, my old comrade Chris Reid, who had worked so loyally with me on many cases, and after leaving the prison – such a very dismal place – we drove to a nearby coffee shop to talk about what we could do for Marie.

Chris said to me, 'I can't work out why the Crown has charged her with murder and not infanticide.'

'I agree,' I said, and then I told him, 'I think we should discuss this case with Laurie Gluckman.'

Laurie was a friend and an eminent psychiatrist; we had spent many evenings at his home discussing forensic defences for clients over the years. Within a day or two, Chris and I met him at his clinic. He had read the briefs of evidence and had come up with a possible explanation for this tragedy that had befallen the woman and her baby.

'From what you have told me and from what I have read of the case,' Laurie said, 'this woman could have been suffering from puerperal fever – childbirth fever. It's not as common as it used to be but it would explain why this woman killed her child. It's a type of infection that causes extreme pain and acute depression. In some cases it leads to psychosis, where the patient may commit terrible acts and then have no recollection of what they have done.'

I asked Laurie, 'What sort of evidence do you think that we should try to find to support a defence of this puerperal fever?'

And he told me, 'Well, there are certain physical symptoms I would have expected the police doctor to have ascertained but I don't see any of these in the doctor's brief of evidence that you have supplied me with. However,' he advised, 'you should examine where she was living. Puerperal fever is an infection that can arise from conditions of poverty and squalor. You should also look for evidence concerning her emotional state, particularly depression.'

Chris and I then went to the address where she had been living. We had not been able to get the key to the place, but when we got there we found other tenants in the dilapidated property to be very cooperative. They showed us the part of the house where the woman had been living with her three children. It was literally just a passageway. Mattresses, children's clothing and blankets seem to almost entirely cover the floor.

I asked one of the tenants, 'How could she have lived in such shocking conditions?'

He said, 'It's worse than that. If you look at the ceiling you can see daylight through it. When it rains the whole place is damp. And outside the house there is no proper drainage, either, so in bad weather the backyard becomes a pool of mud.'

'Why doesn't the landlord fix it up?' I asked the tenant.

He laughed and said, 'He's a wealthy fellow and a member of the ACT Party. He has many houses. He makes all his tenants sign an agreement that they are responsible for the maintenance of whatever property they rent, and as none of us have any money, no maintenance is ever done.'

I asked him, 'Where is Marie's partner?'

'We have never seen him since the death of the child,' he told me.

'What sort of fellow was he?' I asked.

The tenant replied, 'I don't want to be quoted but he spent most of his time at the pub or on the pokie machines. He was rarely home before 10pm. You could hear him shouting and knocking her around. We all felt sorry for her; she did her best to take care of those kids. She had no money and no one to help her. We all believe that in her own way she was a kind and devoted mother. She loved those kids.'

The trial was heard at the Supreme Court in Auckland. Justice Peter Mahon presided and a jury of twelve was selected. Justice Mahon, with his long, distinguished, aristocratic face and his dry sense of humour, was regarded as one of the finest judges that ever sat on the bench. He never wasted a word. He was renowned for his fairness and ability to quickly get to the heart of the case.

In Marie's case, when the registrar read out the charge of murder, she was in such a state of fright that she could hardly answer. She was visibly trembling and I really thought she might have a heart attack, she was so scared.

The trial proceeded and eventually the prosecution doctor took the stand. He had been called to the scene by the police soon after the accused's arrest, and he readily admitted under cross-examination that he had physically examined the accused at the time. He said he had examined her because she looked ill.

I asked him whether he had seen the symptoms of childbirth fever. Again he readily admitted that he had.

I said, 'But there are no details about that in your brief of evidence.'

He retorted sharply, 'I didn't prepare the brief. If you want to know why that information is not there, ask the detective who prepared it.'

The atmosphere in the courtroom had become very tense and I believe it was obvious to everybody present that the wrong charge had been preferred against the woman.

I then asked the doctor, 'Do you believe that at the time of the homicide this woman was suffering from puerperal fever?'

He said, 'Yes, that is highly likely.'

'Is it symptomatic of that illness that a woman may become psychotic and commit a dreadful act, which is entirely inconsistent with her true nature?' I asked him.

He replied, 'Yes, that is well established by the literature.'

I asked him, 'Do you believe it is reasonably possible that at the time this woman killed her child, she was psychotic and unaware of the nature and quality of her action?'

Without any hesitation the police doctor answered, 'Yes, I believe that is highly likely.'

At this point, the judge intervened: 'I would like to see all counsel in my chambers.'

In chambers, Justice Mahon appeared stern and on the borderline of being angry. He asked the prosecutor, 'Why was this information not in the doctor's brief and why was it not communicated to the defence?'

This was long before discovery of documents had been made compulsory by law, but even back then there was duty incumbent upon the prosecution to volunteer any information that might be critical to the defence.

The prosecutor mumbled something about the police having prepared the brief. This explanation was totally ignored by the judge. I knew it was not necessary for me to utter a word.

The judge declared, 'I have no power to dismiss the charge of murder but I do have the power to so direct the jury, and that is what I intend to do. Mr Prosecutor, I wish you to add to the indictment a charge of infanticide. I believe that Mr Williams will advise his client to plead guilty to that charge.' Then he added, 'This woman needs help not punishment.'

Neither counsel addressed the jury, and without leaving the jury box the jury found Marie not guilty of murder but guilty of infanticide.

The judge then sentenced the woman to a term of probation. He included express provisions that she immediately be provided with medical and psychological assistance and that the authorities find for her a satisfactory place to live.

In conclusion, the judge addressed the court, apologising on behalf of the judicial system for the unnecessary stress that the accused had been through. He said that the court would do all in its powers to obtain for her the assistance that she so desperately required.

Sometime later I learnt that Marie had her children returned to her, she had been provided with a state house and had severed her relationship with her violent partner. Justice had finally been delivered by one of our great New Zealand judges.

Justice Mahon had the wisdom of Solomon, and we saw it exercised during this trial. What impressed me was his decisiveness and his seemingly innate ability to remedy injustice with promptitude and judicial fairness.

The Planted Shell-case

Some years ago, the Ryan brothers, Kevin and Gerald, who were both famous lawyers, asked me to take up the role of senior counsel in the case of Arthur Allan Thomas. Arthur had been twice convicted by two juries on a charge of murdering a farmer and his wife in their home at Pukekohe: David Harvey Crewe and Jeanette Lenore Crewe.

I visited Arthur at Auckland Prison, and it soon became apparent to me that he was an innocent man wrongly incarcerated. We sat at a large table in a visiting room, which had been especially provided by the prison manager, Jack Hobson.

The prison staff and the inmates all strongly believed that Arthur was innocent, too, and he was treated with great respect by them all.

As he related to me the details of this terrible miscarriage of justice against him, he began to cry when he told me how his wife, Vivien, had now left him. He said that she would always be loyal to him in respect of his case, and would continue to fight for him to expose the terrible wrongs committed by the police, but in the end she had got to a stage where she felt she must make a life for herself.

The case began to take over my life and the further I investigated, the more I realised the enormity of the police corruption at the genesis of this case.

Pat Vesey was the chairman of the group of people devoted to protesting Arthur's innocence and gathering evidence to support his cause; among this group were Arthur's parents, his brothers and their spouses, and many others. Pat Vesey told me that they had received no cooperation from the police. On the contrary, the police had tried to impede their attempts to obtain exculpatory evidence. For example, when the group had wanted a sample of soil from the Crewe homestead garden so that they could test one of the prosecution's crucial assertions, they were informed by the police that if they entered the farm they would be arrested for trespass.

Dr Jim Sprott was the forensic expert for the defence, and I had long regarded him as New Zealand's premier mind in this field. He was ably assisted by Pat Booth, who was the editor of the *Auckland Star* newspaper (and, as mentioned in the 'Exotic Stripper' chapter, had acted as witness for the prosecution in the Sante Collins case). Another scientist deeply involved in this case was Professor Neil Mowbray, head of the engineering faculty at Auckland University. I spent many hours with these experts and even travelled to Melbourne with Dr Sprott and Pat Booth to inquire first hand at the factory where the shell-case – the Crown's main exhibit against Arthur – had been made. This was the shell-case the police belatedly said they had found outside the victims' house, and which they said had come from a bullet fired from Arthur's .22 rifle.

I say 'belatedly' because initially Thomas's rifle had been excluded as a possible murder weapon, because of inconsistencies with the test bullet fired through it and the lead from the bodies of the deceased. However, many months later, when Thomas became a suspect, a shell-case, fired from his rifle, was surprisingly found outside the Crewe house.

In Melbourne we met Mr George Leighton, from the company that engraved lettering on hobs supplied by ICI. The engraving was carried out on a pantograph machine which enables stock letters, or templates, to be reproduced on the object to be engraved at a given smaller size. He told us that every few months he would, on request, engrave a new head stamp which would then be used by ICI to indirectly produce a new batch containing millions of shell-cases. He said ICI would have copies of the receipts for these new head stamps on their files, and this would give the dates in relation to the production of each new batch of shell-cases.

Because part of the process in making the new head stamp involved manual dexterity, no two of these original head stamps were ever identical. Although the same letters 'ICI' were invariably engraved on the stamp, there were always small idiosyncrasies that made each head stamp unique: these idiosyncrasies were then reflected on the progeny of the head stamp – that is, the batch of millions of shell-cases.

Basically, a completed piece of ammunition suitable for firing in a .22 rifle comprises the shell-case, the leaden projectile, and the gunpowder and wad contained in the base of the shell-case. These shell-cases were manufactured by the million in the ICI factory at Melbourne, and some were exported to New Zealand, where they were fitted with the leaden projectiles and made ready for use.

Apart from the letters 'ICI' stamped on the base of the shell-case, there were other distinguishing features in these completed pieces of ammunition. For instance, in some batches, the priming material was wet, but in others, it was dry. In relation to the leaden projectiles, some batches had the number '8' inscribed upon them, but others did not. By careful microscopic examination and with reference to company records, it was therefore possible to date the manufacture of any particular shell-case within certain parameters. Our object was to try and date the manufacture of the shell-case which was found outside the Crewe house.

Mr Leighton was pleased to see us and very cooperative. He told us how the officer in charge of the case, Inspector Bruce Hutton, together with Dr Donald Nelson, the lead scientist for the prosecution, had a short time previously arrived to interview him in Melbourne. He told us how they had both tried to persuade him to swear a false affidavit. He said they already had the document prepared, and put pressure on him to sign it. He told them that he would not sign the affidavit because it was false and, in particular, it incorrectly stated that all the head stamps made by him for ICI were identical and had no distinguishing details, contrary to fact.

He said that they became quite angry with him when he refused to sign the affidavit. He told them that he was going to take the document to his own lawyer, and later, during our visit to Melbourne, George Leighton gave the still unsigned affidavit to me.

While in Melbourne, I obtained a truthful affidavit from Mr Leighton, which set out how the head stamps were made and why there were small differences in the lettering of each batch. This is because, from the original head stamp, engraved upon a master hob, hundreds of duplicate hobs were made, which in turn stamped out the millions of shell-cases manufactured.

His affidavit also recited the unethical attempts by the police, Hutton and Nelson, to try to persuade Mr Leighton to sign the false affidavit. I attached the unsigned false affidavit to Mr Leighton's new affidavit, which he duly executed. It should be emphasised that Mr Leighton was not an employee of ICI, but an independent contractor, who, for many years, had been entrusted by ICI to engrave new head stamps for the production of shell-cases.

The manufacturer's records clearly showed that the shell-case allegedly found by the police outside the victims' house could not have contained one of the bullets that killed them. These bullets had been recovered from the dead bodies, and inscribed upon each was the number '8'. Because bullets with the number '8' had no longer been used in the manufacture of cartridges at the time the type of shell-case found by the police and the DSIR outside the Crewe house was made, it was not possible for any of those bullets to have had such a shell-case.

Mr Robert Walton, who was then the Assistant Commissioner of the New Zealand police, obtained an affidavit from Dr Nelson, which was supported by a report from Mr Hutton, stating that the individual shell-cases could not be categorised because the hobs that made them were all identical. Dr Nelson said that any small differences were due to wear and tear by the machinery. Mr Walton advised the then Attorney-General, Dr Martyn Finlay, to keep this information confidential, and in particular not to let the defence have a copy.

In defiance of this advice, however, Dr Martyn Finlay sent me a copy of Nelson's affidavit, together with the Hutton report, which I immediately handed over to Dr Sprott and Pat Booth.

The reactions of Dr Sprott and Pat Booth to these documents was that they were both appalled by the patent dishonesty revealed in these false affidavits by Hutton and Nelson. We drafted affidavits in reply, which set out the true situation. We then petitioned the Governor-General to refer the case back to the Court of Appeal in the light of the fresh evidence relating to the shell-case.

Arthur Thomas's case was indeed referred back to the Court of Appeal, but the question formulated for them to answer was framed in such a way by the Solicitor-General that it placed the onus of proof upon the defence.

Further to our disadvantage, the Court of Appeal at the hearing included Chief Justice Richard Wild, who had previously made public statements to the effect that he considered that Arthur Thomas was a threat to the judicial system. He publicly stated that because Thomas had been convicted by two juries, if now, at this late stage, he was granted a new trial, the judicial system would be brought into disrepute.

During my submissions, when I referred to the false affidavit and described how Hutton and Nelson had tried to twist Leighton's arm to get it signed, Chief Justice Wild, to my amazement, laughed and said, 'Don't all lawyers do that?'

I did not join in the laughter and felt my anger rising. As a disciplined barrister, I kept my feelings under control, but not without difficulty.

The Court of Appeal stated in their judgment that we had not satisfied them beyond all reasonable doubt that the shell-case could not have contained one of the fatal bullets, and therefore our application failed. I may say that, years later, one of the judges who had sat on the Court of Appeal at that hearing told me privately that if the question had been framed so that the onus of proof was on the balance of probabilities, he personally would have found for Thomas.

The fervour of Arthur Thomas's supporters was only increased by this legal setback. It was decided that a public meeting would be held at the town hall, and I was to be the main speaker.

When I arrived at the town hall, I found a large queue of people outside on the street. I asked one of the officials, 'What's going on here?'

The official replied, 'Well, the town hall is so packed with people that, according to the safety requirements, we have to stop allowing the public in now.'

When I explained that I was a speaker, he was most cooperative and, once inside, I went up onto the stage and sat with several other people who were to speak, including Dr Sprott and Pat Booth.

I can remember that night quite vividly. I have never had an experience like it and probably never will again. When I spoke I felt like a pop star. Every time I paused during my speech, huge applause would rise from the large audience. It was abundantly clear that, apart from undercover police (who I have no doubt were there), the audience were overwhelming in their desire to express their absolute support for Arthur Allan Thomas. It was a great night and it brought home to me just how important justice is and how it can be found in the hearts of ordinary people. The public understood how Thomas had been railroaded into being wrongly convicted of murders by some very dishonest senior police officers, even if the justice system so far had not exposed this shocking malpractice by the police and DSIR.

There is not sufficient space here to relate all the many details concerning the Thomas case, and I may say there are plenty, but eventually, as a result of this public campaign, the Muldoon government would go on to issue Arthur Thomas with a free pardon.

The Prime Minister, Robert Muldoon, met with Kevin and me in Auckland to discuss the case, and it was obvious that he had studied all the issues involved carefully and assiduously. The then Minister of Justice, Jim McLay, had also studied the case with great care. They dispatched a barrister, Robert Adams-Smith, to make inquiries on behalf of the government into some of the evidence, and his findings supported the innocence of Arthur Thomas.

Arthur himself, though, was not prepared to leave the prison where he had been for nine years until he was satisfied that the pardon now offered to him meant he was declared innocent of the heinous crimes he was alleged to have committed.

The Muldoon government then set up a Royal Commission headed by an Australian judge, Justice Robert Taylor. The Commission was held in downtown Auckland and it turned out to be a very stormy affair.

Within a very short time, Justice Taylor made it very obvious that he had a detestation for Inspector Hutton. When Hutton gave evidence, Justice Taylor was very critical of him. The hall where the Commission sat was packed with spectators, most of them police officers, and every time Justice Taylor criticised Hutton the police would actually boo.

THE PLANTED SHELL-CASE

Justice Taylor was scathing about how the police had taken the planted shell-case exhibit in the dead of night to the Whitford tip and hidden it so nobody could find it. Hutton said he was told to do this by the prosecutor, Dave Morris, but Dave Morris said that was a lie and that it was Hutton's idea.

The evidence in relation to this shell-case was central to the whole inquiry, and the DSIR, headed by Dr Nelson, remained adamant that the date of manufacture of the shell-case could not be ascertained by microscopic examination of its head stamp. Finally, however, the DSIR capitulated, and agreed that Thomas's experts were correct. It had taken the DSIR ten years to come to this conclusion.

Dr Sprott, Pat Booth and Professor Mowbray brought many other factors into play, such as the priming of the cartridges and the degree of corrosion on the shell-case from its alleged period concealed in the soil of the Crewes's garden. They produced insuperable evidence that the shell-case had been planted.

The Royal Commission ultimately found as a fact that Hutton and another senior police officer, Johnson, had indeed planted the shell-case in the Crewes's garden outside the window of the lounge room in which the Crewes had been shot, exonerating Arthur Thomas completely of the crime, and uncovering the depths of police dishonesty in his case.

From the beginning of the Commission, Justice Taylor had ordered that the Crown hand over to the defence, *ab initio*, copies of all documents in their possession. This is what we know today as discovery of documents. In those days, however, it was not obligatory, and senior counsel for the police, John Henry QC (later to become a High Court judge), was most adamant that the documents should not be handed over. Justice Taylor remained equally adamant, and compelled him so to do.

When Kevin and I received the documents, they were given very grudgingly and in a state of disorder. Many of the copies were unintelligible and some had been deliberately placed upside down and out of order. Kevin spent hundreds of hours sorting these documents out and trying to separate the wheat from the chaff. One document we found, however, was quite remarkable. It was a report made by Dr Nelson to the police at a very early stage in the inquiry. This document had never been handed over to the defence before, and was not revealed to Paul Temm QC, who was Arthur Thomas's counsel at the first jury trial. This document by Dr Nelson related to his testing of Arthur's rifle and other .22 rifles which had been collected in the neighbourhood in the aftermath of the murders.

He had compared lead fired from Arthur's rifle with lead recovered from the bodies, and had found there was a significant scarring mark on the test-fired lead, which did not appear on the lead from the bodies. He concluded at that stage that Arthur Thomas's rifle could be excluded on the grounds that it could not have fired the fatal bullets.

At that early stage in the police investigation, Arthur's rifle was returned to him as no longer having any significance, and so Arthur put the rifle away again and considered that he was not the suspect. Indeed, the police were looking at another suspect at the time, a man called Demler.

Sometime later, however, Hutton sent a police officer to Arthur's home and demanded the rifle back. Then, a day or two later, Hutton and Johnson were seen in a police car driving out to the Crewe farm, obviously taking that rifle with them. Witnesses heard shots being fired at the Crewe farm and afterwards saw Johnson and Hutton return in the car.

Within another day or so, Hutton ordered a couple of other detectives to go back out to the Crewe farm and re-search the area of garden near the lounge room of the house, where the Crewes had been shot. This area had been sieve-searched previously without any evidence being found. This time, however, within a short time, the shell-case was found – the one that had been planted there.

Throughout my career, on many occasions I have sensed a favourable bias of judges towards the prosecution and that the word of a police officer was invariably preferred to the word of the accused. But the commission of inquiry into the Thomas case was to restore my faith in British justice. Justice Taylor gave no favour or comfort to the police. He was a man of absolute integrity, completely fearless in his demand for answers to questions. He could not tolerate people whom he believed to be dishonest, particularly those who, in his opinion, had deliberately fabricated evidence to convict an innocent man of shocking crimes. In his sights in this regard were both the mealy-mouthed Dr Nelson and the arrogant, dishonest Hutton.

I record these matters in this account as I believe the Thomas case will go down in history as an exemplar of absolute corruption by both the police and the DSIR. It has become the precedent frequently used by defence lawyers to illustrate how it has been conclusively proved that on occasions both the police and the DSIR, with tunnel vision, can stoop to unscrupulous deception to try to nail a particular accused.

The Girl Who Identified the Wrong Accused

As a young lawyer I arrived one day at my office in the Lister Building to find a Lebanese family waiting for me. The husband, wife and their three sons were ushered into my office and, as they were seated and introduced themselves, I could not but be impressed by their good looks and the careful way in which they were dressed. The father then related their sad story to me, and while he spoke, the mother bowed her head and cried.

What the father said was briefly this: 'We have been recommended to you as a lawyer who gets results. My son Hassim has been charged with rape. I can tell you now that he is innocent and the girl has made a mistake of identification. Money is no object. We have a successful business in Auckland and our reputation is all-important to us. This is a case that you must win and the preliminary hearing is in the Magistrates Court in Auckland next week. Hassim is presently on bail and I had to lodge $5000 with the court to get him out. We know he is absolutely innocent because he was home with us when the girl said she was raped. He told the police this when he was arrested but they just laughed and said, "Of course your family would always stick up for you."'

Hassim then spoke, telling me, 'Mr Williams, I have never met this girl. All I can say is that she must have mistakenly picked me out from photographs at the police station. How they can charge anyone on that evidence I don't know and frankly I am completely bewildered. I cannot sleep and I want you to get me off at the hearing next week. I just cannot bear for this to go on any longer; I cannot bear the pain I am causing to my family. I am so ashamed, even though I am innocent.'

'Well,' I replied, 'the standard of proof at a preliminary hearing is very low. At a criminal trial, the standard of proof is "beyond reasonable doubt", but at the depositions, they only have to prove a "prima facie case". This means that on the face of it there is a case to answer. It's not often that the justices of the peace who preside at these hearings will throw a case out. But on the other hand, now and again they do. As for the alibi, it's customary to file that after the preliminary hearing and, at any rate, if we do file it now, the police may just change the date of the alleged rape!'

The father spoke again: 'There is not much more I can tell you. This case means everything to us. You must give it top priority. We are hopeful that you will get the case dismissed next week.'

After the family left, I sat back in my chair and thought about the case. It was clear that the family expected, and even demanded, that Hassim be cleared of the rape charge at the depositions.

In those days, the preliminary hearing was really a mini-trial. If the accused was committed for trial, he would usually be granted bail and ultimately be tried at the Supreme Court before a judge and jury. However, unlike the law today, it was customary for the prosecution to call all their witnesses at the preliminary hearing, where they would be cross-examined. Perhaps surprisingly, quite a few accused had their charges dismissed by the two JPs who usually presided, and the prosecution seldom brought the charges again. This was despite a dismissal at a preliminary hearing not being a bar to the charge being brought again.

I had not reached the top echelon of the criminal bar at that stage in my career and I felt my responsibilities towards the accused's family very heavily. I considered bringing in another senior lawyer, such as Ronald Davison QC, who later became Chief Justice of New Zealand, or Dave Beattie QC, who later became the Governor-General. These were the two pre-eminent criminal barristers during this period.

I could not get the case out of my mind. I thought about the facts again and again. There was something about the family that was quite remarkable. To an ordinary New Zealander like me, they all looked similar. Naturally, a family usually do look similar, but these people, particularly the brothers, seemed uncannily alike. It has been said that members of another race often look the same to an outsider.

The day came for the preliminary hearing. In those days the Magistrates Court (as it was then called) was located in Kitchener Street and a special room was dedicated for preliminary hearings. This was a somewhat unusual room in that the accommodation for the lawyers and the public was tiered. Below the seating accommodation for the defence was accommodation for the prosecution, and across a small floor space was a table for the registrar and, above that, a table and seats for the two justices of the peace who would be presiding. To the right of them was a witness box and on the floor level a separate door so that the witness could enter and walk to and from the witness room without passing through the public gallery. It was a small courtroom but the furniture was well-made, carefully varnished, and the whole place had an appropriate judicial atmosphere.

We arrived a few minutes earlier than the 10am commencement time. I arranged for the father and one son to sit at the very back of the courtroom. Behind me, but in full view of the witness stand, I placed the accused, and beside me at my table, his brother. Usually, a defendant is seated in the dock, or next to his lawyer. This is, however, subject to the direction of the court. In the present case, no objection was made to the order of seating.

Within a few minutes the various personnel of the court assumed their positions and awaited the justices of the peace to enter and begin proceedings. The police prosecutors took their seats in the front row below the defence table and the registrar placed the various files on his table and then went out to bring in the justices. When the justices entered, everybody stood up and waited for the justices to be seated. The registrar then called out, 'You may be seated!' and the ensemble all sat down.

The registrar then called the name of the accused, and Hassim, seated behind me, stood up, in full view of the court, and was formally charged. He elected trial by jury and pleaded not guilty. He was then given permission to sit down again. The justices made an order for the exclusion of all witnesses and the prosecutor asked for an exception, namely that the officer-in-charge could remain in the courtroom and be seated next to him as an assistant. This exception was granted.

Soon after the proceedings commenced, a reporter came into the courtroom and sat at a table reserved for the news media, and then the justices began the hearing by asking the prosecutor to outline the case against Hassim.

The prosecutor rose and read from a summary of facts, giving explicit details of how allegedly the complainant had been raped by Hassim. He made no mention of the alibi that Hassim had given him at the time of his arrest.

After the prosecutor had finished his opening address, he called his first witness, the complainant. She spoke very firmly and convincingly but at the end of her testimony, when asked to point out the person who had raped her, she pointed to the accused's brother, who was seated next to me. The prosecutor did not seem to notice this error and sat down thinking he had established at least a prima facie case. I asked no questions.

From then on a series of witnesses were called but their evidence was not particularly probative and none of them were asked to identify the accused. Finally, the prosecutor informed the court that there were no more witnesses and that he was closing the prosecution's case.

I then stood up and addressed the justices. 'May it please Your Worships, there is no case against the accused. This is clearly a case of mistaken identification. The only witness who purported to identify the accused was the complainant but she identified the wrong person in this courtroom. As has already been made clear to this court at the commencement of these proceedings when the charge was read out to the person who stood up and pleaded to the charge, the accused is not the person seated next to me but is the person immediately above me. He was in clear view of the complainant when she quite clearly pointed out his brother, who was seated next to me and still is. There is no other evidence of identification and the only course open to Your Worships is to discharge the accused.'

The prosecutor immediately rose to his feet. He demanded that he immediately be permitted to recall the complainant so that she could have the opportunity to identify the accused once more. I rose to my feet and objected, saying that the prosecutor had closed his case. The witness had had every opportunity to make a careful identification, nothing was hidden from her, and she pointed out the wrong person.

'It would be a miscarriage of justice if she was now allowed to patch up her faulty evidence!' I argued.

The justices called for order in the courtroom and asked the lawyers to be seated. They said that they would retire and consider their ruling. The court was adjourned and the justices left to discuss their pronouncement. In the meantime, in the courtroom, the prosecutor became very angry. He accused me of playing tricks on the court and deceiving the witness.

'You have been interfering with the course of justice! If this case is dismissed I am going to report you to the Law Society and the Crown Law Office!' he bellowed.

Hassim and his family remained absolutely quiet and waited for the return of the justices. Eventually the justices returned to the courtroom and gave their verdict. They said that they had discussed the matter thoroughly and unfortunately were both of the opinion that they had no alternative but to dismiss the charges and find that there was insufficient evidence to warrant the case being sent to trial.

Outside the courtroom, the family was overjoyed. The father said it was like a gift from heaven and they could not thank me too much.

Around the town the next day, the newspaper billboards read, 'Professional Man Believed to be Behind Courtroom Identification Switch'. This, of course, was perfectly untrue. No witnesses had been switched. The law had been observed to the letter.

No doubt the Crown solicitors had been consulted by the prosecution but, in fact, no rules had been broken. All that had been achieved was an exposure of the frailties of the prosecution's case. I never received any letters about it from the Law Society or the Crown Law Office. I believe justice had been achieved, and an innocent man relieved of the stress of a jury trial.

The Police Sergeant Who Came to Dinner

In my younger years, as I've already written, I had a fair amount to do with boarding house accommodation in Auckland, and it was a boarding house that was, in a way, responsible for my very existence. Allow me to relate a little family history here.

My maternal grandparents spent most of their years in Ohakune, the centre of the King Country. My grandfather had migrated from Ireland to Tasmania and then to New Zealand, where he married my grandmother. He was referred to by the locals as Big Barney, as in his prime he weighed some 120 kilograms and was the local wood-chopping champion. He managed the local milling company but was in his later years badly injured by a falling tree. After a long convalescence he died, leaving my grandmother to raise six daughters and a son. My grandmother, whose maiden name was Donovan and who also originated from Ireland, in order to provide for her large family, procured and ran a boarding house in Ohakune. My grandmother also taught elocution in Ohakune and gave recitations at the local concerts. And it was at her boarding house that my mother met my father, who stayed in a room there when he was a young teacher in the district.

But to come to the boarding house subject of this narrative, we must go back to Auckland, and a woman called Mrs Ross, now unfortunately long deceased. She was the proprietor of a reasonably commodious boarding house situated on Symonds Street. Opposite her boarding house, on the corner of Alfred and Symonds Streets, was the police barracks, which provided accommodation for young constables. Around the corner on Princes Street, just a few hundred yards away, was the Central Police Station. Because of its central location, Mrs Ross's boarding house was frequently used by transients who were only passing through the centre of Auckland. The charges for her lodgings were very modest and, indeed, she often gave accommodation to destitute persons in exchange for him or her doing odd jobs around the property or helping with the cleaning and washing the dishes. Mrs Ross's reputation for generosity was known to the police and sometimes they would send her people who had no fixed abode and might otherwise have been placed in the police cells.

In those days, the 1960s, boarding houses were commonly used and most of the boarding houses were respectable places. Brothels, on the other hand, were of course illegal, although prostitution was by no means unknown. When I worked in the Magistrates Court, from time to time a group of young girls would appear in the dock, flanked by older women whom the police would refer to as madams. These arrests were often the result of police raids on known brothels and the girls would have been held overnight at the police station, usually to be fined and released by a magistrate the following day.

The madams, however, faced more serious charges, such as managing a place for purposes of prostitution, and sometimes these women would even be jailed. Perhaps the best-known brothel in Auckland then was a large and expensive dwelling house on Ring Terrace in Ponsonby, owned and operated by Flora McKenzie, a woman whom some would describe as notorious. Flora's brothel offered services of a high standard in relatively luxurious surroundings. She had begun her brothel during the World War II years, when the place had mainly entertained American and New Zealand officers. She boasted that her clientele included many men of high status in New Zealand.

Some of the other residents of Ring Terrace took great umbrage at the presence of Flora's brothel and from time to time there were petitions organised to pressure the authorities to close it down. At one stage, the newspaper *Truth* published a long list of car registration numbers and stated that these cars were seen parked outside the Ring Terrace property, with the inference that the owners of the vehicles had been indulging in the services of Flora's prostitutes. This resulted in at least one suicide of an owner of one of the listed vehicles. To be embroiled in such moral scandals in those days, and to suffer the hysterical public reaction that invariably followed, often had devastating consequences, as the infamous case against Stephen Ward in England, referred to in the 'Exotic Stripper' chapter, sadly illustrates.

On one occasion, when Flora was criminally charged with running a brothel, I acted as junior counsel to the great and formidable L P Leary QC, who was then the doyen of the Auckland criminal bar. We successfully transferred the case to be tried at Christchurch on the ground that Flora would suffer undue prejudice in Auckland. The case was heard before a judge and jury, and LP, as he was known, gave one of the finest closing addresses to the jury that I have ever heard. The jury and indeed the judge were laughing loudly at times. LP, apart from being a great advocate, was also well experienced as an amateur actor. During his address to the jury he used humour to cut down the efficacy of the Crown case. Yet, much to our consternation, the jury returned within five minutes of their retirement with a guilty verdict. LP could not quite believe his own ears. But such was the almost puritan public feeling against vice at the time.

As for Mrs Ross's boarding house on Symonds Street, it was definitely not a brothel. This was a hardworking woman who had successfully raised a family and who was now performing an excellent service to the community in providing clean and comfortable accommodation. Unfortunately, her relationship with the police had deteriorated at some point, though. The reasons for this are now obscure but she became the butt of many jokes from the young police officers who lived in the barracks across the road.

Mrs Ross retaliated by denouncing the police and refusing to take any referrals from them as guests in her boarding house. A feud-like state developed between the boarding house proprietress and the police. The culmination of all this came when a posse of police officers arrived at her establishment. The officers first searched the property in a rough and ready manner and then, to the astonishment of Mrs Ross, charged her with running a brothel on the premises. She was absolutely shocked and angered by this and proceeded to loudly proclaim her innocence. She was nonetheless arrested and taken into custody at the Auckland Central Police Station, only to be released the next day by the Magistrates Court on bail.

Predictably, Mrs Ross's case attracted great publicity, particularly in the *Truth* newspaper. When she became my client she bitterly complained to me that her reputation would be ruined regardless of whether she was acquitted or not. She was, however, a born fighter. She was determined to win the case and to expose the malicious malpractice of the police who had generated these charges against her.

When I was finally apprised of all the so-called evidence, it really boiled down to the statement of one young girl who said she had been offered money by Mrs Ross to sleep with guests at the boarding house. The trial was eventually heard at the then Supreme Court before a judge and jury. At the trial, the girl retracted her evidence and acknowledged that the money offered to her by Mrs Ross had not been for the purpose of soliciting prostitution at all. A further feature of this girl's evidence, which emerged during cross-examination, was that, while she had for a short time been a guest at the boarding house herself, once she had returned home to live with her parents, the police officer in charge of this case against Mrs Ross had been a frequent visitor to the girl's home in the period leading up to the trial. In fact, she said that the routine was that each night he would come by and have dinner with her family. Then, after dinner, he would go over her evidence and emphasise to her the main things that she should state at the trial.

Other evidence in the case had little or no probative value. At the time of the police raid, Mrs Ross agreed to show the police through the house. The sergeant in charge said the police found a nineteen-year-old youth with a sixteen-year-old girl, whose overnight bag contained only cosmetics; and, as well, a partly clad man with a young woman wearing only an overcoat in a room where her clothes laid on the floor beside a bed. This evidence had little probative value on the actual charges filed against Mrs Ross.

In due course, the jury returned verdicts of not guilty on all charges. Mrs Ross, however, was insistent that an action be taken against the police for malicious prosecution. With her blessing, I engaged LP Leary to be senior counsel in this case, in which Mrs Ross was claiming damages against the police.

We issued a writ claiming considerable damages and received a statement of defence denying all liability. However, the day before the trial for damages was to be heard before a judge and jury, a settlement was reached whereby the Crown paid to Mrs Ross a substantial sum of money.

Mrs Ross was a fine woman and was well served by the judicial processes. Her case exemplified the dangers of allowing the police to have jurisdiction to bring charges in regard to matters that are merely breaches of certain people's moral codes. In those days, consenting males over the age of twenty-one could be charged with committing crimes for homosexual conduct. Such cases frequently led to gross injustices and humiliation for the people concerned and sometimes led to suicides of young people. A peculiar and bigoted aspect to this was that the young men arrested on these charges of homosexual offences were often badly treated by police officers at the police station. It was also significant that there was a prevalence of disagreements within juries hearing these cases.

Today's society has become more enlightened and these classes of offences have mercifully been abolished. However, there is still much progress to be made to limit victimisation, and unnecessary and unwarranted police intrusion into the private lives of citizens.

As a footnote to this story here, although acquitted and presumed to be innocent, Mrs Ross felt after the trial that her character had been so damaged by the adverse publicity associated with the case that she must leave Auckland. She sold her boarding house, which was then known as Arras House, and moved to a small provincial town.

He Chopped Her Head Off

Henry was an old fellow. He lived alone in a bach at Te Kouma. His lifestyle wasn't too bad – the bach was freehold and he had his pension and relatively good health. He got on well with his neighbours and, because he was an excellent guitar player, he was popular at social functions and always had a cheery word for everybody. Down near the beach he had a small aluminium dinghy, known in those days as a 'tinny', and because the place teemed with fish, he was never short of fresh fish for a meal, and indeed often gave away a few to the neighbours.

He kept a small but productive vegetable garden at the back of his bach and on occasions would make a homebrew that had a hell of a kick. Henry was completely inoffensive and had led an unblemished life. He was a generous person and was content with his lot.

One morning he drove his old Vauxhall car to Auckland because he wanted to get some strings for his guitar. Playing the guitar was his major pleasure, and he often gave lessons to some of the locals. On the way back from Auckland and about to pass Kingseat Mental Hospital, he noticed a small woman on the side of the road with a suitcase. She was waving at him to stop. Henry hadn't had much experience with women for many years and he certainly was not looking for a mate – the life of a bachelor left him quite content and he was past the age of desiring female company.

But, owing to his good nature, he stopped the car and invited her in for a lift. He placed her suitcase on the back seat and treated her with his customary politeness. She was a woman slightly younger than he and was bright and talkative. Within a very short time, she had explained to him her situation. She had been a patient at Kingseat Hospital for some time but was very pleased to be released. The hospital in those days was a large, sprawling complex with excellent amenities. She would have been well cared for there. It had various recreational facilities, including a swimming pool, library and large grounds for the patients to wander around. Indeed, it was looked upon as something of a model institution for the mentally ill.

Back in the car, Henry asked the woman where she would like to be dropped off as he would soon be turning off the main highway in the direction of Thames, on his return to Te Kouma. For a while she prevaricated but then finally said she had told the hospital authorities that she was going to stay with some relatives in Hamilton. That was actually a lie, however. In fact, she hadn't made any arrangements at all to stay with relatives; she had nowhere to go.

She started to cry and Henry was overcome with pity. In a moment that he would come to very much regret, Henry said to her, 'Why don't you come and stay with me for a few days? I have an old bach at Te Kouma. It's nothing flash but Te Kouma is a lovely spot!'

Te Kouma is a small inlet and the people there were easy to get on with. Henry had never known any trouble there. He told the woman that she could sleep in his bedroom and he would sleep in the lounge. He made it clear to her that he was not after any hanky-panky as he was simply too old for that.

'Oh, how great that would be and how kind of you!' the woman beamed in reply, and she told Henry that they would have a few great days together. The woman proposed that they stop at Thames to buy a bottle of wine so that they could celebrate when they arrived at the bach together. Henry agreed and felt the woman's jolliness rubbing off on him. Before long, they were laughing and joking and really enjoying each other's company.

At Thames they stopped at a local hotel and bought a bottle of wine. The woman proposed a drink there and then but Henry replied, 'Oh no, I am driving!' since he was a law-abiding old fellow. At the bach, her good spirits continued as she ran around tidying things up and before long the place looked completely different. She found some flowers outside and put them in a vase, gave the kitchen a much-needed clean-up, and did the dishes. She seemed to have endless energy.

Within a few days, she had tidied up the whole house, washed all the clothes, and generally impressed Henry with her ability to make the place comfortable and homely. The weather was rather cold and windy but the bach was equipped with a Kent wood-burning stove. Henry had a good supply of firewood outside and the stove was kept well lit. At night they would sit around the stove and Henry would play the guitar, and occasionally the woman would sing, although it was clear that she was not musically gifted. They seemed to get on well and before long they had visited the neighbours together and were soon invited there for dinner. She was invariably cheerful and the neighbours thought the two a great couple.

At the bach, Henry had always eaten on one of those chairs with a small, fold-out table attached to the front, like the type of chair that infants are fed in. He found that this dispensed with the need for a large table. Henry bought another such chair for his house guest so that they could both sit in their respective chairs eating their evening meal off the folding tables. It was all pretty cosy with the Kent stove blazing away and sometimes a record or two playing on the old-fashioned gramophone.

On Fridays, Henry would drive his car to Thames to obtain provisions for the week – this had been his habit for many years. While he was in Thames he would have one beer at the local hotel, and only the one because he would have to drive back to Te Kouma and didn't want to be caught driving while intoxicated. The lady from Kingseat loved to accompany him on these trips to Thames; she especially loved going to the hotel. As she wasn't the one driving, she would indulge with the alcohol more copiously. She had also, by this time, admitted to Henry that she had nowhere else to go and now looked upon the bach as her permanent home.

However, after having a few drinks the lady's mood would change dramatically. She could become nasty and derisive towards Henry, and she would chide him for not drinking enough and for being a 'silly old bore'. Henry, on the other hand, took all this in his stride, but as the months went by, he was becoming rather tired of her. Sometimes he would reflect to himself how good it had been in the old days, when he lived his bachelor lifestyle and did not have to put up with all the mood swings, nagging and vituperation from her.

But, as he couldn't find any practical solution to getting rid of the woman, Henry accepted his fate that they were stuck with each other at the bach. As time went on, the Friday excursions to Thames became more elongated – that is to say that when they went into the local hotel for what used to be a solitary beer, the lady insisted on staying for longer and she would habitually become inebriated and, later, when back in the car and the bach, would become a pain in the neck.

Henry would try to get her to leave the hotel at an earlier stage but she would insist on staying. This in turn led to numerous quarrels. Eventually, their routine changed and Henry would go home without her. She had no objection to this arrangement and would spend the night somewhere and turn up at the bach the following day. When Henry inquired of her where she had been the night before, he would be met with sneers and jeers from her. She called him a 'pathetic geezer' and laughed at his lack of physical strength and aging features.

It got to the stage where the lady would stay away for several nights in a row and she would still persist on refusing to reveal to Henry where she had been. There was now not even a semblance of love and goodwill between the two – she neglected all household chores and it was usually Henry who knocked up the evening meal, which they ate in their respective fold-out-table chairs in a state of abject disharmony.

It was after one of her two- or three-day excursions that the climax came. She was obviously hung-over and crueller than ever with her sarcastic and demeaning barbs towards Henry. It was evening time and Henry had lit the Kent wood stove. They were seated in their usual chairs but this time the anger between them became even more bitter than usual. Henry had quietly and politely asked her where she had been in the nights prior, following their Friday excursion to the

Thames hotel. She referred to him in explicit language as a worthless old bastard and told him that there was no way she would tell him anything, except to say that she had a jolly good time without him.

For some reason, Henry could no longer control the anger that boiled inside him.

'If you don't tell me, you bitch, I am going to get the axe and chop your bloody head off!' he threatened.

She laughed out loud and with absolute scorn. She mocked him: 'You couldn't manage that if you tried. You're nothing but a cockroach! You're a dead loss, you old bastard!'

Something inside Henry's head snapped and he lost all self-control. He went outside to the firewood shed and grabbed the axe.

He rushed back into the house and, while the lady was still giggling and slobbering in her chair, without hesitation, he belted her over the head with the butt of the axe and she crashed to the floor with blood flowing profusely from her wound. Henry swung the axe several times more and completely severed her head from the torso. It was only when this macabre act was done that he came to his senses.

It seemed as if the act of decapitating her had assuaged his anger and he now felt a terrible remorse. Henry went to his neighbours' house right away and explained what had happened. The neighbours were aghast and shocked. The man in that house told Henry that they must contact the police immediately, and Henry agreed. Within a short time, Henry was arrested, charged with murder, and lodged in the police cells.

Henry's murder trial was ultimately heard at the then Supreme Court in Hamilton before a judge and jury. Hamilton juries had a reputation for being tough on accused people, but this jury were sympathetic towards Henry. His case relied upon the defence of provocation and the jury were amenable.

It is a great tragedy in New Zealand that we have abolished this defence. Provocation was never a defence to murder but merely a mechanism that allowed a jury, if they so wished, to reduce the charge from murder to manslaughter. This, however, made a great difference to penalty. Generally speaking, without going into all of the legalities of the defence, if the situation was such that it made the jury sympathetic to the accused, even to the extent that they might have seen themselves in the same circumstances doing the same thing, provided that the judge considered there was a basis for raising the defence, the jury could be merciful and bring back the lesser verdict of manslaughter. This is what occurred in Henry's case.

The presiding judge sentenced Henry to a relatively short prison sentence that did nonetheless recognise the gravity of his offending, and he was duly lodged at Waikeria Prison to serve his sentence.

Two or three years later, I happened to be at Waikeria to visit another client. I asked a warden if I could just quickly see Henry, 'the old fellow who cut his girlfriend's head off'. The warden told me that I could not as I had made no prior arrangement. He explained that Henry would have to be escorted into the visiting room and they did not have time to arrange this. I asked the warden whether it was really necessary to have guards accompanying Henry, who was now over eighty, and questioned whether he was in a physical condition to run away. In any event, the warden relented and Henry was soon brought to the visiting room.

When he came in, he looked better than I had ever seen him – he seemed to have put on weight and had a most pleasant demeanour about him. He was genuinely glad to see me and we shook each other's hands with vigour. I asked him how his life was and he told me that he was happier than he had been for a long time. He explained that he did not have to worry about his meals, and the inmates in the block treated him well. He told me that he had his eighty-third birthday the week before and the boys in his block had put on a party for him. He gave some of them guitar lessons and often they had sing-songs in the evenings.

'I now feel at peace with the world!' Henry explained.

He never mentioned the deceased and I never raised the subject, either. He was indeed a happy old man.

Mr Uganda

On 24 July 1968, Richard Burr entered the office of an accountant, Alick Faine, and shot him at close range. As a result of his injuries, Faine died. Burr was later tried and convicted of the accountant's murder.

At Burr's trial, the defence of automatism – where the accused acts without premeditation and has no memory afterwards of what he did – was relied upon but was unsuccessful.

The facts of the case, however, were very unusual and the defendant himself had none of the hallmarks of the archetypal murderer. Murder is an offence that contains a mental element. Usually that element is an intention to kill. This subjective ingredient must be proved by the Crown if a conviction for murder is to be obtained. Even when a murder is unprovoked and premeditated, it is open to the defence to submit that at the actual time of the killing the accused was acting subconsciously and that he had no conscious awareness of his actions. A corollary of this, if proved, is that the defendant has no criminal intent. He must, however, establish a basis for this and usually calls psychiatric evidence to establish that he was acting automatically.

The problem with Burr's case was that he acted with much preparation and, after the event, was able to recall in detail precisely what had occurred. On the other hand, without doubt, Burr was acting under hypnotic influence and completely and absolutely out of character.

Burr was an intensely religious man. As a child he regularly attended the All Saints Anglican Church, and at the Green Meadows public school he had received religious instruction from the visiting minister and won a Bible for his devotion. Later, for about seven or eight years, and because of ill health, he was cared for in a Catholic convent where the nuns and priests were very good to him and engendered in the young Burr a longing to be a Catholic. Later still, he became associated with the Salvation Army and played third cornet in the Napier Citizens Junior Boys Band. When he was about twenty, he attended the Youth for Christ at the Baptist Tabernacle, of which he said, 'At the Tabernacle we had many gatherings and sang religious chorales and hymns and would hear from evangelists and visiting missionaries. I attended every week.' He married a Catholic and regularly attended mass with his wife, eventually becoming a fully pledged Catholic.

His marriage was successful and they had four daughters. His health, however, was never good. He was not a strong person physically and his family background was tragic. His father returned from World War I with severe injuries and remained an invalid, unable to work, and died prematurely. His mother, on the other hand, was a very domineering person and tried to control every aspect of Burr's life right up to the time of his marriage. She detested his wife, as she had his previous girlfriends.

Burr was described by all who knew him as a very likable person, although some would say weak and ineffectual. He had developed his musical abilities while in the convent and was a popular pianist at social occasions and at church services. His ability to work was hampered by his ill health but at times he seemed to make progress. He purchased a home for his family and at one stage he even bought a brand-new Holden car. He deeply loved his wife and did all he could to please her and make her life happy.

He was described as a peace-loving man, never violent, and always kind to his family and his friends. The question was, how did this likable and devoted Christian become a murderer?

The courts of law quite definitely said that his killing of Mr Faine was clearly premeditated and deliberate. Justice North, when delivering the opinion of the Court of Appeal, said, 'The evidence must be sufficient to lay a proper foundation for the plea that the accused person acted through his body and without the assistance of his mind, in the sense that he was not able to make the necessary decisions and to determine whether or not to do the act. Now in the present case all the facts show that the appellant knew what he was doing, and knew what he was doing was wrong. This being so, in my view there was no room at all for the defence of automatism. It is not sufficient that the medical evidence suggest that the appellant's mind was not fully functioning and that he had an imperfect appreciation of the nature and quality of his act. To allow such a plea to be submitted to a jury in a case like this would be dangerous in the highest degree.'

So, let us now look at the facts leading to the murder.

In 1963, Mr Faine advertised that he wanted someone to sell women's clothing on credit. Burr answered the advertisements and not only successfully sold knitwear and crockery for Mr Faine, but became something of a confidant to the accountant.

But then things started to go downhill for Burr. His mother took ill, and he had to take time off work to care for her. Then his wife gave birth to a stillborn baby and was hospitalised afterwards; this meant he had to take time off to stay home and care for his four daughters. His financial position became hopeless.

It was about this time that he was introduced to spiritualism. He had met a woman called Mrs Taylor and, after telling her of his financial and other troubles, she referred him to a spiritualist called Mrs Stillman. When he consulted Mrs Stillman, she went into a trance and told him that the world of spirits would be helping him. After that his business seemed to improve.

Later, Mrs Taylor introduced him to another spiritualist, Mrs Nola Webb. Mrs Webb said she could look into the future and used cards to make prophecies. She started off by telling him, in a high tone of voice, 'That car of yours in the drive, you will be selling that very soon.' Within a few weeks Burr had sold his car, and the money went to reduce his overdraft.

At this stage, he was no longer selling directly for Mr Faine, but was making pelmets and installing them in people's houses. He still, however, owed Mr Faine for a series of loans secured by post-dated cheques. Mr Faine kept these cheques in a safe in his office. When Burr realised he couldn't meet his commitments to Mr Faine, he went to see him, taking with him a schedule of his commitments.

As the dire state of Burr's finances became clear, Faine said to him, 'I thought you owned your car.'

To which Burr replied, 'Yes, I did, I had owned it, but now I'm leasing it.'

Burr later said to me of this encounter with Faine, 'He pushed all the papers aside and seemed to froth at the mouth ... It was as though suddenly a man who was my friend was no longer my friend. I was very shocked, so shocked I was crying.'

After that, Burr went to Mrs Taylor and told her what had happened. 'She said not to worry, and that she would take me to a man who would know what to do. She said his name was Uganda and that he was the greatest spiritualist in the world.'

Burr described his visit to Uganda in Ponsonby, Auckland: 'I walked into a room where there were two men, one was Uganda. He was standing in a white tunic in a corner with his arms folded and his eyes closed. They asked first what I wanted. "Do you want a health diagnosis or a business consultation?" I was asked to strip down to the waist and to get onto a bed like a doctor's room. Uganda came forward and unfolded his arms. He then proceeded physically with his hands to examine my legs and my whole body while he was sort of moaning and saying things to the attendant. He asked me if I had my own teeth, and I said, "Yes." They then poured warm oil on my body, and then Uganda massaged my body for twenty or thirty minutes. Uganda then said he would discuss my business problems. I told him that that day I had received a terrible shock and that my mind was terribly worried. I said I was close to a breakdown. Uganda said he would give me medicine to help me; it was called Nervine. After the consultation, I started taking this medicine. I kept coming out in heavy sweats and my head kept thumping.

'A few days later I went again to see Uganda. The people in the room were Uganda, his wife, Mrs Taylor and myself. Uganda said he would give me a card reading. He produced a set of cards and said for me to shuffle them carefully. He told me he first fell into a trance when he was fourteen and that both his mother and father were mediums. On his mother's side they went back generations as mediums; he said his parents gave him the gift. Uganda told me that his ancestors had been given the spirit of a Zulu warrior who had lived over a thousand years ago, and was a Zulu chief. He said that Uganda was seven feet tall and was so powerful that if anyone stood in his road, he would walk straight at them and knock them over.'

The medium had then read the cards, dividing the pack into four lots. When he picked up the first lot, he proceeded to turn each of the cards face up, and the third card he flipped over was the ace of spades. He said to Burr, 'You are going to be experiencing death.'

To which Burr said, 'Could it be my mother?'

'No, it's to do with your business,' Uganda replied.

After that, Burr said he took the medicine at home again and that it gave him a hot burning feeling. He felt thumping and banging in his head once more, too.

He told me that although he had previously been a non-drinker, he now had a craving for wine. He played the piano a lot and there were times he didn't know he was actually playing. At night-time he was not able to escape the vision of the ace of spades in his mind and it haunted him in his dreams.

Burr then spoke about buying a rifle and getting a police permit. He said that he could remember going to Faine's office but only as if someone had told him that this was what had happened. He could not actually recollect killing Mr Faine, nor could he recollect pouring petrol through his office and then igniting a match, but knew that he had done these things. A day or two later he went to see Mrs Taylor and told her what had happened, what he thought he had done. In the meantime, the murder had been reported in the newspapers. Mrs Taylor said to Burr that he was very ill and that she would take him back to see Uganda. After the usual preliminaries, Uganda told Burr not to worry. But he said that God was very angry with Burr and on no account was Burr to give himself up to the police. He gave Burr four more bottles of Nervine instead.

The next day, Burr went to his mother and told her how it had seemed to him that he had been taken over by another person and committed this terrible crime. Burr then visited a priest and confessed it all to him. The priest gave him a drink of brandy and, with the consent of Burr, called the police.

He then made a full confession to the police.

As defence counsel, I was able to confirm all the details of what Burr had told me. I believe that Burr had been hypnotised by Uganda and did not have control over his own mind at the time of the shooting.

Not without some difficulty, I interviewed Uganda. At first, he refused to see me, but later agreed to meet in the foyer of the Intercontinental Hotel. I found his true name was Arnold Richards and he described himself as a healer. He had a pronounced Pommy accent and seemed very nervous. However, he confirmed all the details that Burr had told me. I also consulted Henry Bennett, a medical superintendent, and

Henry Bethune, a psychiatrist, both of whom gave evidence that Burr had been hypnotised and his reasoning powers had been dethroned.

The trial was held in Auckland before Justice Clifford Richmond and jury, and a large number of witnesses were called on both sides.

The Crown was represented by Mr David Morris and Mr David Baragwanath (who later became a Court of Appeal judge). They both successfully argued that there was far too much evidence of conscious premeditation for lack of intent to apply.

Burr was sentenced to life imprisonment. He was, however, a model prisoner, popular with both staff and prisoners at Mount Eden, and his actual time served in prison was comparatively short. His wife was completely loyal to him and visited him regularly.

But I may say in retrospect that although the letter of the law was correctly followed, I still believe that Richard Burr was not master of his own mind when he shot Mr Faine, his mind instead being clouded by Mr Uganda and the ace of spades.

Yelash Sues the Prime Minister

This is a strange case that involved two men I had known for many years, both extroverts with very strong personalities.

I met Dover Samuels many years ago and he has continued to be my friend. Dover is definitely a man's man. He is renowned as a diver and fisherman, and indeed it is reliably reported that, on one occasion, when a man was seized by a large shark, Dover dived down with a spear and shot the shark through one of its eyes, thereby saving the man's life.

Dover came from a large family and was brought up according to Maori custom, soon becoming a leader among Ngapuhi. Dover speaks fluent Maori and is well respected, particularly throughout the Maori community, for his determined stand on issues, his oratory, and his leadership generally. On a personal level, I have always enjoyed Dover's company. He is a fine raconteur with a great sense of humour and an eclectically down-to-earth philosophy of life, who is in turn always supportive of the common folk.

For many years, Dover ran a motel at Matauri Bay with his then wife Jacqui and their family. My partner, Heeni, and I were often guests at the motel, the restaurant at which offered such delicacies as fresh crayfish and tarakihi caught on the day. Evenings would be spent in all manner of boisterous political argument, although these were always amiable affairs and accompanied by the odd bottle of good wine.

Dover's political career would ultimately establish him as a Cabinet minister in the Helen Clark government, where he was highly respected. But Dover Samuels and Helen Clark were inherently different personalities. Helen was definitely a socially progressive Prime Minister. She introduced controversial anti-smacking legislation and was a champion among campaigners of women's rights. She also introduced civil unions for gay and lesbian couples. Dover, on the other hand, came with a strong indigenous belief in male dominance. Maori traditionally barred women from speaking on the marae and indeed, on occasions, Maori women were required to sit behind men in formal situations at the marae.

With this background, it was not surprising then that, when some groundless sexual allegations arose against Dover, which later proved to be absolutely false, Helen described them as 'rumours swirling around'. Instead of giving Dover support and standing him down as minister until these were resolved, she abruptly sacked him from his ministerial posts and adopted an almost adversarial role against him.

One of her junior whips, Chris Carter, made a phone call to another friend of mine, John Yelash, seeking damaging information about Dover. John had recently published a book entitled *Jail Song*, which described his experiences in prison as an inmate. He had given a reading from this book in a public performance at Titirangi, which Carter had attended. Chris Carter, supported by Helen and her then Attorney-General,

Margaret Wilson, denied that he had ever made the phone call. What Chris Carter had overlooked, however, was that, when he phoned John, he had left a message on the answering machine. What Chris Carter was recorded to have said (in a rather plummy voice) on this answering machine was as follows:

'Hi John, it's Chris Carter here. John, I'm just ringing up on a little bit of detective work. I'm just wondering if among your many circle of friends and acquaintances you have ever come across any information about my colleague Dover Samuels [pause]. I want to sort of discuss this in a sort of non-controversial way and of course a confidential way.

'So, [pause] I'd really like to have a chat to you about one or two things. If you get the chance, could you ring me on my cell phone? I'm going to be out tonight but I'll have my cell phone with me [recites the number]. Really appreciate having a confidential chat with you. Thanks very much, John, bye bye.'

To my mind, the recorded words definitely supported John's version of events, namely that it was Chris Carter who initiated the phone call. I expressed this view emphatically, both on television and to the press generally, and received in reply a barrage of criticisms, particularly from the Labour MPs of the government. I was threatened with defamation by Helen Clark and even received an aggressive letter from one of her secretaries, referring to a certain radio interview I had done during this period.

I made reference during that radio interview to the fact that a former Commissioner of Police, Peter Doone, had been employed by the Office of the Prime Minister, and I said that this was unconstitutional, as it gave Prime Minister Clark possible access to police intelligence.

Helen Clark's reply, through the Chief Executive of the Department of the Prime Minister and Cabinet, rebutted my allegations stating, and I quote:

- Peter Doone does not work in Helen Clark's office but works in the Crime Prevention Unit of the Department of the Prime Minister and Cabinet.
- Peter Doone's work does not bring him into any direct contact with the Prime Minister.
- Peter Doone has assured me that he has had no discussion of any sort with any person connected to the inquiry into Dover Samuels, nor does he have any information on the process of the inquiry.
- The Police have not provided any reports on the progress of the inquiry to myself or anybody else in my department. As you know, the Prime Minister has already made it clear that neither she, nor any member of her office, has received any report on progress in the inquiry.

The involvement of Peter Doone arose during public debate concerning the Dover Samuels affair. However, I am still of the opinion that it is unwise for former senior police officers to be seen as being employed by the Prime Minister. The Colin Moyle incident during the Muldoon government was a gross example of a Prime Minister having illegal access to police intelligence.

(The so-called 'Moyle Affair' happened in 1977 when the then Prime Minister, Robert Muldoon, stated in parliament that Colin Moyle MP, a Labour Party politician, according to police intelligence, had been interviewed by the police concerning an alleged sexual assault. Police intelligence is prepared merely for the purposes of confidential police files, and is not intended for the public domain. What Muldoon did, on that occasion, was absolutely reprehensible, but because his statement was protected by parliamentary privilege, the press were able to report it as a consequence. Mr Moyle resigned from parliament.)

A political furore erupted involving the issue of whether it was Chris Carter or John Yelash who had initiated the taped phone call to dig up 'dirt' on Dover. In a public interview, Helen Clark said that she preferred to take the word of Mr Carter over that of a murderer, in reference to John Yelash.

This was indeed a rather cruel remark by Helen Clark, which I have no doubt she later regretted. John Yelash had been convicted of manslaughter in a controversial trial many, many years ago but since that time had led an exemplary life, and was a committed member of Alcoholics Anonymous. John had not touched liquor for over thirty years and had built up for himself in the community an excellent reputation, particularly as a prisoner reformer, writer, actor and reciter of poetry.

I have known John personally for many years. His knowledge of classical music and opera is encyclopaedic and his extensive reading of literature makes him a great conversationalist. I believe he is probably the greatest exponent of James K Baxter's poetry in New Zealand. He has published several books, and was the principal actor in the International Film Festival winner *Barney Flanagan*. He has appeared in numerous other plays and public performances. John, I and others had been involved with several theatrical productions, performing as part of a troop in various provincial centres.

My part in these performances was to recite poetry and give the audience detailed descriptions of several famous trials in New Zealand. We played to good houses in a three-day season in Hamilton and later to a packed house in Kerikeri. The Kerikeri performance had promised that two Auckland opera singers would join us and that the Mayor of West Auckland, Bob Harvey, would also make a contribution. Unfortunately, the opera singers failed to appear and Bob Harvey (who at the time had achieved notoriety for dropping his trousers during a public event) also failed to appear. When we arrived at Kerikeri, patrons were offered their money back but the show proceeded and eventually ended successfully.

John also had a tendency to make sexually explicit references during his performances and was indeed reported by the *New Zealand Herald* to have caused a hapless elderly attendee at a National Party luncheon (to which John was invited to speak following the Chris Carter brouhaha) to faint following a recital from his book, *Jail Song*, which was apparently peppered with references to masturbation and homophobia. John, however, denied this and said he was merely reciting Wordsworth.

In any event, the Helen Clark, Dover Samuels and John Yelash saga attracted a great deal of publicity and eventually, after John issued court proceedings, he received a very favourable settlement. But the saga didn't quite end there.

At the conclusion of these matters, John was able to purchase for himself a modest vehicle (after being car-less for many years), and parliament itself bubbled on to its next crisis.

The tape on the answer phone clearly established that Chris Carter had made this phone call to John. Helen Clark made the mistake of believing that Carter.

In fact, Dover and John had never met, but even though Dover was cleared on all the false allegations against him, including rape, he never again regained his position in Cabinet. True, he was given several portfolios outside Cabinet, but Helen Clark never gave him again the proper respect to which he was entitled. Today Dover is still, however, well valued in the Maori community, and although not an MP, he is seen as a great leader and champion of indigenous causes.

I may say that although I am not a member of the Labour Party, generally speaking I have always been sympathetic to its objectives, and some years later, I had cause to have dealings with Helen Clark, sitting around a table with her and her secretaries. I found her to be sincere, indeed even charming, and a very good listener. She has my warmest regards.

The Careless Accountant

Many, many years ago an elderly man came to see me. He was shabbily dressed but had obviously made an attempt to be presentable. His suit was faded and shrunk and failed to conceal his pot belly. His shirt was yellow at the collar and the tie clumsily knotted. His well-wrinkled face reflected a life of hard work with plenty of hardship. He smelt of the land, the river and the sea, and exuded an honesty that was far removed from that of the business leaders of the city. His faded blue eyes still had a twinkle and he carried a comfortable affability.

He said to me, 'Peter I've come to you as a lawyer of last resort.'

I immediately thought to myself, why don't I get the so-called respectable clients with a ton of money and cases that will inevitably succeed? He's obviously been to half a dozen lawyers and been turned down because he has no money and his case is all uphill. I did not, however, express those thoughts to him.

Instead, I said, 'Okay, tell me what your case is all about.'

He leant back in the leather chair and began: 'I've been farming all my life. I had little schooling and even in those days I spent more time doing farm work than attending lessons. As soon as I was old enough, I left school and took up farm work fulltime. Eventually, I bought a small farm at the bottom of the Bombay Hills, near the Waikato River, and I've concentrated on growing vegetables and dealing in whitebait.'

I asked him, 'Is that your small shop on the Bombay Hills where I often notice a sign advertising fresh whitebait for sale?'

He smiled broadly and said, 'Yeah, that's the place. But really I don't own anything now. I had a mortgage on my farm, and when things got tough, the only way I could get money to carry on with was to get a loan from my accountant, a man named Smith. He is well known in the Pukekohe district, and is a pillar of the local church.'

'Where did you get your whitebait from?' I asked him, as a keen fisherman myself. 'I've tried to catch whitebait in the Waikato River, but have had very little luck.'

'What part of the river did you place your nets in?' he asked me.

And I said, 'Down by the river mouth, where the delta is.' We chatted about that area for a moment, where a number of people lived in small baches on the tiny islands at the river mouth. They seemed to be happy enough. Apparently they paid no rates, because nobody owned the land, and they virtually lived on fish, mainly mullet and kahawai. The farmer told me that among them there was even a sly grogger who made homebrew, which he swapped with the others for fish and provisions.

'They all have small boats around there,' he told me, 'and at times they gather together for parties and drinking sessions.'

'Anyway,' I asked him, 'where did you get your whitebait?'

'I've been buying whitebait off the fishermen on the river during the season for many years,' he told me. 'They all know me and trust me. I've got a couple of boats down there on a jetty and, during the whitebait season, I motor up and down the river buying whitebait. I don't usually pay the fishermen in money. They usually prefer provisions and I swap things like tinned meat and bread with them. Then, of course, I used to sell the whitebait at my shop on the Bombay Hills, but now that's all gone. My farm's gone, too. Peter, it was a terrible year. It was a financial disaster.'

I could see moisture gathering in his eyes and suspected a tear might roll down his cheek. Quietly I asked him, 'What happened?'

'The whitebait didn't run,' he said. 'For a whole season the fishermen hardly saw any whitebait at all. They had nothing to sell me, so I had none to sell in my shop. I felt sorry for some of them who really depended on whitebait sales and gave a few fishermen supplies on credit. But that's not the end of the story. I also lost my crops on the farm. I had put all my work that year into growing beans and, by Jove, they were growing well. I had acres and acres of beans and was just about to harvest them when the river flooded. I grew them near the river, because that's where the best soil is. I've known the river to flood before, of course, but never as bad as it flooded that year. I lost the whole crop. I could've cried. Apart from the money, I put hundreds of hours of work into that crop, all ruined by the flood.

'I think I have already told you, I had borrowed money from Smith, my accountant, but as a security for the loan, I had given him power to sell all my assets if I defaulted. There is no doubt I defaulted. I had no alternative, as I had no money. So Smith sold up everything, including my shop, farm, livestock, tractors and farm equipment – every bloody thing. He sold up the lot.'

I said, 'Well, I can't see we can do much about it. He was acting quite lawfully, wasn't he, under the security documents?'

The farmer leant back in his chair and an angry expression came across his face as he said, 'I haven't told you the whole story. When he sold my belongings, he didn't get the best prices for anything. Let me explain. Take the livestock – most of the animals had a pedigree but he sold them without disclosing the pedigree and only achieved abattoir prices. I've also got written statements from people who wanted to buy the farm – who made higher offers than the price he accepted. He didn't maintain the farm machinery, either – it was left outside to rust. He didn't even put covers over the tractors and the rainwater got down the exhaust pipes. There was a large stack of pumpkins in one shed, and they were just left to rot. Surely there's some law that prevents this type of poor conduct against a man?'

Somehow I knew that this farmer was telling the truth.

I said to him, 'Well, you'd better make a list of all these things and I will write a letter to Smith, holding him liable in damages.'

'That'll be no problem,' the farmer replied. 'And I can tell you now, I've got plenty of witnesses that can prove all I've said.'

'Okay,' I said. 'Bring them to me and we will get signed statements.'

He was true to his word. Within a few weeks, he had introduced me to a variety of people, mainly farmers, who gladly attested to the negligent way the accountant had acted.

We issued proceedings in the then Supreme Court at Auckland and the case was heard by a judge and jury. Smith was represented by a leading Queen's Counsel who took a haughty attitude towards us, virtually indicating that the writ had been maliciously issued.

The farmer gave evidence well and I could see that he favourably impressed the jury. He was highly regarded by the local community at Bombay and all the local farmers who gave evidence not only deposed to the shocking way the estate had been handled, but also to the excellent reputation of the plaintiff himself. After two weeks of trial, the jury returned ordering substantial damages in favour of the farmer.

The irony was, however, that when confronted with payment of the damages, Smith said he had no ready money and the farmer would have to take a deed of arrangement. The money was eventually paid and, I am content to say, the farmer resumed his farming, as well as his trips up and down the river buying whitebait.

Among the Poets

One of the last people to be hanged in New Zealand was a man named Edward Thomas Te Whiu. He was a twenty-year-old with mental deficiencies when he was sentenced for killing an old lady in the course of a burglary. Many objected to his execution, including the Howard League for Penal Reform, but politicians, including the then Prime Minister, Sid Holland, ruled that the execution must go ahead.

In his poem entitled 'A Rope for Harry Fat', James K Baxter exposed the shallowness and hypocrisy of men like Holland. The last two stanzas read:

The butcher boy and baker boy
  Were whistling in the street
When the hangman bound Te Whiu's eyes
  And strapped his hands and feet,
Who stole to buy a bicycle
  And killed in panic blood.
'The parson won his soul at length,'
  Said Harry Fat the good.

Oh some will kill in rage and fear
And some will kill in hate,
And some will kill in foreign lands
To serve the master State.
Justice walks heavy in the land;
She bears a rope and shroud.
'We will not change our policy,'
Says Harry Fat the proud.

It was a few years before the hanging, about 1951, that I first met Jim. I was boarding at Weir House in Wellington, next to the Kelburn cable car – I mentioned the place early on in 'The Bloodbath'. Weir House had formerly been a boarding establishment for servicemen returned from World War II who were attending Victoria University. The place had acquired certain notoriety for excessive drinking and womanising, as might be expected from soldiers who had endured the suffering of war.

I found the place quite comfortable. Most of the student-occupiers shared apartment-like accommodation for two. My companion was Gordon Cruden, who later became a judge in Hong Kong and was related to the All Black, Aaron Cruden.

The food at Weir House was notoriously bad and the place suffered a disadvantage of having to support both a matron and a padre, who to my mind were both parasites. One day, I saw on the noticeboard a request from the Harbour Authority for waterfront labour and responded accordingly. It was not unusual for places like woolstores and other industries, suddenly needing temporary labourers, to advertise at institutions like the Weir House, and a few days later, I found myself working in the hold of a ship at the Wellington docks, unloading cement. The work was dusty and monotonous but, by my standards at the time, well paid. This extra cash allowed good restaurant fare to supplement the miserable meals at Weir House.

After I had been working there for a while, I became acquainted with a fellow labourer who introduced himself as Jim. From time to be time we would have a break and I soon found Jim to be a great conversationalist. He was a few years older than me, a smallish man who was slightly tubby but with piercing blue eyes and a great sense of humour.

I did not know at the time that he was in fact James K Baxter, who had already established himself as one of New Zealand's leading poets and was to become our greatest.

We had not studied New Zealand poetry at Feilding Agricultural High School, where I had been educated, although the English teacher there – a Welshman named Rees – often read us poems from the classics with great passion, sometimes even with tears streaming down his cheeks. We boys would make snide remarks to each other behind our hands, failing at the time to appreciate his genuine love of poetry.

At the school, we also had frequent oratorical contests and, in preparation for these, I learnt a certain amount of poetry by heart. When the conversations with Jim turned to poetry, I recited a few of these poems, such as Henry Newbolt's 'Drake's Drum'. Jim's face would immediately brighten and he would respond with recitations from what I would later learn to be his own poetry. All this was accompanied by plenty of laughter and interspersed with periods of loading out cement.

One afternoon, at the end of the working day, after washing ourselves at the waterfront toilets, Jim suggested that we have a few beers at the National Hotel. The National Hotel was situated on Lambton Quay, an easy walking distance from the wharves. I soon found out that Jim was a highly regarded customer at the hotel, known to all the barmen and indeed many of the patrons. I began to realise that I was in the company of a distinguished intellectual and poet.

Jim took an avid interest in all the issues of the day and, although he spoke with a somewhat plummy accent, he was never condescending. In fact, he never treated me as the callow adolescent I obviously was. I should emphasise here that I was a first-year university student at the time and had come from the Manawatu, which was not then regarded as a centre of culture.

From then on, I became a frequenter of the National Hotel and met there several of New Zealand's leading poets, including Anton Vogt, Louis Johnson and Denis Glover. I also met a few of the acolytes, including Brian Bell, who was a likable bohemian, and a fellow named Rhodes, a somewhat sombre character who invariably wore a very long brown overcoat. Rhodes was said to be a descendant of the famous Cecil Rhodes, who provided the trust money for the Rhodes scholarships.

The distinguished poets, of course, usually held the floor and would at times recite their latest compositions. I was in awe of all this and somewhat mesmerised by the galaxy of wit and intellect.

At a later stage, Jim invited me to his home for dinner and it was there that I met his wife, Jacqui. She seemed a very quiet woman but served us a substantial meal. She, too, wrote poetry but, again, Jim was the leading light of the household.

I became further acquainted with Bell and Rhodes, who seemed to be at a more modest artistic level, and sometimes after six o'clock in the evening, we would repair to a church on Lambton Quay. Bell apparently knew the caretaker who kept a key to the church and would let us in. Because I was flush with money from working at the freezing works over the Christmas holidays and from other casual labour, I would purchase beer and fish and chips, and we would merrily feast sitting on the pews, while being entertained especially by Bell, who was definitely a raconteur.

Bell had been educated at Palmerston North Boys High School at the same time my brother, James, was a pupil there. Even at that early stage, Bell was regarded as a radical. He refused to play sports and wrote left-wing articles for the school magazine and opposed military training, which was then compulsory at all secondary schools. Post high school, he worked for a while at Smiths Bookshop in Wellington, which was then one of the finest second-hand bookshops in the country. He had an encyclopaedic knowledge of current events and for many years kept a catalogue of police brutality in New Zealand. He was also an avid photographer with a huge private collection of photographs depicting personalities and unique buildings. In particular, he liked to photograph corner dairies and milk bars with his Brownie camera. Bell lived in a caravan with a young lady and we regarded him as a true hippie.

Rhodes, on the other hand, was quietly spoken and something of a philosopher. At times he could become somewhat pompous. Although he was impecunious, he could not resist occasionally booking into an expensive hotel and conducting himself as a man of affluence. These events at times would cause him problems with the authorities.

My difficulty with associating with the great poets of the day was that I was not a poet myself and was perhaps too young to realise that I was out of my depth. An example of this occurred at one poetry reading that took place in one of the great halls of the university – the hall was pretty well packed but when I caught sight of Jim Baxter and some of his compatriot poets seated in the front row, I thought that I should sit there, too. To my embarrassment, I was soon shunted away by the ushers and, somewhat sheepishly, I took my place among the proletarian audience.

As the years went by, I became more and more engrossed in my studies and, during the winter, rugby, and no longer associated with the poets.

Not until years later, as a barrister, would I become reacquainted with Jim. I was conducting a murder trial in Dunedin for a young man called Paul Morrison. Morrison and another youth, Thomas Wilson, had tried to escape from the Dunedin Central Police Station, and during the attempted escape, Wilson had struck a police officer with a scrubber, a type of broom used to clean concrete floors. Unfortunately, the police officer died of his injuries, and both young men, after being given the customary beating in these circumstances by the police, were charged with murder and held in custody. Paul Morrison, it turned out, had been a close companion of Jim Baxter's daughter.

Jim felt a deep sense of loyalty towards the young Morrison, and during our lunch hours throughout the trial, Jim would join me and my junior on this case, Brian Nordgren, for a snack. Over those conversations, I began to realise that Jim was more than just a poet but a man of great compassion and a disciple of humane principles. Both Morrison and Wilson were convicted of murder and sentenced to life imprisonment.

Some years later again, I met Jim in Auckland, when he was staying at the Newman Catholic Hostel on Waterloo Quadrant. My old friend Kevin Ryan, who was also a Catholic, was acting for Jim in relation to his matrimonial affairs. On one occasion, the three of us had a beer together at the Kiwi Hotel on Symonds Street, during which Kevin asked Jim if he would write him a poem. Jim smiled modestly but immediately wrote an exquisitely beautiful poem dedicated to Kevin Ryan on the back of a menu.

The change in Jim, however, from the man I had previously known, was quite dramatic. He now wore a tattered priest-like full-length robe, and a set of rosary beads and no shoes. He had grown a somewhat ragged beard and in some ways looked like the common perception of Jesus of Nazareth. He appeared also to be quite emaciated, his features drawn, prematurely aged, and his eyelids were blighted with some type of fungus.

I was very concerned about his health and invited him to stay with me at my home on Remuera Road. Jim did stay for a while and I appreciated his company, but because I was heavily involved in litigation, I could only spend a limited amount of time with him.

Jim eventually slipped away and a year or two later died at the age of 46. Sometime afterwards, I visited the place on the Wanganui River, Jerusalem, where he was buried next to a small Catholic church. Within the church, there was a small plaque commemorating the life of James K Baxter.

Jim has been written about extensively. However, what impressed me about him, his writings and poetry, was not only his powerful social conscience but his determination to personally help those in distress. He was a pacifist. Jim's father had been a conscientious objector during the First World War and suffered severely for his principles, and in a poem entitled 'To My Father', Jim placed in poetry his father's philosophy. These ideas struck a chord in me. As a person who detested nuclear weapons, I personally protested at Mururoa against the detonation of nuclear devices there; Jim also took an anti-nuclear stance and vividly expressed his views in the poem entitled 'For a Child at Nagasaki'. In his poem 'A Bucket of Blood for a Dollar', he exposed the massive cruelty and unnecessary violence of the Vietnam War.

Throughout his work, he accused the New Zealand police of unnecessary violence, particularly against the down-and-out. Jim tried to establish a refuge for drug addicts at Boyle Crescent, Auckland, but this place became the consistent target of police harassment. He wrote about this in his poem 'Ballad of the Junkies and the Fuzz'. In Jerusalem, he also established an asylum for those who needed help but again he was ultimately defeated by the bourgeoisie – farmers and local council members – who objected to his endeavours.

And here I pay my tribute to Jim Baxter, not just a great poet with a worldwide reputation, but a good man – a true fighter for justice on earth.

Fishing with Joe

Some time ago, a friend of mine, Joe Miles, would pick me up in his old Bedford truck and we would drive to Muriwai Beach to catch mullet. The Bedford truck was excellent for this purpose because it was relatively light and did not sink into the sand and become stuck, as heavier trucks might have done.

At the back of the truck, under a canopy, a large variety of goods were stored in anticipation of the requirements of these trips. It was a bit like an Aladdin's cave. These items included equipment needed to pull the truck out of the wet sand should it become immobile, such as ropes, spades, sacking, jacks and wooden planks. And then, of course, there were the fishing nets and the manuka poles for dragging them. Joe also kept a rather large range of culinary equipment in there, including a petrol stove, large kettle, pots, and all the usual implements for making tea and cooking toheroa.

We would drive along the beach slowly, looking for concentrations of plankton that the mullet fed on. The plankton is a fairly bright, yellowy green colour and is easily observable from the beach, often appearing fairly close in. As the mullet feed, their heads can be observed poking out of the plankton, probably also on the lookout for any predators, including humans.

Mullet have excellent hearing and, therefore, to catch any requires stealth. At the same time, Muriwai Beach is known for its dangerous water sweeps that can suddenly burst upon the beach and submerge an unwary motorist, whose vehicle may even at times be dragged into the water by the fierce rips. Many vehicles have been lost in this way over the years. Joe, however, was a very experienced mullet catcher and when we had spotted the plankton, he would park the Bedford high up the beach next to the sand dunes and we would carefully carry the net to the water's edge.

Joe was a big man and very strong. In his youth, he was an Auckland wrestling champion and had maintained his fitness well into middle age. We would stretch the net along the beach and carefully make sure that there were no holes or debris caught in it, before attaching one manuka pole to each end. All this had to be done very quietly, so that the mullet would not hear us and swim away out to sea.

Muriwai is also infamous for the holes on the ocean floor that lie under the breakers. A fisherman can be wading in knee-deep water one moment and then step into a hole and become totally submerged the next. Together with the ferocity of the currents and rips, it all made netting for mullet a rather exciting activity.

To stop the mullet from escaping to the open sea, one person must take the deep end of the net and stride right out through the breakers behind the feeding schools without disturbing them. Joe always took the deep end of the net and he would slowly wade out into the sea and entrap the mullet. When he was confident that the mullet had been trapped, he would give me a signal and we would then slowly bring the net onto the beach.

We would quickly see the flapping mullet, with their large scales shining in the sun. They are a vigorous fish that would flap energetically. After disentangling them from the net, we would place them into hemp sacks brought from the back of the truck. In this way, on a good day, we caught a pretty large quantity of mullet. Before returning home, however, we would quickly dig up a few toheroa, a very succulent shellfish, and place them in boiling water heated on Joe's stove. As soon as the toheroa opens with the heat, the flesh is extracted and doused in a dressing of vinegar and onion and then eaten sandwiched between heavily buttered pieces of fresh white bread. Gorging on toheroa in this way provides one of the most magnificent gastronomic delights that a discerning eater can enjoy. And of course, all this would be accompanied by large mugs of hot tea. I thoroughly enjoyed these trips with Joe. They provided a scintillating and healthy exercise.

Later, Joe would smoke the mullet in the smokehouse at the back of his home at New Lynn and would drop off as many at my place as I wanted. Smoked mullet is indeed a fine delicacy and Joe would sell most of it at his local hotel, making a small but well-earned profit.

In those days, the public were permitted to take toheroa from Muriwai Beach, although the numbers were regulated and carefully monitored by fishing inspectors. Some people would try to take excessive amounts by devious means, such as placing them in the hubcaps of their cars, but the inspectors soon wised up to these tricks and the toheroa numbers were able to be maintained. It has been said, however, that the heavy vehicular traffic on the beach probably destroyed most of the toheroa beds and eventually their collection was prohibited altogether.

But Joe, being the keen fisherman that he was, unfortunately continued with a career of poaching toheroa. This took immense manoeuvring on his part, as the fishing inspectors, equipped with two-way radios and powerful binoculars, carefully monitored the beach and they all recognised Joe's truck.

Behind the sand dunes at Muriwai is a labyrinth of roads and tracks, some of which sit behind padlocked gates. Part of the art of a toheroa poacher is to know all these roads intimately and when the gates across them would be shut. High-speed chases between inspectors and poachers frequently took place over these roads, which at times traversed dense bush. The bush was also home to wild animals, such as rabbits and deer. Once a poacher knew that a fishing inspector was in hot pursuit in his four-wheel-drive vehicle, an escape was possible only with daredevil driving or by hiding the catch in dense bushes, to be retrieved later. Joe knew all these roads and tracks, and was probably the best toheroa poacher ever.

Over a period of years, Joe was caught once or twice and duly fined. However, there came an occasion when Joe was wrongly charged. Joe had been well up the beach, with his daughter, catching snapper on a set line near what was called 'the lagoon'. The lagoon was a place where, in the old days, ships would come in to collect cargoes of logs. It certainly had a very wild and dangerous bar and I doubt whether any ocean-going yacht or launch today would cross the bar and come into the lagoon.

After catching a few snapper on the long line, Joe and his daughter made camp high up in the sand dunes. The night was particularly dark and they sat around the stove, about to prepare a meal.

Then suddenly, out of the darkness, a four-wheel drive approached them at high speed. Joe's daughter was certain they were going to be run over and she screamed. The four-wheel drive stopped, however, and two uniformed fishing inspectors jumped out. One was a Maori and the other an elderly Pakeha in his mid sixties.

'What the hell is going on?' Joe demanded. 'We thought you were going to run us over and you nearly did! What's the idea?'

The Maori inspector immediately said that he and his partner had been watching Joe and his daughter through their binoculars, and they had clearly seen them digging for toheroa.

'That's a lie!' Joe said and questioned how the inspectors could have seen them from the sand dunes some three hundred metres away. 'You could hardly see your hand in front of you and look at how you nearly ran us over!'

The Maori inspector ignored Joe's complaints and announced that they would search Joe's truck. There and then, with torches in hand and the headlights of the four-wheel drive, the inspectors made an intense search but found neither toheroa nor evidence of the same. Instead of being apologetic, the inspectors then announced that Joe would be charged with disturbing the toheroa beds.

When the case was eventually heard at the Helensville Magistrates Court, Joe defended himself to cut costs. He was able by simple cross-examination to establish a major conflict between the two inspectors. The younger inspector said it was a moonlit night and that was why they could see it all so clearly. The senior inspector was, however, more truthful and admitted that the night was very dark. Joe submitted to the magistrate that it would have been impossible for the inspectors in those conditions to have witnessed anybody three hundred metres away allegedly digging in the sand.

The magistrate was, however, completely unimpressed. He had bright red cheeks and seemed to be suffering from high blood pressure. Joe said the magistrate completely disregarded what he had said and seemed only too eager to convict him and to impose a fine.

After the courthouse had closed, Joe sat in his truck and watched the magistrate leave the courthouse through a back entrance. Joe said he quite clearly saw the senior fishing inspector approaching the magistrate and, after a short conversation, he saw the fishing inspector place a dripping sack of toheroa into the boot of the magistrate's expensive car. Joe was very angry about this and contemplated following the magistrate's car, cutting him off, demanding his boot be opened and the sack of toheroa exposed.

However, he soon thought better of this and did not do so. Joe was so chagrined with this experience, though, that he continued to poach toheroa 'on principle'. On a later occasion, he was caught with a rather large cargo of toheroa and brought before a magistrate at the Auckland Magistrates Court. On this occasion, he engaged my services because he was a bit worried that he might be imprisoned.

I explained to the magistrate that Joe was a person of excellent reputation and was regarded by many as a pillar of the community. Because he was an outdoorsman, to send him to jail could have a very deleterious effect on his health. The magistrate, however, said that the toheroa had to be protected and that, in any event, Joe had not paid his previous fines. I realised then that I must do everything to help my old friend and, with a rush of blood to my head, I said to the magistrate that I would personally guarantee the payment of any fines. The magistrate gave me a smile and opined that it was a rather unusual submission. However, he accepted my undertaking, although it was made clear that Joe's fines had to be paid immediately.

After payment of the fines, Joe was released and in due course he repaid me. Joe and I have remained firm friends to this very day, except now we catch flounder and not toheroa.

The Highest Court
in the Country

In 1995, I sailed a yacht I then owned, *Aquila d'Oro*, to the Mururoa Atoll as part of a protest against the French government resuming the testing of nuclear devices there. On the way to Mururoa, we tied up at Rarotonga, where protests against the nuclear explosions by the French were also being held. During the few days that I stayed at Rarotonga, I found that the main topic of conversation, apart from the actions of the French government, was in relation to a forthcoming inquiry into the activities of a company named European Pacific Investments (EPI).

Many of the local hotshots involved in dealings with this company seemed to expect that they would be arrested and indeed imprisoned as a result. The situation was this: a company owned by EPI, called Magnum, had paid the Cook Islands government $2 million and received a tax certificate, which had then been presented to the Inland Revenue Department in New Zealand, whereby EPI received a tax credit for the same amount. Meanwhile, back in the Cook Islands, another entity in the EPI group received a refund of

$1.95 million from the government, the net effect being that the EPI group had paid the Cook Islands government $50,000 but received a New Zealand tax credit of $2 million.

The directors of EPI, which was incorporated in Luxembourg, were David Richwhite (Chairman), Paul Collins, David Lloyd and Francis Hoogewerf, a Luxembourg native. Mr Lloyd was responsible for convincing the Cook Islands government to establish a tax haven. It suffices to note that, towards the end of 1986, EPI increased its capital, and two of its entities, Brierley Investments and Capital Markets (Sir Michael Fay and David Richwhite being the major shareholders of the latter), were issued large quantities of shares at a certain price for each share.

A short while later, Brierley Investments and Capital Markets sold in quick succession large share parcels in EPI, first to the Bank of New Zealand and then the New Zealand public for considerable profit (in the tens of millions). The shares in EPI were clearly sold to investors on the premise that EPI was '... an international network combining trustees and banking services' in the Cook Islands. In the words of the esteemed business commentator, Brian Gaynor, EPI was established as a tax avoidance company.

It is not even debatable, in my opinion, that the tax avoidance activities of EPI were a scam and totally immoral, in that they denied New Zealand taxpayers of millions of dollars in unpaid taxes, which in turn should have gone into worthwhile projects; for example, education and health.

The reluctance of the Serious Fraud Office in New Zealand to take any action in response was hard to fathom. At the later commission of inquiry (colloquially known as the 'winebox inquiry') presided over by Sir Ron Davison, the then head of the Serious Fraud Office, Charles Sturt, attempted to justify the inaction of that office and, while doing so, had a breakdown in the witness box. In his book, *Dirty Collars* (Reed, Auckland, 1998), Mr Sturt described his reaction when reading the winebox inquiry documents as follows:

> *I soon realised that I was examining the work of several clever men who were intent on getting round our tax laws ... I quickly came to the conclusion that what they were doing was decidedly immoral, and I would later be criticised for not viewing this immoral behaviour as illegal. But I was not head of the ethics or moral police. My job was to catch law breakers, and getting round the tax laws is only a crime if you break the law. I could find nothing in the winebox that indicated criminal activity.*

The fact that there was an inquiry into the activities and unconscionable actions of the so-called winebox group of companies was due almost entirely to the actions of one man, the Right Honourable Winston Peters MP, leader of the New Zealand First political party.

It is clearly an indictment on the government of the day that this huge rort on the taxpayers of New Zealand was not contested by other so-called honourable members of parliament. However, the government of the day was a National Party government and perhaps they had too many friends among the architects of these money-go-rounds to allow them to act objectively and honestly. The Labour Party opposition was also pretty impotent.

During the course of the winebox inquiry, the commissioner, Sir Ron Davison, gave the impression that he was certainly out to nail the perpetrators of this huge tax avoidance scheme. However, at the end of the inquiry, to the shock and surprise of everyone (and no doubt to the relief of the accused), he refused to hold that the schemes involved were illegal. He even criticised Winston's motives for initiating the inquiry.

It is noteworthy, however, that in November 1998, the Court of Appeal upheld Winston Peters's right to contest the findings of Sir Ron's facile report and in a subsequent High Court decision, the criticisms of Winston personally by Sir Ron were ruled invalid as these were based on various erroneous findings, including the view that the Magnum transaction was not potentially fraudulent. The Court of Appeal expressly found that there was a basis on which to contend '... that by only telling half the story', the Fay-Richwhite affiliated company in question (EPI) 'misled the New Zealand Inland Revenue', and gained the immediate advantage of the $2 million tax credit without '... the risk of having to withstand a tax avoidance investigation by the [Inland Revenue Department]'.

The Court of Appeal which heard the judicial review comprised five judges: Justices Richardson, Henry, Thomas, Keith and Tipping. All these judges concurred that Sir Ron Davison's decision was based upon wrong reasoning on his part. In his judgment, Justice Thomas said:

It is difficult to accept that the Commissioner would have reached this conclusion if he had proceeded on a proper appreciation of the law. Most people, including many lawyers, would be surprised to learn that, whatever its shortcomings, the law was so deficient. At the point European Pacific presented the tax certificate

> to the Inland Revenue Department, it knew that the
> tax which it represented had been paid by it to the
> Cook Islands Government had been paid on its behalf
> by an associated company which had then received
> the amount of the tax back from the government (less
> $50.000). Most people would expect such conduct to
> constitute tax avoidance, if not tax evasion or fraud,
> At the very least, these possibilities required serious
> consideration on the basis of established law.

Without doubt, Tony Molloy QC is the pre-eminent expert in relation to matters of New Zealand tax law, and in an article which appeared in the *New Zealand Herald* on 21 July 2008, he wrote: 'The Court of Appeal definitively quashed Sir Ron Davison's whitewash.'

Although Winston's victory in the winebox affair was pyrrhic, in that none of the illegally obtained tax credits had to be disgorged, nor any of the participants prosecuted, there can be no doubt that he (almost alone) achieved a great victory. And in doing so, Winston procured for himself a legacy of wealthy and powerful enemies.

Winston Peters is essentially a man of the people, renowned as parliament's best *ex tempore* speaker. Over the years, he has worked strenuously to protect the rights of the elderly and the disadvantaged.

He has been my friend for a long time. On one occasion, when he was staying for a few days with me at a bach I owned at Port Fitzroy, Great Barrier Island, I awoke early one day upon hearing the sound of someone chopping wood outside. To my amazement, I found Winston had already risen to attend to the requirements of our wood stove. Later, when I introduced him to the local fishing club, he immediately went around every member present and politely introduced himself.

On another occasion, I took him to Paremoremo Prison so that he could witness the shocking conditions in the infamous D Block where about thirty prisoners were habitually kept in small cages. The management tried to deter him from entering by claiming that it was too dangerous, and that he would be attacked by the 'hostile prisoners' incarcerated there. He, however, waved aside their entreaties and personally entered each cage, having lengthy and friendly conversations with each prisoner. When he left the block, the prisoners, contrary to prison regulations, loudly performed a haka in appreciation of his visit.

In 2008, I, along with Heeni Phillips, my lawyer partner, appeared before the Privileges Committee as legal counsel for Winston. The Privileges Committee discharges a judicial function when investigating allegations of breach of parliamentary rules by members of parliament. The Committee exercises power of recommendation to the House. At the end of its deliberations, it reports to the House, which then considers the Committee's findings and recommendations.

The allegation against Winston was that he knew about a payment of $100,000 that an expatriate, Sir Owen Glenn, had paid to a lawyer, Brian Henry, as legal fees, and that he should have declared these monies to the Register of Pecuniary Interest as a party donation. The legal fees were paid to Mr Henry as his fee for representing a group of petitioners in the High Court, who were complaining that the result of the Tauranga elections should be annulled on the grounds of alleged misconduct by the successful candidate, namely Bob Clarkson, a member of the National Party.

Winston, on the other hand, stated quite firmly that this professional work carried out by Mr Henry had nothing to do with wooing or pursuing voters, but was based on an alleged failure of Bob Clarkson to keep to the rules of election expenditure. Our argument therefore was that Mr Henry was representing a number of people in the community committed to reversing that election result. Winston had unsuccessfully stood as a New Zealand First candidate for that seat.

It was evident that it had never been previously suggested that the legal expenses in regard to such a petition should be regarded as election spending. Election spending is money spent by a candidate to try to persuade voters to vote for him or her and includes such expenditure as election advertising, placards and so on. We further submitted that money so described should not be regarded as donations to a political party, as the money is neither paid nor received by a political party.

We also submitted that there had, in the past, been at least five such petitions. With each petition there had been a respondent who was an elected member of parliament. Therefore ten politicians recently had been involved either as petitioners or respondents, but none of these ten people had previously been required to register a pecuniary interest in regard to legal expenses incurred for such a court case.

There was therefore no legal precedent to support the allegation against Winston and the allegation reeked of political jealousy. What concerned me about the inquiry was that some of the members of the Privileges Committee had already made statements during their speeches in the House condemning Winston and it was clear that they had prejudged the issue. The second matter was that the members of the Privileges Committee seemed to form their views on party lines. Winston's support came from some Labour Party members but his main detractors, which were the majority, were from the National and ACT parties.

The chairman of the Privileges Committee was the National MP Simon Power, and the National Party Minister Jerry Brownlee seemed to act as prosecutor.

One of the main antagonists against Winston was Rodney Hide, who had initiated the complaint. He sat behind us during the hearing and actively displayed his feelings to all and sundry with his body language and facial expressions.

At the outset of the hearing, Simon Power made an announcement that I could only address on matters of procedure but not on the factual matters in issue. Every time I tried to develop an argument, Simon Power ordered me to stop, and our exchanges became very testy, although on my part, at least, liberally laced with such words as 'with respect' and 'obliged'. Finally, with the assistance of the Labour spokesman on justice, Russell Fairbrother (recently made a Queen's Counsel), I reached a truce with Simon Power whereby my written submissions would be tabled.

The Privileges Committee is said by some jurists to be the highest court in our country. I was appalled, however, to find that it did not recognise the most fundamental rules of natural justice. In fact, it reeked of bias, predetermination and voting on party lines. In this regard, in my written submissions, I quoted from Lord Bingham of Cornhill, a senior Law Lord in England, who wrote as follows on the issue of fairness:

> *First and foremost, I suggest, that decisions are made by adjudicators who, however described, are independent*

and impartial: independent in the sense that they are free to decide on the legal and factual merits of a case as they see it, free of any extraneous influence or pressure; and impartial in the sense that they are, so far as humanly possible, open-minded, unbiased by any personal interest or partisan allegiance of any kind.

My submissions in this regard were like water poured on ducks' backs.

The morning after the conclusion of the hearing, the *Dominion Post* published an article headed 'Points Win to Winston's Lawyer'. At least I had been able to table our written submissions, albeit with the help of Russell Fairbrother.

The one thing I want to state here quite clearly is that none of the Owen Glenn money ever went to Winston Peters personally, nor to his political party. The charges against him relied upon convoluted and politically motivated claptrap.

One of the problems that the committee had in realising their determination to find the charges against Winston proved was the fact that he had no pecuniary interest in the Owen Glenn money. Finally, after several drafts, the committee settled this difficulty on the basis that if the petition had been successful against Bob Clarkson, then Winston would have benefitted because he would have had the opportunity to stand for the vacant seat in Tauranga, thereby becoming eligible for funds available to such a candidate.

Not only was this reasoning remote and nebulous, it was certainly not supported by precedent. Furthermore, the committee had relied very heavily on a leaked email from Sir Owen Glenn, in which Sir Owen said he had made the donation to New Zealand First. But only very recently, the former president of the New Zealand Labour Party, Mike Williams, in an article published in the *New Zealand Herald on Sunday*, agreed that Winston was in fact telling the truth when he said neither he nor his party had received the Glenn money.

In his article, Mike Williams wrote that, in 2005, he had travelled to Sydney and visited Sir Owen at his 'beautiful Double Bay property'. He wrote that they had discussed how 'Bob the Builder' (aka Mr Clarkson) had won the Tauranga electorate by a mere 730 votes. Mike Williams claimed that Sir Owen had inquired of him whether an electoral petition to unseat Bob Clarkson might be successful because of Clarkson's heavy campaign overspending. Williams claimed that Sir Owen then resolved to make a payment towards Brian Henry's fees in support of the petition, writing in his sorely belated article:

> *The transaction did not involve Peters and no money even went near him or the New Zealand First party. However, the Privileges Committee and media chose to believe the leaked email – and the rest is history.*

It seems to me that to be a politician in this country, one needs the hide of a rhinoceros and the heart of the famous racehorse, Phar Lap. I believe Winston has both of those qualities in abundance.

The View from the Penthouse Suite

Some years ago, a lawyer whom I had known in my student days said to me, 'The next time you are in Wellington, Peter, call in and see me.' A month or two later, I was in Wellington, so I went to the building where his office was to pay my respects.

It was an old building, and his office was on the sixth floor. I walked down the corridor and, by mistake, entered the wrong room. When I opened the door, I immediately knew that I was not in my friend's office. A small, bespectacled man with a hooked nose sat at a large table, which had about six telephones upon it. He looked at me like a startled owl, and I made a hasty retreat.

Further down the corridor, I found my friend's small office, and after his warm greeting, I said to him, 'Michael, I went into someone else's office. There was a chap there sitting at a table with a whole lot of phones. What the hell does he do?'

Michael laughed, and said, 'Oh, he's a currency trader. He gets information from all around the world. If there's a major catastrophe somewhere, he knows their currency will fall.

But on the other hand, if they strike oil or gold somewhere else, he knows their currency will probably rise. But currency traders have to get that sort of news early. Sometimes he's there all night, and I suppose every now and again he makes his plunge – usually with somebody else's money. Not a job I'd want myself,' he added. 'But we live in a very strange world, and there are some very peculiar ways that people at times may earn fantastic sums of money.'

Over a cup of tea, he told me about his latest case. 'I've just had this very unusual brief,' he said. 'This person just appeared in my office. I don't even know how he got on to me. He was a tall, skinny fellow, with a bit of an evil look. Quite frankly, I felt a bit nervous about him, but he insisted on paying a good retainer, so I couldn't turn him down.

'He told me that he wanted to apply for an offshore licence to drill for oil. I told him that it was really out of my territory, but I had heard, anecdotally, that those licences are hard to get. I said to him that, generally speaking, they were only granted to the big, well-known oil companies with political connections, and that the first thing to be proved is that you are not a trader in licences, and have a record of financial stability and the means to exploit the licence.

'Well, the fellow just laughed and said, "Look, leave the detail to me. All I want you to do is file the documents. I can assure you that the rest will be okay."'

A week or two later, Michael said, he met again with this client (whom we shall call Elias) and they filled in the application forms together. Michael said that he soon found out that Elias was an Australian con man with a list of convictions, mainly for fraud, but that he had recently formed a company with its main object being oil exploration.

Michael repeated to me his remarks to Elias: 'I told him again and again that he had no hope of getting a licence and that all this was a waste of time and very expensive.' But Elias, according to Michael, would only smile in a condescending manner, and politely say, 'Just get on with the job.' Michael then told me that in the end, to his amazement, the licence was granted. 'I don't know how or why,' he said, 'but it was.' Within a very short time thereafter, Elias had sold the licence, and made a very fat profit.

To this I said, 'Quite frankly, nothing surprises me. There is a top echelon in this country who get away with things that the public wouldn't even know about.'

Michael agreed, and said that Elias obviously had political connections: 'There are some lawyers in Wellington, you know, who do practically nothing else except lobby politicians on behalf of clients, and by God do they make a big quid.'

A day or two later, I received a telephone call from Michael, and he said, 'You know, I got a call from Sydney a day or two ago from Elias. He's the chap I told you about – the one who bought and sold the offshore drilling licence. He said that he'd heard about you and your success as a criminal lawyer, and if you were ever in Sydney, he would like to meet you.'

I said, 'As a matter of fact, I'm going to Sydney for business, in a week or two, and if he'd like to have a cup of coffee, that's okay.'

When, in due course, I alighted at the Kingsford-Smith Airport in Sydney, I found, in the foyer, that I was being welcomed by a man dressed as a chauffeur, holding a placard with my name on it. He greeted me warmly as I approached him, and said to me, 'The boss is looking forward to meeting you.'

We drove back to central Sydney in a Rolls-Royce: I sat in the back seat, and the chauffer had little to say.

On the directions of the chauffeur, I alighted at a large building in the centre of the city, and he said to me as I got out of the car, 'The boss owns this building, and they'll be waiting to have coffee with you at the penthouse on the top floor.'

I took the lift to the top floor.

The door to the penthouse was opened by a tall, elderly man with grey hair, dressed in a red dressing gown. He knew who I was, and cordially welcomed me. On entering the penthouse, I noticed a large number of empty wine bottles on various tables, and obviously the place had been a venue for partying the night before.

The elderly gentleman said, 'You know, I'm a lawyer too, but unfortunately I've been struck off. I advise the boys, and they're doing very well at present.' He then asked me, 'How many times have you been to the Privy?'

For a moment I didn't know what he meant, but then it dawned on me that he meant the Privy Council. This was, in those days, the highest court in the British Commonwealth, and was situated in London. I said, 'Well, I haven't been there very often.'

He said, 'I regularly went there in the old days, before my career became a disaster.'

Within a short time, Elias appeared with one or two other dubious-looking rascals. He said, 'I'm going to take you to the best restaurant in Sydney.'

The maître d' greeted us like long-lost friends at the restaurant. The place was extremely sumptuous, and immediately wines appeared of superlative quality. The lunch comprised at least eight courses, including caviar, Moreton Bay bugs, and salad so fresh it could have come straight out of a garden.

This was one of the more delicious meals of which I have ever partaken, but there was something scary about the whole business.

During the meal, Elias said, 'Peter, we would like you to come over and practise in Sydney. I have a lawyer friend here who wants to meet you, and he's going to make you an offer you won't be able to refuse.'

The next day, by arrangement, I met the lawyer at his Sydney office.

The place seemed to be in great turmoil: there were several clients in the waiting room, but the physical space of the office was very small. I said to my new lawyer friend, 'You do seem to be a bit cramped here.'

He said, 'Yes, but office space in Sydney is very expensive. Most of our typists work from their homes. I'm sure we'll find room for you when you join the firm. Come on,' he continued, 'I'll introduce you to some of our contacts.'

That afternoon, after a hotel counter lunch, he took me around a series of bars in Sydney. In each bar we would meet with a senior police officer. These officers were well known to my new lawyer friend, and indeed they seemed like old mates, always delighted to see each other.

At the end of the afternoon, I was beginning to feel quite affected by the liquor, and I was becoming very puzzled as to why we were meeting all these police officers.

I finally asked the Sydney lawyer, 'Tell me, how come you know all these police officers? And why are we meeting them, one after the other?'

He gave me a very furtive look, and replied, 'Peter, where the hell do you think we get most of our work from? These are our contacts in the police force – every time they arrest somebody who has a good roll of money in his pocket, they ring us, and we get a steady supply of good paying clients. Of course, we've got to arrange for the police officers to be paid as well, but that's just part of the territory.'

That night, I made a resolution: Sydney was just not for me. It was too complicated and too dangerous. Give me good old Auckland any day – I have never heard of any police officer being paid in Auckland for sending a lawyer a wealthy client. And that's how it should be.

I have some niggling doubts about our offshore oil drilling bureaucrats, though.

Death by Fire

Between 5 and 6pm, on Friday, 13 February 1998, a man called William Annear burnt to death in his cell in D Block, Paremoremo Prison. When his body was discovered, the sight was so ghastly that the wardens immediately closed the door of his cell again. It was said that it was as if his body had been barbecued, and his flesh was literally falling off his bones.

William Annear was a 32-year-old Maori man, who had been sentenced, on 18 July 1989, to life imprisonment for murder. Over the years in prison, he had rehabilitated, and already a decision had been made to transfer him to a medium-security prison as part of a plan to release him on parole. He had been looking forward to this; indeed, the night before his death, he had written a very encouraging letter to his sister, his only living relative, and it was certainly not the letter of somebody contemplating suicide.

William was devoutly religious, and read from his Maori Bible every evening. He was also deeply involved in Maori language and culture, and was well liked by his fellow prisoners.

He had fallen out, however, with the wardens, who insisted that he made too many complaints. He wanted more exercise, better food, and more facilities for his religious and cultural studies.

The prison authorities deliberately frustrated him by delaying information about his imminent transfer, and generally showed resentment concerning his tendency to make complaints.

The conditions in D Block were inhumane: William and the others were each kept in separate cages within the prison walls, but had no aperture to the outside world. These inmates were locked up alone in their individual cells for at least nineteen hours a day, and were given no encouragement whatsoever to rehabilitate or do anything at all that was useful. At this stage, following a ministerial direction by Corrections Minister Nick Smith, all educational and cultural visits to the prison had been cancelled. Generally speaking, the inmates were not treated as human beings, but rather as dangerous insurgents.

Annear had come to the end of his tether, and really was close to becoming mentally ill. He could no longer stand the jibes of the wardens, and was looking for ways to retaliate.

It is clear that in these circumstances, he hatched a plan to light a fire in his cell.

His plan was to do this as a form of protest, but he did not realise the fatal consequences that would follow.

I never knew William Annear, but after his death, I was approached by his sister to act on the family's behalf at the inquest.

The inquest was held at the Coroner's Court in Auckland, and presided over by a coroner who is now deceased. The Corrections Department was represented by two eminent counsel, who were dedicated to protecting the department from adverse criticism.

When there is a death in a prison, a prison inspector makes a report. I may say that I have appeared at several of these inquests, and have found these reports to be very objective and often highly critical of the prison staff. In William Annear's case, the inspector was Simon Gibson, who wrote a devastating report criticising the prison staff.

The public are not fully aware of the absolutely wretched conditions and soul-destroying routines imposed upon many prisoners in New Zealand. The conditions that prevailed in D Block (and still do) are examples of these inhumane restrictions.

When William Annear threatened to the prison wardens that he was going to light a fire in his cell that afternoon, the wardens scoffed at him, and said, 'Go ahead.' They even shifted some of his belongings, which had been outside his cell, back into his cell, giving him more fuel.

An outsider may wonder how a prisoner, locked in a small, virtually bare cell can light a fire. First, he may ask, 'Surely the cells are patrolled by officers?' And secondly, 'Where would the inflammable material come from?'

Annear's cell was fitted with a fire sprinkler. He knew this and placed a blanket over it, thinking that, while it would not stop the sprinkler operating, it could certainly slow things down. But when we engaged a forensic expert, Ronald Selkirk, he gave evidence that the sprinkler was inoperative at any rate.

All the cells in the prison were supplied with alarm buttons, and when these were pressed, bells were set off in the prison's central office. After Annear had lit his fire, and the smoke had become threatening to the other prisoners, they all pressed their alarm buttons, and it was admitted that the bells rang at the central office. There was, however, no response by the prison authorities. They later said they thought the prisoners were joking, and decided to ignore the alarms.

The real reason for the fatality, though, was the mattress that Annear had been supplied with. This mattress was inflammable and, when burning, emitted cyanide fumes. This, of course, was not known to him. The prison authorities were well aware of the dangers provided by these mattresses, but because they were cheaper than fireproof mattresses, they had persisted in their use. An experiment carried out later by burning one of these mattresses ascertained that it generated heat of between 500 to 600 degrees centigrade, and emitted dense, acrid smoke.

When the fire got out of control, Annear screamed for help. He was screaming from the pain of the intense radiated heat in his small cell. He plugged his hand basin and turned on his taps, and got under the hand basin so the water would flow over him. But within a few minutes, he suffered an agonising death by fire.

The smoke from Annear's cell spread down the D Block landing, and across the passageway between the lower East D Block unit into the lower West D Block unit. This was a distance of at least fifty metres.

All the other inmates in D Block, about thirty of them, were yelling and banging on their steel grilles – they could hear Annear screaming as he burnt to death.

The alarming circumstances of William Annear's death included the following: by chance or design, no warden was on duty in D Block at the time of the fire; by chance or design, the automatic film taken by the cameras, which would have shown the inception of the fire, was later made unusable by the prison staff; by chance or design, it took 24 minutes from the time Annear lit the fire until his cell door was opened by prisoner officers; by chance or design, Annear had been supplied with a mattress, known to the prison authorities to be lethal at times of fire; and by chance or design, no alarm bells were answered.

Fires are not uncommon in prisons, and are often lit by prisoners when rioting.

On a previous occasion, I was summoned to the prison by the superintendent, together with Kevin Ryan and Barry Littlewood, both well-known lawyers, to help quell a prison riot. Fires were burning in virtually every wing of the prison, and the prisoners had taken hostages. Eventually, over a period of many hours, we were able to assist in the restoration of order.

When Mount Eden Prison burnt down years ago, as a result of an insurrection by the prisoners, many prisoners would have died had it not been for the actions of Ron Jorgensen, as mentioned in my chapter on him, 'He Laughed with the Wind and the Sky', and others who bravely went back into the flames and opened cell doors.

To be locked up in a cell, without any means of escape, to know that the cell is being filled with poisonous smoke and being heated like a huge oven, would be one of the worst experiences a human being could ever go through. The account of William Annear's death by fire at Paremoremo Prison is an example of incompetence on a terrifying scale. It exemplifies, with clarity, the pettiness of some prison officers who will deliberately provoke prisoners and indeed encourage the dangers of revolt.

The tragic outcome of the absolute neglect shown by the Corrections Department and the failure to keep to the rules at

Paremoremo Prison should be a warning to that prison and all other prisons.

The punishment of imprisonment is to deprive a man or a woman of his or her liberty, but it should not extend to exposing that person to shocking dangers.

I hope that William Annear has not died in vain, that D Block will be abolished, inflammable mattresses will no longer be provided, sprinklers will be routinely maintained, and cell wings will be properly patrolled. Prisoners should not be encouraged to light fires, and central officers should respond promptly to warning bells.

The ghastly case of William Annear should never be forgotten in the annals of penal history. The report of the coroner was, in my opinion, a 'Uriah Heep' whitewash.

The Fijian Escape

Ballu Khan was an icon in Fiji. As a successful businessman, he sponsored many charities, including the Nadi Muslim College Rugby Academy. The interim military government that took over in 2006, however, detested him and regularly arrested his employees without cause, taking them to the barracks and subjecting them to wrongful imprisonment.

On 3 November 2007, Ballu had, together with other friends, organised a farewell dinner at Lautoka for a team of heart surgeons from Auckland, who had come to perform free heart surgery. With his usual flair and generosity, he engaged one of Fiji's premier bands and a dance group to provide entertainment for the occasion.

The evening was a great success, and the next day they drove back in three vehicles to Suva. As they approached the Delainavesi police post, a mile or two from Suva, their vehicles were stopped by a roadblock.

Ballu was ordered from his vehicle by a military officer who was at least six feet, four inches in height and weighed about 120 kilograms: he was a big man, wearing a white shirt and pants. Ballu later learnt that he was Mr Korovou, one of the military's top martial arts instructors.

The military man aggressively pulled Ballu by his shirt and threw him into the police post. In the post were other military persons with martial arts experience, and another policeman. At this point, one of the soldiers punched Ballu on his jaw.

When Ballu protested, he was beaten again, this time by three military officers. He was hit so hard about the head, he feared he would lose his eyesight. However, Ballu did not resist, but yelled in pain and tried to protect his eyes with his hands.

The military martial arts instructor led the attack and continued to concentrate on Ballu's head, belting it into the wall of the police post, and at the same time, repeatedly bringing his knee up into Ballu's face.

The attack went on for at least ten minutes, and by this time Ballu was bleeding profusely and was virtually unconscious. The police inside the post did not participate, but did nothing whatsoever to stop the brutal attack by the military officers, either.

The beating only stopped when an off-duty police officer, who witnessed the beating from the roadside, intervened. He warned the military officers that they would kill Ballu if they did not stop.

Ballu was taken to the Central Police Station at Suva, where he was subjected to verbal assault and abuse. He kept blacking out, and was still bleeding copiously. Later, an army doctor put a plaster on his face but this did not stop the bleeding.

Throughout the night, his assailants would come to his cell and keep threatening him, saying things like, 'This is the start of the journey, we are going to take you from here and finish you off.' They also said, 'We are going to take your girlfriend tonight and do some nasty things to her.' Ballu could smell alcohol on the military officers.

The police officers at the Central Police Station were concerned about the critical state that Ballu was in, though, and had numerous arguments with the military officers, insisting that Ballu should be hospitalised for treatment.

Finally, he was taken to the Colonial War Memorial Hospital where he was treated for twelve days, and remained under 24-hour military guard. Each day at the hospital, military personnel tried to interrogate him and continually threatened him.

During this period, Ballu could not walk and had to use a wheelchair. He could not eat or drink, either, as his jaw had become locked. His injuries also included a base of skull fracture meted out by the martial arts expert. He was not allowed any privacy and his family members were not permitted to visit him. He was, however, interviewed by a senior member of the New Zealand High Commission, who was escorted into the hospital by one of his assailants.

After the military insisted that he be discharged from the hospital, they immediately conveyed him to the Criminal Investigations Department (CID) headquarters at Toorak, Suva.

At the CID headquarters, this time the police attempted to interrogate him but his medical condition deteriorated and he continued to be seriously ill.

It was at this stage that I arrived from New Zealand with another lawyer, Chris Reid. We immediately demanded that Ballu be placed in a private hospital. At the Suva Private Hospital, however, Ballu was refused access to most of his visitors. No criminal charges had been brought against Ballu but he was not free to leave his hospital room, and two uniformed police officers were stationed outside his bedroom twenty-four hours a day. From time to time police officers would enter his room and take away his personal papers. In the space of twelve days, Ballu had lost fourteen kilograms in weight.

Ballu later found out that on the night he was arrested at the roadblock, the women members of his group were taken to a police station where they were taunted and stripped naked, on the pretext that they might be concealing weapons.

The defence learnt that the State was planning to charge Ballu and eight or nine of his alleged accomplices with conspiring to assassinate virtually all the hierarchy of the interim government, including their head, Commodore Frank Bainimarama.

Meanwhile, Ballu remained seriously ill as a result of the brutal treatment he had received from the military at the time of his arrest.

It was just prior to my departure back to New Zealand, in late November 2007, that the defence team held a press conference at the Holiday Inn in Suva, not only extolling the virtues of democracy and the rule of law, but announcing that a writ had been served against the Attorney-General, representing the military and police. We sought compensation of $40 million on behalf of Ballu for the battery and assault, wrongful imprisonment and wrongful detainment that he had been subjected to. We released a six-page statement to the media, detailing the events that transpired on the afternoon of 4 November 2007. The case of Mr Ballu Khan, I told the media, was 'emblematic of the exercise of excessive and ill-controlled police and military power against the individual and therefore it was of great constitutional importance to the international reputation of the Republic of Fiji'. Furthermore, Mr Khan had good reason to suspect that there were certain persons of high status, particularly in the interim government and the military, who were hostile towards him and were partisan to other business enterprises in Fiji, which in some respect were Mr Khan's business rivals.

In late December 2007, I returned to Fiji, this time with my partner Heeni Phillips, and we issued a writ of habeas corpus so that Ballu could be brought before the court and we could apply for either his release or bail. By now, Ballu had been in effective police custody without charge for fifty-seven days.

By Monday, 31 December 2007, the hearing was to be called at the High Court before Judge Jocelyn Scutt from Australia. The State opposed the issue of the writ and filed an affidavit stating that, as Ballu was in hospital, he was not controlled by the police but was in the custody of the doctors.

We knew this was absolute nonsense as Ballu, although in hospital, was under heavy police guard, not only outside his room, but at all the hospital exits. In light of this, myself, Heeni, two local lawyers, Graham Leung and Semi Leweniqila, Ballu, and Agnes (his then partner) drew up a plan to get Ballu out of the situation he was in. In furtherance of our plan, I approached the senior doctor at the hospital and obtained a letter stating that Ballu was free to leave the hospital whenever he wished.

The next day, we arranged for two getaway vehicles to arrive at the front entrance of the hospital. Heeni meantime contacted Kate Lynch at TV3 in Auckland, as Heeni was concerned our safety could be compromised when we exited the hospital with Ballu and throughout all that was to follow later. TV3 in turn contacted local Fiji television to record our departure from the hospital. We thought this might obviate violence.

All dressed in formal suits, we marched defiantly out of the closely guarded hospital room.

Two police officers, one at Ballu's hospital room door and another plainclothes one in the corridor, protested in vain as we marched confidently to the front entrance. I brought the doctor's release note to the attention of the police officers but they chose to ignore it, threatening us all the while in Fijian.

At the entrance, for a moment it was difficult to ascertain who was military, who was media, and where our transport was, but we quickly found the getaway cars and piled into them. I was in the front car with Ballu and Graham Leung, and before we got anywhere, a large police officer strode in front of our vehicle, waving his hands and demanding that we stop. I jumped out and showed him the letter from the hospital, telling him, 'You have no legal right to stop us.'

Then I jumped swiftly back into the car. Our driver, fearing that bullets might be fired, had got down below the dashboard, and I was concerned that he might not be able to steer the vehicle properly, but he managed well enough.

We took off in convoy. Ballu's residence was only a few miles away, and we made it there in good time. Police cars soon arrived behind us, their sirens wailing.

Ballu's magnificent home was surrounded by a high steel fence and the entrance gate was electronically controlled. After we had all driven through the gate, it was closed, preventing the police from entering the property. I noticed at this stage that Ballu was absolutely exhausted and quite ill, and I advised him to go to bed.

A large number of police officers had arrived by this time outside Ballu's house, and indeed the whole area had been blocked off, with media being told to stay right away. By arrangement, we allowed one police officer to enter into the property, so that we could discuss Ballu's position.

For many hours, Heeni, Graham Leung, Semi Leweniqila and myself sat around a table on the veranda with the police officer, trying to work out an agreement.

What we opposed was for Ballu, who was weak and ill, to be taken back to the police station for more of what they called 'interrogation'. The police, however, were adamant that Ballu was to be arrested and taken back into custody for a further grilling. We argued for hours without any resolution. The police officer concerned spent most of his time speaking to his superior on the phone. It was apparent to us that it was not the police but the military who were controlling the situation. Finally, it was agreed that Ballu would not be further interrogated, and he was then formally charged and taken to the Magistrates Court, where, after a prolonged bail application, he was granted bail. The court itself opened for this special sitting, which came to a conclusion at approximately 11.30pm.

During this application, the prosecution misrepresented a number of things to the magistrate, saying that Ballu had ocean-going boats secreted at various inlets around the coast of Fiji so that he could escape if bail was granted. I made strong oral submissions in support of bail and was pleased to note that the magistrate carefully recorded what was said and conducted the proceedings in a very judicial manner. The magistrate reserved his decision but, after an hour or so, came back on the bench and granted bail.

We took Ballu home again, and for the first time I saw him relax.

A few weeks later, Heeni and I again flew to Fiji to prepare the case. While we were at Graham Leung's office, the police telephoned and said they had a warrant to arrest Ballu for breach of bail. Their allegation was that when Ballu had driven his car to Nausori Airport to pick us up, he had breached the terms of his bail.

Graham Leung tried to explain that Ballu had not acted outside the terms of his bail, but to no avail. Almost immediately, several police officers arrived at Graham's office, demanding to arrest Ballu for his bail breach. Ballu argued that he could not go to the police station as it was nearly 6pm, and under the curfew terms of his bail he had to be at his home by that hour.

They let us go, and we then drove to Ballu's home, where his brother had prepared a delicious meal. Afterwards, in the presence of a police officer whom we had allowed in, we telephoned Magistrate Katonivualiku, who had originally granted bail. The magistrate agreed with us that Ballu had not breached the terms of his bail by driving to the airport, and so we asked him if we could hand the phone to the police officer present so that he could be informed of this, too. Magistrate Katonivualiku obliged, but in the meantime, a large contingent of police had assembled outside Ballu's electronically controlled gates. They were led by a senior police officer named Tabakau. A television crew had also arrived and the police were ordering them to move further down the road.

I went outside with Heeni and spoke to Tabakau through the gate, telling him what the magistrate had said.

He was not at all receptive, so I then addressed the row of armed police officers behind him, telling them that they were acting illegally and that there could be serious repercussions for them. I also told them that they were not being given the true story from Tabakau.

By this time, Tabakau was clearly enraged and he yelled out to his men, pointing at me, 'Arrest the old man!'

Heeni then called out beside me, 'What for? What for?'

'For obstruction!' Tabakau shouted back at her.

And Heeni then told him, 'If you arrest Mr Williams I will be accompanying him to the cells, too.'

Mercifully, none of the police officers moved. Tabakau, however, threatened to call in the military's bulldozer to smash down the gate.

At this stage, Ballu had arrived on the veranda and called out that he would come down to the police station voluntarily.

Ballu later told me that, while I was at the gate, one of the rank and file policemen outside the gate had telephoned the police headquarters. He had expressed his concerns about the legality of what they were being ordered to do by Tabakau.

Subsequent to the phone call, the police had withdrawn from the gate and were hovering around further down the street.

Ballu and I then left the house together, and as the electronic gate opened, again Tabakau said, 'Arrest that old man!' But nobody moved.

Tabakau then ordered Ballu into a police car, and I went with him voluntarily. We were driven to the police station, with Heeni following in a private vehicle.

At the police station, Ballu was detained all night but refused to enter a cell because of the stench. Instead he sat up all night in an armchair. The next day in court, the breach of bail allegation was dismissed and Ballu remained free on bail.

At a later date, Ballu and his alleged accomplices appeared at the Suva High Court charged with conspiring to assassinate three senior members of the interim government, namely

Commodore Bainimarama, Minister of Finance Chaudhry, and Attorney-General Sayed-Khaiyum.

On behalf of Ballu, we applied for a stay, which in Fiji has the effect of an acquittal. We were lucky that the case was presided over by an eminent lawyer from Australia, Justice Andrew Bruce. I was very impressed by his judicial demeanour and fair attitude.

Justice Bruce, after a lengthy argument, granted the stay on the basis that the State had acted unconstitutionally in detaining Ballu so long without bringing a formal charge. The judge declared that the detention period was illegal. Under Fijian law, a suspect can be discharged if the State's agent, such as military personnel or police, has been guilty of such gross misconduct. The stay is a clear expression of the court's disapproval of the unconscionable actions by the authorities.

We were scheduled to fly back to New Zealand the following day and urged Ballu to do the same. Given the numerous malicious incidents during this case it was unwise for Ballu to remain in Fiji, and so he decided to come with us. Even then he was still suffering from the injuries so cruelly imposed upon him by that despotic regime.

Ballu has never fully recovered from his ordeal, but is now successfully practising as an accountant in New Zealand.

In Cruel Solitude

On 9 March 2012, I parked my car outside Paremoremo Prison, Albany. My friend Kevin Brett took my two labrador dogs for a brief walk while I visited an inmate, Arthur Taylor. I was visiting Arthur in my capacity as president of the Prison Reform Society, as Arthur was complaining that he was being unlawfully kept in solitary confinement for an undue period of time.

Walking from the car, I surveyed the prison exterior. It was well manicured, with lawns and flower gardens. It granted a deceptive facade to the claustrophobic bleakness within the prison itself.

As I approached the front entrance, memories of past incidents came to me. I remembered the night of the terrible fire in the prison, responding to the telephone call from the superintendent, and arriving here with Kevin Ryan and Barry Littlewood, as I mentioned in 'Death by Fire'. Among us, we divided the prison into sections, and then each of us went from wing to wing, trying to calm the prisoners and abate the riot. Every inflammable object was on fire. Some prisoners had taken wardens hostage and most were releasing their suppressed emotions by screaming and yelling, burning and smashing. The Minister of Justice had also arrived but, too frightened to meet with the prisoners, he stayed in a well-guarded office. Finally, after many hours, the rioting ceased, but the prisoners in D Block successfully urged us to stay until morning because they said they were afraid they would be beaten by the wardens.

Another memory resurfaced, of the time I had taken the famous member of parliament and icon of human rights, Winston Peters, to the prison, so that he could see for himself the disgraceful condition in D Block. As I recounted in 'The Highest Court in the Country', the superintendent tried to persuade Winston not to enter D Block, saying the prisoners there were too dangerous and violent. Winston, however, persisted and eventually went into every single cage, speaking and joking with the inmates. As we left, the prisoners performed a haka in his honour, and in brazen defiance of the prison rules. To me, that showed the collective, insuppressible spirit in D Block.

I had now reached the front office of the prison. After completing the formalities, I entered through the electronically controlled sliding steel doors, went down a metal staircase and into a corridor which led through the main body of the prison.

This corridor is at least fifty metres long and the floor is lined with faded green linoleum. On either side, the slit windows are heavily barred, and generally the atmosphere is foreboding and repressive.

The warden who accompanied me on this occasion chuckled and said, 'I often see a change in the expression of the prisoners when they first enter the prison and have to walk down this corridor. I see fear appear in their eyes.'

After being escorted past many sally ports and grilled doors, I was ultimately directed to enter a small lock-up compartment. There was barely room for one chair, and when addressing the communication window my shoulders were jammed against the opposing walls. Behind me a grilled door slammed shut. I was told to wait there for the prisoner, Arthur Taylor.

The chamber was airless and extremely claustrophobic. When Arthur arrived, I could barely see him through the small, thick glass window and could hardly hear him through the internal microphone.

I found the confines of this hellhole suffocating and immediately decided that I would not put up with these conditions.

After shouting, rattling and banging on the door, finally a warden arrived. I graphically informed him of my displeasure. Immediately adjacent was a large visiting room that was equipped with security arrangements but was not so claustrophobic. I asked the warden, 'Why can't the visit be there?'

He replied nonchalantly, 'I've had a direction from the top that the interview is to be where you are.'

'Well, you'd better go back and get fresh instructions,' I replied, 'because I'm certainly not going to sit in this cattle pen.'

Eventually, permission was given to use the larger room, but all this reminded me just what an inhumane prison Paremoremo is. It was designed to crush human spirit and breed psychosis.

Now, sitting opposite Arthur, even through the thick glass partition between us, I could see the anaemic, pallid puffiness of his features and the unnatural whiteness of his skin. He did not conceal, however, his pleasure in seeing me, and I took some comfort in the fact that I had, for a short time, brought him out of his isolated misery.

He told me he had been, for the last nine months, under directed segregation, which meant he was kept in isolation, away from all the other prisoners.

'This means,' he said, 'I have no one to speak to or be with. I think they're trying to send me mad. Before, I was in D Block, which was bad enough, but at least in there I was able to talk to other prisoners and work on my legal papers.' Arthur was well known as New Zealand's best 'jailhouse lawyer', and had successfully, from jail, argued several cases relating to prisoners' rights in the High Court.

'Last June,' he explained. 'I took proceedings against the manager here, Mr Beal, for inhumane treatment. My cell was searched and they found my cell phone and some tobacco. And then I was moved into this "directed segregation". I'm locked up in a small cell twenty-three hours a day and released for one hour only, when I am taken to a small yard – but again I don't have access to any other prisoners there.

'I've already complained to the Inspector of Prisons and the Ombudsman but to no avail. I've also been visited by the Chief Inspector at the Ombudsman Office, Greg Price. He told me he specialises in the national prevention of torture under the Crimes of Torture Act 1989. He was sympathetic but he can't help me, either. He doesn't have the pull to get anything done.'

I asked Arthur, 'What do you do all day?'

And he told me, 'In the one hour I am released I have to shower and make phone calls – I'm restricted to two phone calls a week, too, and my mail is deliberately delayed by the prison.'

'What do you do for the other twenty-three hours?' I asked.

He said, 'My cell is very small, hardly big enough for me to lie down. All that's saving me from going nuts is reading books. The librarian here, Barbara, has been good to me, and provides me with reading material. Without her I would have lost my sanity completely. I just lie all day on my bunk, reading and sleeping, that's all I can do. When I was first put in that cell, they placed sacks over the window to destroy any natural light, and there's a camera in the corner that watches every inch, twenty-four hours a day.'

I asked him, 'Do you think you are being punished for having tobacco and a cell phone in your cell when you were in D Block?'

He said, 'No. I was punished by a Visiting Justice for that, her name is Sally Sage. Ten days in the pound and thirty days off privileges. I had no quarrel with that and served that sentence a long time ago. But I've been in this punishment of directed segregation now for all these months, since June 2011.'

I asked him what the physical conditions were like in his cell, and he told me, 'This part of the prison they have put me in has not been used to house prisoners for at least five years. It used to be the place where mentally disturbed prisoners were kept, especially those who were high suicide risks. Sometimes prisoners can't take it anymore, they bang their heads on the walls, shout, scream and go into convulsions. Those prisoners used to be taken here and strapped down for their own safety. More recently the unit has been used for urine testing to find out whether a prisoner has been taking drugs.'

'How is your health, how are you standing up to it?' I asked him.

And he said, 'I know I have already been damaged psychologically. I would like to be counselled by an independent psychologist. The loneliness is getting to me. I like to play chess but now there is no one to sit down with. The food's crap and I have lost a lot of weight. They give me dinner at about 3pm, which includes one plum for dessert, and I'm not fed again until 8.30 the next morning, when I receive two Weetbix. I can't even make a cup of tea, as there is no hot water in the cell. I'm also concerned about the effect of having no sunlight on my body.

'But,' he added, 'when they heard you were coming a couple of days ago, and that you were bringing a Member of Parliament, Phil Twyford, they became quite concerned. Yesterday I received a television set and this morning a radio.'

I asked him, 'Why do you think they are picking on you?'

He sighed deeply and said, 'Well, they think I'm a troublemaker because I stand up for my rights, because I've brought an action against the prison over the abolition of tobacco and they believe I leaked information to the *Truth* newspaper about the shocking conditions here.'

I asked him, 'Why don't you apply to do some type of rehabilitation course?'

He chuckled and told me, 'No high-security prisoner in New Zealand is able to do any course of study to prepare himself for release.'

'I don't know how you stand the claustrophobia,' I said. 'I certainly wasn't prepared to sit in that rat-hole visiting room they first put me in this morning.'

'Of course,' he mused, 'they would have done that deliberately.' A lawyer from Wellington was directed to submit to the same conditions; they even turned the lights off on him and he had to complete his interview in the darkness. I was told this by a warder, who thought it was funny.

About this time, the warden came in and said our time was up. Through the glass barrier I farewelled Arthur. Trekking back through the prison, through the corridors, grilles and sally ports, I reflected once more upon just how inhumane and cruel parts of New Zealand prisons are.

I observed the depressing prison interior, garish yellow paint peeling off the bars, the rusty iron. It was a place desolate of art, culture and humanity, designed to crush and reduce prisoners to automatons.

Walking away from this wretched place I felt some satisfaction that Arthur had been brought some slight respite from his solitary confinement.

The Ombudsman has since declared, in an official report, that keeping Arthur so long in solitary confinement amounted to 'torture'.

PS: Research has shown that sleep-enhancing and desire-destroying medications, freely and copiously available in New Zealand prisons, not only destroy parts of the human brain, but have disastrous long-term effects. Claustrophobia cannot be logically controlled. It is fundamental to our human psyche that we have an abhorrence of being placed in inescapable pits or underground tunnels where freedom is deprived by steel grilles.

The Great Evangelist

Back in the 1960s, Brian Edwards, who held a doctorate in literature and whose thesis dealt with the writer Kafka, became prominent as a television interviewer. I acted for him in a libel case in Wellington, where he was successful in obtaining substantial damages against the *New Zealand Truth*.

The modus operandi of Brian's interviews was that he would question some individual of importance, and in this questioning he would be assisted by a panel of three commentators. The show was very popular.

Around this time, Billy Graham was probably the world's best-known religious crusader, and he and his entourage came to New Zealand in the 1970s, holding successful meetings throughout the country. These gatherings were attended by thousands of people and probably comprised the largest evangelical crusade in the history of New Zealand. At the climax of each meeting, after Graham's hellfire and brimstone sermon and much soul-stirring music from the large choir, people from the audience would come forward and give themselves to the Lord.

The Reverend Graham had written several books, which gradually mellowed somewhat in their content, but the early ones, at least, advocated such things as castration of sexual offenders. All his books prophesised a hellish Armageddon would soon be visited upon us because, according to him, evil was triumphing in our materially obsessed western world.

Graham himself was an imposing figure, and always immaculately dressed. His oratory was of the old-fashioned damnation variety, inspired by the great preachers of the past, such as the Presbyterian John Knox and the Methodist John Wesley.

His approach to evangelism was very lavish. He travelled in great style and always demanded opulence. With his large entourage, he stayed in the most expensive hotels, where he tipped the staff generously. He was renowned for gifting expensive cars to the heads of state in countries where he was crusading.

Paradoxically, he was an intimate friend of the then President of the United States of America, the notorious Richard Nixon (although the Watergate incident, which exposed Richard Nixon as a criminal, had not then yet occurred). Graham spent lengthy periods as a live-in guest at the White House, and was a close confidant of 'Tricky Dicky'. In view of the fact that Nixon was probably the rottenest and vilest of all the American presidents, it would appear somewhat incongruous that these two were attracted to each other.

However, in New Zealand, among the Protestant churches at least, Billy Graham was regarded as almost a saint, and it was hoped that attendance at our churches would be substantially increased by his New Zealand crusade.

Brian Edwards, as it happened, invited me to be on the panel questioning Billy Graham, so I put some time into researching the Reverend.

I was shocked at the contents of his early books and soon realised that Graham was a bigot and, in my view, an unsavoury person who was able to lead the lifestyle of some royal personage by his mastery of emotional religiosity.

There was a plethora of books, either written by Graham or written about him, that were invariably praiseworthy of him. But I discovered one book, a biography, that was heavily critical of Graham and his crew.

This book contained photographs of the Billy Graham team counting up buckets of money with gleeful expressions on their faces after one of their meetings. It also contained information about substantial trust funds created by Graham for his family, commenting that this was inconsistent with Graham's protestations that he was a 'man without means'. The book furthermore exposed Graham's pandering to people of authority and high status, in order to obtain advantages for his own organisation. It was suggested that he increased his own popularity and status by being photographed with presidents, kings and prime ministers.

On the night of the Brian Edwards interview, I met with Billy Graham at the television studio in the makeup room. I had brought with me some of the books I had read in preparation, and one of these was the exposé biography. Billy Graham presented himself well: dressed in an expensive suit, with silvery hair and piercing blue eyes, he obviously was a force to be reckoned with. I saw that he immediately recognised the exposé biography I was carrying, and his attitude towards me changed abruptly. A flame of detestation lit up in his eyes.

The interview turned out to be quite tense. Graham disliked the critical questions I put to him, and retaliated by accusing me of being a 'sinful person', making veiled references to my private life. He referred to my agnosticism, as well as my support for decriminalisation of medical abortions and consenting acts between adult homosexuals.

After the interview, any initial comity between myself and Billy Graham was completely annihilated, and we parted in a demonstrably unfriendly manner.

Some days after the interview, however, an article appeared in a nationwide newspaper, stating, quite incorrectly, that I had been at one of his meetings, and had come forward and given myself to God. I had never attended any of his meetings, and this propaganda was completely false. Ridiculous, actually.

But a certain truth would soon be revealed to me.

In those days, I had a friend called Gus Urlich, who sadly is now deceased. Now, Gus was a professional gambler, and he arranged poker, crown and anchor, and manila games around Auckland and elsewhere. He had a close associate, a bookmaker, Charlie White, and together they would attend places like factories and freezing works on pay day, and hold games for employees.

Gus was a physically well set-up man and had been, in his earlier days, a professional boxer. When Eddie Cotton, a contender for the world light-heavyweight championship, came to New Zealand to fight in a boxing match, one of the persons he sparred with was Gus. On a previous occasion, I had seen Gus fight in a bar room brawl. His opponent was a large man, who was boasting that he been a soldier in the Vietnam War, and had been taught not only how to fight, but how to kill people with his hands. Gus demolished him very quickly in the brawl, by grabbing the veteran's hair and pulling his face violently down, at the same time as bringing his own knee up, smashing the man's nose into a gory mess. When he fell to the floor, Gus quickly finished him off with a few well-directed kicks to the head. The ex-marine was carried out.

It was somewhat bizarre, then, that Gus should be approached by one of Billy Graham's entourage to arrange a gambling night for the staff during that New Zealand crusade. Gus was told that the members were bored, as the nightlife here was, to use their words, 'quite pathetic'.

As a footnote to this story, a few days after the television interview, a youngish man called at my office. It was an old school mate, from Feilding Agricultural High School, and he told me he was in Auckland for a few days, and had decided to look me up. I was pleased to see him, and my secretary brought in coffee as we chatted about the old days at Feilding Ag. Soon it became apparent, though, that he really wanted to talk about the Billy Graham interview. I remembered then that he came from a family in Feilding who were very religious. He asked me particularly about the biographical exposé I had referred to during the interview. Then he asked me if he could borrow the book, and by chance I had it in my office. I lent it to him, but after he departed, I never saw him or the book again.

Over the years, when the opportunity has arisen, I have looked in second-hand bookshops for this book, but I have never been able to obtain a copy.

The Howard League

In the eighteenth century, John Howard devoted much of his life to prison reform. He not only travelled around Britain but almost every other country in Europe, including Russia, carrying out his inspections of prisons. What he found was that prisoners were ill and rules went unobserved and that prisons were the antithesis of Christian charity.

He travelled nearly 80,000 miles on horseback, and spent some £30,000 of his own money in his efforts to investigate and reform prisons. He discovered that the Europeans were much more advanced than the United Kingdom, and one consequence of a book he wrote was to expose the English to other prison practices and to suggest that England lagged behind other countries.

Published in 1777 and entitled *The State of the Prisons in England and Wales*, his book captured public attention and, not too long afterwards, individuals including William Blackstone were drawing up the Penitentiary Act 1779, which saw many of the Continental institutions' features incorporated into the English system.

John Howard died in Kherson in the Ukraine in January 1790 of jail fever, a form of typhus, but his legacy would continue to travel. The Howard League spread to many countries, including America, Australia, Canada, England, Wales, Scotland and New Zealand. Founders of the Howard League in New Zealand were mainly women, and the League soon established for itself a reputation of integrity and respect.

Over the years, the League in Auckland has been led by Frank Haigh, a well-known civil rights lawyer, Mr Bob Goodman, a bookseller extraordinaire, and then by Mr Arthur O'Halloran. I remember attending meetings at Mr O'Halloran's residence at Parnell. As well, Fred Jordan, an Auckland lawyer, and then President of the League later, held meetings at his office in High Street, and frequently presented submissions to parliamentary committees dealing with penal matters. Those were days of fierce campaigns by the League against shocking jail conditions, and of calls for the education and rehabilitation of prisoners.

About thirty years ago, at the urging of Fred Jordan, I was democratically elected as president of the Howard League, and was fortunate enough, for the next eighteen years, to have David Hagar as the League's secretary. David worked assiduously for the League, never accepting any payment and indeed paying for incidental expenses out of his own pocket. When a New Zealander, Lorraine Cohen, was sentenced along with her son Aaron Cohen to death for drug offences in Malaysia, David and I travelled there to help her and, with the assistance of Karpal Singh, a famous Malaysian lawyer, we successfully had her death sentence commuted to imprisonment.

During my time as president, the majority of the meetings were held at my house. The League membership came from all walks of life: family members of prisoners, lawyers, accountants, ex-prisoners, and people generally interested in justice and injustice. We were a voluntary organisation and no one expected to be paid. We considered ourselves politically neutral, too, an independent voice, and as a matter of policy, we opposed the following:

- Corporal punishment
- The death penalty
- Prosecution of consensual adult homosexual conduct
- The borstal systems
- Young prisoners in adult jails
- Overcrowding in prisons
- Lack of habitation centres and bailhouses
- Violence in prisons
- Multiple prisoners in one cell
- Solitary confinement
- Gross miscarriages of justice (such as occurred in Arthur Allan Thomas's case)
- Keeping prisoners in cages (as was done in D Block of Auckland's Paremoremo Prison, and the Waikeria Prison following the Mount Eden Prison fire) and
- The prevalence of suicide in prisons.

Our activities were wide ranging and included preparing and filing submissions in a commission of inquiry into the New Zealand penal system and violent offending. David Hagar was in particular responsible for insightful submissions, for which he was complimented by Sir Clinton Roper, chairman of the commission.

In 1985, David Hagar designed a computer-assisted inmate rehabilitation programme, which was translated into French,

German, Spanish, Italian and Portuguese, and distributed worldwide. This computer programme was exhibited at the annual congress of the American Correctional Association held in New Orleans in August 1987, and was subsequently upgraded in consultation with the Californian and Los Angeles Probation Service to meet American requirements, and put into general operation there. In 1988, the United Nations requested and was provided with copies of the programme for distribution to interested member states for use as a prototype.

Frustratingly, however, the New Zealand Corrections Department has never implemented this programme, notwithstanding that it was perfectly aware of its worthiness and acceptance overseas.

The League also organised public protests and protested outside the Auckland District Court against the use of court and police cells to accommodate prisoners. Another protest was held outside Mount Eden Prison concerning the lack of washing machines for remand prisoners. And yet another protest was staged there against the political refugee Mr Ahmed Zaoui's detention in custody without trial. To heighten public awareness and support for families of prisoner deaths in custody, the League organised meetings at the Methodist Hall in Queen Street. The aim of all this protest activity was to bring these issues to the attention of government institutions and politicians, who might change their policies as a result.

Furthermore, the League assisted families involved in prison suicide inquests and civil damages claims against the Department of Corrections for deaths in custody cases. In the case of one young boy, who committed suicide at Christchurch Prison, he told the guards that he had suicidal thoughts, and the guards for inexplicable reasons then gave him a piece of rope, by which he hanged himself a short time later. David Hagar relentlessly pursued this matter until the boy's mother was compensated by the Corrections Department.

A further case concerned a young Maori boy in Mount Eden Prison, whom we shall call Rangi. He was suspected by some of his fellow inmates as being an informer against his co-accused. Rangi became so panic-stricken by intimidation and taunting by fellow prisoners that he killed himself by hanging.

When the 'Three Strikes' legislation was being moved through Parliament we, in conjunction with the Canterbury branch of the Howard League, invited the Head Prison Chaplain of Californian Prisons, Reverend Givens, to New Zealand. He gave speeches in various centres throughout the country strongly opposing this legislation.

As president of the League, I gave hundreds of television and radio interviews on topics relating to penology and justice issues. We received numerous letters from prisoners, too, which we always endeavoured to respond to in a timely and considered manner.

These activities and meetings, across the last eleven years of my presidency, would not have eventuated, though, without the valuable contributions of League secretaries Heeni Phillips and Tina Wilson, both Auckland lawyers, who provided the additional drive and determination required to see these things happen.

It is with sorrow, however, that I recall recent events at the New Zealand Howard League in Auckland which, in my view, have changed the nature of the organisation. Mike Williams and Tony Gibbs are now at the helm, though neither had been involved previously. I was personally ill with cancer and was receiving debilitating radiation treatment at the time. This affected my ability to manage the organisation.

Tony Gibbs, as the new patron, introduced the League to two commercial lawyers, whom he said would act pro bono in the interest of the League. The League was advised by them that it should change its constitution so that it could obtain charitable status and therefore be amenable to corporate funding. Tony Gibbs also brought to the League Mike Williams, whom he said had been a fundraiser for the Stellar Trust and had previously been President of the Labour Party. We were told that he had corporate connections and would be an excellent fundraiser.

The League in Auckland, however, had never looked for funds before and had always acted on a voluntary basis. In a 1950s broadsheet entitled *What is the Howard League*, Arthur O'Halloran wrote:

> *During the past thirty odd years the Howard League has advocated an enlightened penal system for New Zealand. When flogging was a punishment permitted by statute law, the Howard League fought for its abolition ... to all those who want a better penal system and in particular to all who believe that hanging should be abolished, we appeal for your support. We need new members (5 shillings per year) and donations. The League's work is done voluntarily.* <u>*We have no paid officials.*</u> (My emphasis.)

At a meeting of the League at my home on 30 June 2011, Mike Williams presented to the members what he said was the new constitution. This had been prepared by Tony Gibbs's pro bono lawyers. He told the members at the meeting that this constitution would enable corporations that donated money to the League to have their gifts treated as tax deductions. What he did not announce to the members was that the so-called new constitution contained a clause granting effective control of the League to himself and Tony Gibbs.

We all signed the document in good faith, not realising that we were essentially handing over management of the League to Tony Gibbs and Mike Williams.

At that stage, according to the document, I remained president of the League, but the effective control was granted to Mike and Tony. A week or so after this meeting, the League learned that Mike Williams was now its paid CEO. I was given a further document to sign, whereby the League would borrow $100,000 from Tony Gibbs's family trust. Tony Gibbs then told me that the money was to enable the Howard League to pay a substantial income to Mike Williams until the money from donations arrived. He said the loan would then be repaid to his family trust. I refused to sign, and resigned from the League, as did other long-standing members. We had never considered that anybody would want to take over the Howard League. It still astonished me.

I personally must accept a large degree of culpability for signing these documents without first perusing them thoroughly. My signing induced other members to similarly sign, none of us ever dreaming that we were signing away leadership and the altruistic spirit of the New Zealand Howard League.

I decided against litigation, but basically have always blamed myself for simply not reading over these documents before signing. I can only say, in mitigation of my own negligence, that I was suffering from cancer, and indeed that day had received radiation treatment at the Mercy Hospital. That treatment leaves the patient extremely tired and listless.

For all that, I am still proud today of the achievements of the New Zealand Howard League for Penal Reform. It had built up a reputation for integrity, honesty and altruism over a period of almost one hundred years. I hope that its long struggle will one day bear fruit in the form of a more enlightened and humanitarian penal system in this country.

He Saw the Stars

Throughout my career, I have held concerns for the welfare and rehabilitation of people imprisoned. There is a grave danger that a competent lawyer may become obsessed with money and large fees, and forget his obligations to the general public.

In many ways, a criminal lawyer has freedoms and privileges not shared by the rest of the community. He does not have to kowtow to an employer, or the rigid rules of a corporation, but is free to express independently his views on current affairs. He also has the advantage of being able to obtain a public profile through his representation of clients and the courts, particularly if he has conducted highly publicised trials.

After practising mainly in the field of criminal law, by the time I was middle-aged, I was in this position. I lived with my family in a commodious home in Remuera, where the New Zealand Howard League held its monthly meetings to discuss ways and means of rehabilitating prisoners.

There was something slightly patrician about the League, and in those days, most of the members, though devout and idealistic, came from what might be called the 'upper crust'. The meetings at my home on Remuera Road would conclude with a tea trolley being rolled in, and the members partaking of cake and tea – no alcohol was ever served. But these were good people. They carried out prison visits to prisoners who did not have loved ones to visit them. They opposed cruel punishment, and other harsh forms of retribution. Generally speaking, they formed a solid rebuttal to the cries and shrieks of the rednecks and the equivalent of today's Sensible Sentencing Trust.

I knew the superintendents of the Auckland prisons quite well at the time, being a frequent visitor to those institutions for the purposes of taking instructions from clients. In those days, superintendents of prisons were much more open-minded and accessible than today, and, I believe, in many ways more humane. Mount Eden Prison had an annual concert, where all the participants were inmates, and indeed the superintendent's wife helped them prepare to deliver their performances. There was the prisoners' choir, accompanied by the prisoners' orchestra. There was always a play put on by the prisoners, too, and individual recitations – of poetry, singing or instrumental pieces.

I would always attend these concerts, with many other members of the public. They were thoroughly enjoyed, and gave great encouragement and self-esteem to the inmate performers, and I can never remember the least bit of trouble.

To give you an example of the humane attitude of some, the superintendent at Mount Eden would take Juliet Hulme – the young girl who had been convicted of the notorious murder of her girlfriend's mother – to his home on a Saturday night where she would join his family for dinner. This was never adversely commented on at the time, but imagine the howl that would come from the talkback radio hosts if that had occurred today.

One day I was at the prison, visiting a client, and as I was walking through the corridors, past the sally ports and grilles, a warden approached me and said, 'Peter, the old man would like to see you. He's got something on his mind.'

I was then taken to the superintendent's officer, where I was courteously received, and provided by an inmate with a cup of tea. This was not unusual in those days. The superintendent and I knew each other quite well, and I had respect for him, as I knew he did his best for his prisoners.

He offered me a cigarette, which I declined good-naturedly. Cigarette smoking was common in the prisons then, and indeed the Justice Department issued free tobacco every week to each prisoner.

After some small talk, he said to me, 'Peter, we've got a prisoner here who has been an inmate for twenty years. I'm trying to help him get parole, but he's institutionalised now, and it will be very difficult for him to deal with the outside world. He committed a bad murder twenty years ago, but he was only nineteen then, and I believe now that, really, he's a totally different person.'

I said, 'Yes, I can understand that. But how can I help? They don't allow legal representation at the Parole Board.' (Now, in some circumstances, the offender may be represented by legal counsel.) I told him, 'I don't see how I can contribute.'

The superintendent leant forward with a gleam in his eyes. 'I believe you can help,' he said, taking a puff of his cigarette. 'The prisoner's name is Jim Brown, and what I want to do is to get one of my wardens, in the near future, to take him out of the prison and drive him to your home on an evening that suits you, so he can spend the night at your place and know what it's like to feel free. We'll come and pick him up again in the morning. We'll give you a telephone number to ring if there's any trouble. Peter, you are one of the few people I know that I can trust and can handle this situation. You've got a bloody big house in Remuera, you are a well-known penal reformer – so how 'bout it?'

He and I looked each other straight in the eye, and I knew this was a bit of a challenge. Not everybody wants to take a murderer into his home overnight. I thought for a moment, and then replied, 'I'll tell you what. I like the idea, but in fairness I'll have to discuss it with my wife, Patricia. You know we have a young family. She's a good woman, but not quite as radical as I am. I'll ring you tomorrow and give you my reply.'

The superintendent replied, 'Fair enough. I can understand that. I think I would do the same if I was in your position.'

That evening, at dinner, I did discuss the proposed visit by the prisoner to my home with my wife. She was an artistic woman, having been a successful ballerina, and not altogether au fait with penal matters. At first she was indecisive, but finally agreed.

It was a Saturday night when the prisoner arrived, about 5pm. He was a smallish man, middle-aged, dressed in a faded suit that did not fit him too well. He was obviously on edge, and carrying a small bag with his overnight gear inside.

My family made him very welcome. He was not given alcohol because that had been prohibited, but he was taken around the gardens and generally made to feel at ease and relaxed. He was not a great talker. My children, however, took an immediate liking to him, and soon engaged him in a chorus of childish chatter.

That night we had a gorgeous dinner, several courses of the best food, and Jim really seemed to have a good appetite. His table manners were impeccable. It was clear that he was trying to be friendly, but his nervousness restrained his conversation.

The rest of us were in great form, though, and soon had the prisoner laughing and joking, and he was really enjoying himself. After dinner, we sat in the lounge before a huge fireplace with the fire roaring. The house had been a club to the American officers in World War II, and the fireplace had the American eagles engraved around its frame. I produced a box of Cuban cigars, and we both sat back in big lounge chairs, smoking those cigars, feeling the warmth of the fire, with Frank Sinatra playing on the radiogram in the background. My wife brought in coffee on a tray with petite coffee cups and chocolate biscuits.

Eventually we all retired to our respective bedrooms. The bedrooms were upstairs and Jim was shown to his, then left alone for the night.

And that's how it was. Everybody in bed, and apparently sleeping.

At about five in the morning, my wife and I heard a noise. 'What's that?' she said. 'I'm sure I heard someone walking down the hall.' We both sat up and listened intently. We heard the stairs creaking.

'Why would he be going downstairs at five in the morning?' my wife wondered.

Within a minute or so, we heard the front door opening.

'For God's sake,' my wife then exclaimed, 'we've got to do something! He's escaping! Ring one of those telephone numbers the prison gave us!'

I was very concerned, but was not prepared to make a phone call at this stage. There was dead silence, no noise coming from the veranda. My wife told me that I should, at the very least, get dressed but I remained completely still as if I had some sort of premonition that things would be all right.

Finally, after about thirty minutes, we heard the front door open and close again. We heard the footsteps of the prisoner climbing the stairs, the creaking of his footsteps along the passageway, and finally his bedroom door closing.

My wife and I hugged each other with relief, and relaxed back under the sheets.

I said, 'Thank God for that – he's back.'

'You were right,' my wife replied. 'We had to trust him. It would have been awful if we had phoned the authorities.'

A little while later, we were all sitting down for breakfast in the big farm kitchen around the large table. Again, there was plenty of food. The prisoner was again dressed in his faded and ill-fitting suit. He had packed his overnight bag, and again his behaviour was beyond reproach. He, however, volunteered nothing about his nocturnal adventure.

Finally, I could not restrain myself, and said to him, 'We heard you go out early this morning. We were a bit worried there for a while.'

The prisoner then looked up at us; his eyes were lit with a warm glow, and a beautiful smile came on his face.

'Yes,' he answered, 'I did go outside. I couldn't help myself. I just had to see the stars in the night sky. They were so beautiful – I hadn't seen them for twenty years.'

Acknowledgments

I would like to thank Ian Ko, Arthur Tse, Eddie Kym and Filipe Batiwale, who assisted me in the preparation of this book and without whose assistance the manuscript would never have been completed.

I would also like to thank Moana Maniapoto for her comments on the manuscript.

I particularly wish to thank my partner, Heeni Phillips, for her encouragement, research and patience during the book's gestation. I also pay tribute to my long-standing friends John Yelash and Christopher Reid, who read drafts of this book and provided numerous thoughtful comments.

A tribute must be paid to my publisher, Finlay Macdonald, whose stimulating encouragement has kept the book on track.

Lastly but certainly not least, I wish to thank my sagacious and venerable friend, Bernie Brown, for his flattering foreword.

Index of Names

Adams-Smith, Robert 67, 180
Annear, William 257–62
Asia, Mr 9–10, 153–61
Astor, Lord 114
Awatere, Peta 137–45

Bainimarama, Commodore 266, 272
Banks, John 110
Baragwanath, David 213
Barrowclough, Harold 150
Baxter, James K 226–33
Beal, Mr 276
Beattie, Dave 186
Bell, Brian 228–30
Bennett, Henry 12, 212
Bethune, Henry 212
Bingham of Cornhill 248–49
Booth, Pat 113, 174, 178, 179
Boyle, Des 39
Brett, Kevin 273
Brown, Bernie 114
Brown, Jim 293–98
Brown, Lloyd 135
Brown, Mick 69
Brownlee, Jerry 248
Brownlie, Alan 65
Bruce 83–7
Bull Jr 103–9

Burr, Raymond 164
Burr, Richard 206–13

Cairns, Frank 124
Carter, Chris 215–20
Cartier, Link 133
Chaudhry, Minister of Finance 272
Chauhan, Sam 39
Clark, Helen 215–20
Clark, Terry 9–10, 153–61
Clarkson, Bob 247, 249–50
Cleal, Stan 105–8
Cohen, Aaron 286
Cohen, Lorraine 286
Collins, Paul 242
Collins, Sante 112–19
Cotton, Eddie 283
Crewe, David 173–83
Crewe, Jeanette 173–83
Cruden, Aaron 227
Cruden, Gordon 227

Darrow, Clarence 96
Darwin, Charles 17
Davison, Ronald 186, 242, 244–45
Demler 180
Dickson, Jimmy 54
Dods, Simon 162–65
Doone, Peter 216–17

Drake, Ben 39
Duffy, Ailsa 20
Dunne, John 130

Edwards, Brian 280–84
Ennor, Stuart 82

Faine, Alick 206–13
Fairbrother, Russell 248, 249
Fay, Michael 242, 244
Finlay, Martyn 145, 177
Firth, Julian 98
Fleming, Lola 127
Frank the Tank 146–52
Fulcher, Peter 13

Gaynor, Brian 240
Gibbs, Tony 289–92
Gibson, Simon 259
Gillies, John Frederick 123
Glenn, Owen 246, 249–50
Glover, Denis 229
Gluckman, Laurie 12, 167–68
Goodman, Bob 286
Graham, Billy 280–84
Gresson, Terrence 20, 107, 109, 127

Hagar, David 286, 287, 289
Haigh, Frank 20, 55, 67, 286
Hakaraia, Mrs 141–44
Hardie Boys, Reginald 114
Harvey, Bob 219
Hassim 184–90
Henry 198–205
Henry, Brian 246, 247, 250
Henry, John 181, 244
Hide, Rodney 248
Hobson, Jack 173
Holland, Sid 226
Hoogewerf, Francis 242
Howard, John 285
Hubbard, L Ron 67

Hughes, John Rex 124
Hulme, Juliet 57, 294
Hutchinson, Heather 125
Hutton, Bruce 176–83

Isabelle 44–51

Jasper the Gypsy 118–22
Johnson, Louis 229
Johnson, Morris 81, 82
Johnson, senior police officer 181–83
Jordan, Fred 286
Jorgensen, Ron 14, 125–38, 261
Joseph 77–82

Katonivualiku, Magistrate 270
Kearney, Dick 163, 165
Keeler, Christine 114
Keith, Justice 244
Kemp, Detective Sergeant 133
Khan, Ballu 263–72
Knox, John 281

Lange, David 7
Leary, LP 193–94, 196
Lee, Gypsy Rose 112
Leighton, George 175–78
Leung, Graham 267–70
Leweniqila, Semi 267, 269
Littlewood, Barry 261, 273
Lloyd, David 242
Lynch, Kate 267

Mahon, Peter 169, 171–72
Mason, Chief Registrar 20, 53
McCarthy, Fred 123
McCormick, Eric 128
McKenzie, Donald F 135
McKenzie, Flora 193–94
McLaren, Roger 83–4
McLay, Jim 69, 136, 180
McMullin, Duncan 20

Meade, Colin 125
Menninger, Karl 17
Miles, Joe 234–40
Moller, Lester 162–63
Molloy, Tony 245
Morris, Dave 181, 213
Morrison, Paul 231
Morsley, Eric 54
Mowbray, Neil 174, 181
'Mr Asia' 9–10, 153–61
Muldoon, Robert 180, 217–18

Nelson, Donald 124, 176–78, 181–83
Ness, Eliot 112
Newbolt, Henry 228
Nicholson, Colin 125
Nixon, Allen 7
Nixon, Richard 281
Nordgren, Brian 231
North, Alfred 11, 144, 208

Oates, Titus 10
O'Halloran, Arthur 286, 290
Ongley, Joseph 154, 156, 164

Parker, Pauline 57
Pearce, Barney 37
Perry, Clifford 81–82, 135
Perry, Graeme 124
Peters, Winston 241–50
Peterson, Bryan 126
Phar Lap 250
Phillips, Heeni 214, 246, 267, 269–71, 289
Power, Simon 248
Price, Greg 276
Profumo, John 115

Rae, Opie 150–51
Rapira, Mere Veronica 125
Rau, Roy 140–41
Reid, Chris 167–68, 265

Rhodes 229
Rhodes, Cecil 229
Richards, Arnold 212
Richardson, Ivor 244
Richardson, Ken 125
Richmond, Clifford 213
Richwhite, David 242, 244
Robertson, Geoffrey 115
Robinson, Michael 62–64
Roper, Clinton 287
Ross, Mrs 191–97
Ryan, Gerald 173
Ryan, Kevin 9, 10, 66, 125, 126, 160, 173, 180, 182, 232, 261, 273

Sage, Sally 277
Samuels, Dover 214–20
Savage, Dr 141
Sayed-Khaiyum, Attorney-General 272
Scutt, Jocelyn 267
Selkirk, Ronald 259
Shadbolt, Maurice 128
Singh, Karpal 286
Skelton, George 20
Smith, Nick 258
Soich, Karen 69
Speight, Graham 76, 125, 140, 144, 155
Speight, Kevin James 124
Sprott, Jim 174, 178, 179, 181
Stacey, Roy 81, 82
Stillman, Mrs 209
Sturt, Charles 243

Tabakau, police officer 270–71
Tapper, Garth 128
Taylor, Arthur 273–79
Taylor, Mrs 209–12
Taylor, Robert 180
Te Kanawa, Kiri 123
Te Whiu, Edward Thomas 226

Temm, Paul 104, 182
Thomas, Arthur Allan 10–11, 173–83
Thomas, Edmund 20, 244–45
Thorpe, Tom 162, 163
Tipping, Justice 244
Tirikatene-Sullivan, Whetu 67
Toofat 146–52
Turner, Alexander 11
Twyford, Phil 278

Uganda, Mr 206–13
Urlich, Gus 283

Vesey, Pat 174
Vogt, Anton 229

Walker, George Frederick 124
Walton, Robert 124, 126, 177
Ward, Stephen 114–15, 193

Webb, Nola 209
Wedgwood, Emma 17
Wesley, John 281
'Whisky Bill' 53
White, Charlie 283
Wild, Richard 178
Williams, Jim 21–32
Williams, Mike 250, 289–92
Williams, Zelda 59, 60
Wilson, Dr 13
Wilson, Margaret 216
Wilson, Thomas 231
Wilson, Tina 289
Wiseman, Jack 69
Woodhouse, Owen 20

Yelash, John 214–20